The Evolving Professional Self

WILEY SERIES IN PSYCHOTHERAPY AND COUNSELLING

Series Editors

Franz Epting
*Dept of Psychology
University of Florida*

Bonnie Strickland
*Dept of Psychology
University of
Massachusetts*

John Allen
*Dept of Community
Studies
Brighton Polytechnic*

Self, Symptoms and Psychotherapy
Edited by
Neil Cheshire and Helmut Thomae

Beyond Sexual Abuse
Therapy with Women who were Childhood Victims
Derek Jehu

Cognitive-Analytic Therapy: Active Participation in Change
A New Integration in Brief Psychotherapy
Anthony Ryle

The Power of Countertransference
Innovations in Analytic Technique
Karen J. Maroda

Strategic Family Play Therapy
Shlomo Ariel

Feminist Perspectives in Therapy
An Empowerment Model for Women
Judith Worell and Pam Remer

The Evolving Professional Self
Stages and Themes in Therapist and Counselor
Development
Thomas M. Skovholt and Michael Helge Rønnestad

Further titles in preparation

The Evolving Professional Self

Stages and Themes in Therapist and Counselor Development

THOMAS M. SKOVHOLT
University of Minnesota

and

MICHAEL HELGE RØNNESTAD
University of Oslo

JOHN WILEY & SONS
Chichester · New York · Brisbane · Toronto · Singapore

Paperback edition first published January 1995

Copyright © 1992, 1995 by John Wiley & Sons Ltd,
Baffins Lane, Chichester,
West Sussex, PO19 1UD, England

Telephone: National (01243) 779777
International (+44) 1243 779777

Reprinted July 1995, October 1997

All rights reserved.

No part of this book may be reproduced by any means,
or transmitted, or translated into a machine language
without the written permission of the publisher.

Other Wiley Editorial Offices

John Wiley & Sons, Inc., 605 Third Avenue,
New York, NY 10158-0012, USA

Jacaranda Wiley Ltd, 33 Park Road, Milton,
Queensland 4064, Australia

John Wiley & Sons (Canada) Ltd, 22 Worcester Road,
Rexdale, Ontario M9W 1L1, Canada

John Wiley & Sons (SEA) Pte. Ltd., 37 Jalan Pemimpin #05-04,
Block B, Union Industrial Building, Singapore 129809

Library of Congress Cataloging-in-Publication Data

Skovholt, Thomas M.
    The evolving professional self : stages and themes in therapist
and counselor development / Thomas M. Skovholt and Michael Helge
Rønnestad.
       p. cm.—(Wiley series in psychotherapy and counseling)
    Includes bibliographical references and index.
    ISBN 0–471–92456–3 (ppe)
    ISBN 0–471–95393–8 (paper)
    1. Psychotherapy—Vocational guidance. 2. Counseling—Vocational
guidance. 3. Psychotherapists—Psychology. 4. Counselors—
—Psychology. 5. Psychotherapists—Attitudes. 6. Counselors—
—Attitudes. I. Rønnestad, Michael Helge. II. Series.
    [DNLM: 1. Counseling. 2. Models, Psychological. 3. Professional
competence. 4. Psychotherapy. WM 420 S628e]
RC440.8..S57 1992
616.89´14´023—dc20   91–35787
                                                                                   CIP

British Library Cataloguing in Publication Data

A catalogue record for this book is available from the British Library

ISBN 0–471–92456–3 (ppe)
ISBN 0–471–95393–8 (paper)

Typeset in 11/13pt Garamond by
Mathematical Composition Setters Ltd, Salisbury, Wiltshire
Printed and bound in Great Britain by
Biddles Ltd, Guildford and King's Lynn

This book is dedicated to
Our Parents
Joseph Skovholt and Elvera Meyer Skovholt
Michael Rønnestad and Helga Rønnestad
and
Our Doctoral Advisors
Joseph Johnston
and
Norman Gysbers

Contents

Series Preface		ix
Preface		xi
Chapter 1	Perspectives on Professional Development	1
Chapter 2	Conventional Stage	17
Chapter 3	Transition to Professional Training Stage	22
Chapter 4	Imitation of Experts Stage	30
Chapter 5	Conditional Autonomy Stage	42
Chapter 6	Exploration Stage	50
Chapter 7	Integration Stage	62
Chapter 8	Individuation Stage	74
Chapter 9	Integrity Stage	87
Chapter 10	Themes in Therapist/Counselor Development	100
Chapter 11	Stagnation versus Professional Development of Therapists and Counselors	124
Appendix A	Research Methodology and Sample Description	143

Appendix B	Themes in Interviews with Three Senior Informants	166
References		205
Author Index		213
Subject Index		217

Series Preface

The Wiley Series in Psychotherapy and Counselling was created to promote the scientific development of professional psychology. In the series this has taken many forms, all of which have been focused on the product of the therapeutic enterprise. For the most part this has been a presentation of books examining and expanding particular theories and techniques, books examining major problem areas, books dealing with specific populations of clients, and books examining emerging strategies. However this book offers, for the first time in the series, the opportunity to become self-reflexive and use the science of psychology to examine the professional helpers as they go about the business of developing their professional lives. The aim of the book is to examine the entire life span of the helping professional.

Professor Skovholt from the United States and Professor Rønnestad from Norway have combined their long-standing interest in the development of the professional therapist to produce a truly comprehensive view of professional development which goes far beyond books which concentrate only on supervision. Most importantly, they have made every effort to include the person of the therapist in their description of the stages and themes involved in understanding what it means to become a professional therapist or counselor. Following an outline which has been carefully thought through, the authors present not only their own model of professional development but also provide an analysis of a hundred interviews with students and professional workers in the field. In combination, the formal model and interview data provide a most engaging beginning for the mapping of the professional's world. This map is well illustrated in personal dialogue and includes the rough terrain of professional stagnation as well as the description of professional fulfillment.

The authors see their work as providing not only an initial structure, but, most importantly, also a way to generate hypotheses about this most important developmental process. The authors have been very careful to document their work as they present both their model and their data. This is accomplished, however, without interfering with central themes. This book will be of interest to every professional who cares to take the time to carefully examine his or her own professional development and would be most useful in the instruction of beginning therapists. It would not be unrealistic to expect that this book will set a new standard for what it means to take a comprehensive view of professional development.

FRANZ EPTING
Series Editor

Preface

This book is intended for a wide audience including *students* in programs which train therapists and counselors, *practitioners* who have already received training and are actively working in the field, supervisors of students and practitioners, *teachers* of courses in the therapy and counseling professions, and *researchers* who are actively pursuing research questions within this domain. Since one author is an American and the other a European, we hope this book will have appeal to individuals in both of these places as well as other continents and countries.

The purpose of this book is to focus on the development of therapists and counselors over the career life span. We hope by focusing on this topic that we will help enhance the professional development and professional competence of therapists and counselors. The book consists of an introductory chapter describing development, eight chapters which present our stage model of development, a chapter which presents 20 different themes of development and a final chapter which contrasts development versus stagnation. The appendices include our research methodology as well as extensive interviews with three senior informants in the field.

When two individuals work together on a project, it often takes effort to make the collaboration work. However, when these two individuals spend six years on their collaboration and live 4,036 miles apart, they face a much more difficult task. It is important to us to acknowledge all the support and help we have received from numerous individuals. We are most thankful to the 100 informants who gave of their time, many for a second interview, and also to the many other people who shared their own developmental issues with us. We are grateful to our editor, Franz Epting, for his perseverance and support of our work. Appreciation goes to the two anonymous reviewers in the United States and Britain selected by Wiley. We acknowledge John Dagley for his help in clarifying our ideas.

In the United States, we thank James Morgan and Roger Barrett for their reviews of the content. We are grateful to Terry Collins for a review of our writing style. For administrative support in the early days, we are thankful to Thomas Brothen. We wish to express appreciation to Darwin Hendel for his research consultation. We are grateful to Bill Cuff, who made extraordinary contributions to this project, Janet Schank, Mohammad Razzaque, and Kevin Herrington for conducting the first set of interviews along with the first author. Thanks to Elisabeth Horst, Patti Neiman, Kay Thomas, and Charles Boudreaux, who conducted the second set of interviews along with the first author. For their assistance with the composition and typing of the manuscript, our thanks go to Carla Hill, Jennifer Franko, Elisabeth Nealy, and Elizabeth Garvey. We appreciate the financial support this project has received from the Division of Social and Behavioral Sciences, the Office of International Education, and the Department of Educational Psychology at the University of Minnesota. Tom Skovholt appreciates the support and encouragement of Cathy, Rachel, and David.

In Norway, we thank the following institutions for financial support: the Institute of Psychology of the University of Oslo; the Norwegian Research Council for the Social Sciences, the Norway-America Association and the Norwegian Marshall Fund. Helge Rønnestad is thankful for the inspirational dialogues with Erik Larsen and Mats Marnell. The support and encouragement of Annette, Elisabeth, and Kari-Brith are greatly appreciated.

THOMAS SKOVHOLT
University of Minnesota
MICHAEL HELGE RØNNESTAD
University of Oslo

15 August 1991

CHAPTER 1

Perspectives on Professional Development

Individuals are entering professional careers in increasing numbers. After an intense period of study, the individual enters as a novice into a professional field such as law, therapy/counseling, medicine, teaching, engineering, ministry or architecture. The period of time from the beginning of academic preparation to retirement may last up to half a century! What happens during all of this time? This is the question we are addressing here. We are particularly focusing on the careers of practitioners in the psychotherapy and counseling professions.

Psychotherapy and counseling have taken on greater and greater importance during the last decades of the twentieth century. Increasingly, these occupational fields hold a central place in the solution of many of the complex and important concerns people face. In our two countries of the United States and Norway, the number of mental health services is increasing steadily and projections are for continued growth over the next decades. A central reason for this increased popularity is the positive response of individuals after receiving counseling and mental health services. People generally value the professional work they receive from therapists and counselors in such diverse areas as reducing anxiety, managing depression, coping with loss, resolving relationship conflicts, developing positive organizations, finding satisfying work, learning new interpersonal skills, stopping addictive behaviors, struggling with meaning and purpose in one's life, and reducing family problems.

In recent years, there has been a growing interest in the *development* of the professional therapist/counselor. This is so partly because the field has increasingly come to realize the intertwining of the personal and professional aspects of the functioning of the therapist/counselor (Guy, 1987).

Realizing our common interest in the topic (Rønnestad, 1985; Skovholt, 1985), we began a research project in 1986 in order to understand the elements that make up development over the career life span of therapists and counselors. We wanted to construct a research based model of professional development. In this process, we have asked a variety of questions, such as: How is professional development enhanced? How does a person progress and improve her/his competence in this field? What is the value of supervision? As a beginning question we decided to ask: What is normative development for therapists and counselors? By answering these questions, we hope to enhance the professional expertise of therapists and counselors and, thereby, also contribute to the increased usefulness of the field in alleviating human suffering. We believe that answering these questions may also advance counselor/psychotherapy education and improve the quality of supervision. Perhaps a clearer understanding of the developmental process will be helpful in establishing realistic demands in graduate education. We assume that some of the theoretical controversies in therapy and counselor education and supervision can be resolved through refining what we know about professional development. Supervisor and supervisee will be able to establish more effective learning contracts if professional developmental paths are better understood. We also think that it will be possible to better arrest the negative avenues of professional development such as incompetence, impairment, burnout, and disillusionment if a more accurate and comprehensive conceptualization of therapist/counselor development is attained.

On the Concept of Development

Few concepts in psychology have such diverse content as the concept of development. Development is a theoretical rather than an empirical concept (Lerner, 1986). An empirical study of development is initiated with developmental postulates (Kaplan, 1983) which provide a reference point for determining if a given empirical finding can be classified as developmental or not. If the preconceptions are few and distinct and the empirical findings are simple and well defined, it is relatively easy to determine if changes under investigation can be labeled developmental. However, if the preconceptions are many and complex and the findings are similarly complex and diverse, it is more difficult to determine if changes can meaningfully be described as developmental.

Lerner (1986) has provided a comprehensive review of the concept of psychological development. Although the theoretical nature of the concept of development allows for great variability in concept attributes, Lerner (1986) has pointed out that there are certain minimal features to the concept of development regardless of philosophical and theoretical orientation. These are: development always implies change of some sort; the change is organized systematically; and the change involves succession over time. The elements of *change, order/structure and succession* are thus basic elements of a concept of development. In their definitions, developmental psychologists may specify further prerequisites for concept inclusions. Examples here are: changes must serve an adaptive function (Schneirly, 1957); changes must be organized so that systems change from a global to a more differentiated, integrated, hierarchical form (i.e., the orthogenetic principle [Kaplan, 1983]); change must be of a qualitative, not only a quantitative nature.

Within therapist/counselor development and supervision, a comprehensive body of perspectives and knowledge has been developed to answer the questions of *what* changes, *how* does what change, and *why* does what change (description/explanation). More emphasis has been placed on the questions of the "what" and the "how," questions that lend themselves more readily to empirical investigation and logical analysis, than on the "why."

It has only been during the last twenty years that the developmental paradigm has dominated the study of therapist/counselor professional functioning and supervision. The developmental paradigm has explicitly or implicitly influenced the study of issues such as: relationship aspects (Cross & Brown, 1983; Hess, 1987; Lambert, 1980; Heppner & Handley, 1982; Worthington, 1984; Worthington & Stern, 1985), expectations (Friedlander & Snyder, 1983; Heppner & Roehlke, 1984); didactic/instructional aspects of supervision (Friedlander & Ward, 1984; Miars, et al., 1983; Worthington, 1984), the role of feedback and support (Rønnestad, 1977; Heppner & Roehlke, 1984; Worthington & Roehlke, 1979; Worthington & Stern, 1985); process issues (Ekstein & Wallerstein, 1958; Stoltenberg, 1981); and concerns such as goal definition, assessment of learning/developmental needs, and conceptual level (Borders, 1989; Borders, Fong-Beyette & Cron, 1988; Hillebrand, 1989).

The Stage Perspective and the Concepts of Continuity/Discontinuity

Lerner (1986) has provided a useful overview of the continuity/discontinuity issue. This is highly relevant for the study of professional development, particularly if one assumes a stage position (Loganbill, Hardy & Delworth, 1982).

Continuity exists if the variables under investigation remain the same in the ontogenetic development of the individual. If variables change, discontinuity exists. A distinction is often made between descriptive and explanatory continuity/discontinuity (Lerner, 1986). Descriptive continuity exists if behaviors at two different points in time can be described in the same way. The description of the behavior of supervisors who do not change the way they supervise as they get more experience is an example of descriptive continuity. Explanatory continuity exists if behaviors at different points in time can be explained similarly. Explanatory discontinuity exists if behaviors, same or different, can be explained by different reasons. In professional development, these concepts direct our understanding of factors which impede and encourage change. It is our understanding that the concept of explanatory discontinuity, in particular, focuses on the many different ways professionals can arrive at the same level of functioning. We may also label this perspective the alternate path perspective (Hilgard, 1970).

The classical theories of development, as represented by Freud, Erikson, Kohlberg, are generally named stage-theories. The richness of literature that entertains a perspective of qualitatively different functioning at different points in time, generally seen as a characteristic of stage (Lerner, 1986), provides us with similar and related concepts such as phase, sequence and level. The stage concept may be regarded as the most stringent concept which, in the classical perspective, denotes an invariant ordering of universal stages, i.e., a hierarchical sequential ordering of qualitatively different functioning/structures.

Critiques of the stage concept will generally question the universality, the hierarchical nature, the invariance, or the qualitatively different nature of changes. However, qualitative difference can also be understood as discontinuity. This is important because there is a shift away from looking at the continuity/discontinuity issue as primarily an empirical issue, towards looking at this issue as primarily theoretical. Lerner (1986) has argued that the main reason why researchers interpret a given change in contrasting ways is that they maintain different theoretical positions. He stated:

> If one adopts a theoretical position stressing the progressive, hierarchical integration of the organism (e.g., Gagne, 1968), one will necessarily view development as essentially continuous. On the other hand, if one stresses the progressive differentiation of the organism, one will view development

as essentially discontinuous. For example, a given theoretical position might lead one to interpret a given piece of empirical evidence in one way (e.g., as consistent with a continuity position), while someone with a different theoretical position might interpret that same empirical fact in another way (e.g., as consistent with a discontinuity position). (p. 188)

The same logic can be applied to "abruptness of transitions' (Flavell, 1963).

Models of Psychological Development: an Overview

A number of developmental model builders have been influential and have influenced us. Freud's psychosexual stages are now so much a part of the conceptual ground we all walk on that it is easy to neglect mention of his four stages—Oral, Anal, Phallic, Genital. Erikson's (1968) four adult stage related tasks—Individuation, Intimacy, Generality, and Ego Integrity—have been valuable expansions within the Freudian tradition. Through a long-term study, Vaillant (1977) has contributed the idea of a Career Consolidation task between Erikson's Intimacy and Generativity concepts.

In the area of cognitive complexity, Perry (1981) formulated a four-stage model of cognitive change—his progress is from Dualism to Multiplicity to Relativity to Committed Relativity. Kohlberg (1979) and Rest *et al*. (1986) have charted growth and change in the area of moral development. Super (1980) and Levinson *et al*. (1978) have developed career focused stage models that are driven by age. Super's (1980) five career stages are Growth, Exploration, Establishment, Maintenance, and Decline. Levinson *et al*. (1978) stages are: Leaving the Family, Getting into the Adult World, Settling Down, Becoming One's Own (Person), Making a Midlife Transition, and Reestablishing and Beginning Middle Adulthood. Gilligan (1982) has provided useful criticism and elaboration of many of these developmental models in her critique of them as biased toward male development and neglectful of interpersonal connectedness as a critical adult development issue.

A developmental model that concentrates on increases in expertise has been formulated by Dreyfus and Dreyfus (1986) (Benner, 1982). This model hinges on experience as well as education differentiate levels of skilled performance. The five professional development levels (Novice,

Advanced Beginner, Competent, Proficient, Expert) vary by functioning on two general dimensions: (1) The shift in time to using one's own work experience rather than abstract principles for paradigms to guide one's performance. (2) Perceptual changes in the use of only certain elements of a complex situation rather than many equal parts.

The *Novice* is described as an individual who must rely on context-free rules because he/she has no experience to guide practice. The Novice can become lost when encountering exceptions that the learned rules do not cover. *Advanced Beginner.* The individual has accumulated some experience to guide practice. This experience enables the person to have some "aspect recognition." Aspects are overall, global characteristics that an individual can use for decision making. *Competent.* This is the highest level of performance using textbook rules. The individual has had enough work experience so that he/she knows how to anticipate events and know what to look for. *Proficient.* Aspects are replaced by Maxims. Maxims are characteristics of a situation that, to a Novice, are only unintelligible nuances of a situation. Maxims provide direction as to what is important in a situation. *Expert.* The individual at this level has the richest experience base. This enables the individual to operate from an intuitive level regarding the important elements of a demand situation. The Expert operates from such an embedded experience base that he/she at times has difficulty describing why a particular action was the right one.

An important element of the Dreyfus and Dreyfus (1986) formulation is the replacement of the theories of experts with one's own relevant experience as the essential guide for practice.

Models of Therapist/Counselor Professional Development

In this section, the developmental approaches of Fleming (1953), Hogan (1964), Hill, Charles, and Reed (1981), Blocher (1983), Grater (1985), Hess (1987), Loganbill, Hardy and Delworth (1982), and Stoltenberg and Delworth (1987) will be described. Other models of therapist/counselor development, but not described here, include Ard (1973), Friedman and Kaslow (1986), Herroid (1989), Jablon (1987), Littrell, Lee-Borden and Lorenz (1979), Patton (1986), Stoltenberg (1981), and Yogev (1982). Although not described in detail here, the work of Jablon (1987) is important because it contradicts the common assumption that experience and age tend to promote increased professional development.

The Psychoanalytic Learning Model of Fleming

A classic developmental model that has been highly influential within the domain of dynamic psychotherapy is the model of Joan Fleming (1953). It is surprising that not more references are made to her model within the field of counseling psychology and the human service fields. The reason for this may be that she does not explicitly use stage, level or phase terms. If she had, her model would also probably be regarded as the classic model for the counseling psychology field. Fleming proposed three different methods that characterize the learning process of students at different experience levels. They are *imitative learning*, *corrective learning*, and *creative learning*. During *imitative learning*, also called the jug-mug model (one pours from the jug to the mug), learning occurs primarily through imitating the supervisor. There is a teaching and didactic focus where emphasis is on suggestion and demonstration. Lacking professional self-confidence necessitates a supportive attitude from the supervisor. In *corrective learning*, where the supervisor assumes the role of the potter (the supervisor forms an unfinished piece of clay), emphasis is on correction and less on support as the therapist has more self-confidence. In *creative learning*, where the supervisor assumes the role of the gardener, emphasis is on preparing the soil and nurturing the seedling, metaphors which convey the facilitative function of the supervisor. This last supervisory mode presupposes that the basic skills of psychotherapy are mastered.

The Four-Level Model of Hogan

The model of Hogan (1964) has been the most influential within the area of therapist/counselor development. Over twenty-five years ago, he published a brief article describing four stages (levels) of psychotherapist development. During *Level 1*, psychotherapists are insecure, "neurosis bound," and dependent. They have little insight into their own motivation for being a psychotherapist. They can be highly motivated for their work, frequently rely on one method, and learn through imitation.

During *Level 2*, psychotherapists struggle with a dependency-autonomy conflict. In their quest to find their own adaptation, they vacillate between feeling overconfident and being overwhelmed. During this stage, motivation fluctuates considerably. Hogan recommended psychotherapy at this stage.

During *Level 3*, a conditional dependency level, there is heightened professional self-confidence and more insight into one's own motivation for the work. Motivation is also more stable than at the preceding levels.

During *Level 4*, the master psychologist level, there is personal autonomy, and a higher level of insight into one's own motivation which is stable. There is a personal security at this level and a recognized need to confront personal and professional problems.

For each level, Hogan recommended different supervisory interventions such as teaching, interpretation, support, awareness training (*Level 1*); support, exemplification and ambivalence clarification (*Level 2*); sharing, exemplification, and confrontation (*Level 3*), and sharing and mutual confrontation (*Level 4*).

The Counseling Student Model of Hill, Charles and Reed

As part of a more extensive study of counseling doctoral student development, Hill, Charles and Reed (1981) described a four-phase model. *Sympathy* is the first phase. Sympathetic involvement with the client, consisting mostly of constant positive support, is the essential counselor focus. If the client improves, the new counselor feels successful. *Counselor Stance* is a second phase. Here the search is for a method to use for understanding and intervening with clients. The focus is on mechanical mastery of the chosen method. *Transition* is next. Here a breakdown occurs in the use of the one method because of new input from theory, clients and supervisors. The last phase is *Integrated Personal Style*. At this phase, there is a preliminary combination of techniques and theory into a consistent personal style. Feedback from clients is now thought of in a more objective way than earlier.

The Cognitive Developmental Approach of Blocher

Blocher (1983), who bases his supervision model on the psychology of learning and behavioral change and on human cognitive development, sees supervision as a teaching-instructional process aimed at higher levels of cognitive functioning. These increasingly higher levels of cognitive functioning provide a stage-like model. He defined supervision as follows:

> Supervision is a specialized instructional process in which the supervisor attempts to facilitate the growth of a counselor-in-preparation, using as the primary educational medium the student's interaction with real clients for

whose welfare the student has some degree of professional, ethical, and moral responsibility. (p. 27)

Blocher criticizes model "straw man" categories, such as those described by Hess (1980), i.e., lecturer, teacher, case reviewer, collegial-peer supporter, monitor and therapist. According to Blocher, these categories have limited utility as schema for categorizing goals, he argued that the ultimate focus should be "on the acquisition of new more complex and more comprehensive schemas for understanding human interaction" (p.29). He delineated relationship and communication conditions as process goals of supervision. He emphasized the importance of communicating trust and respect through clear and honest feedback and in creating communications processes which allow for two-way, broad band channels of communication on a wide range of topics.

Blocher argued for a continually changing contract-based interchange where goals and objectives are made explicit. Early in practicum, he suggests that these goals frequently focus on interview skills, relationship conditions, personality constructs and on issues such as confidence, comfort and authenticity. Later, the focus is on broader issues: implementation of process goals, overall case management, and clarification of professional roles.

A rich contribution from Blocher (1983) is his description of the developmental learning environment. He conceptualized this developmental learning environment with the seven basic person-environment dynamics of Challenge, Involvement, Support, Structure, Feedback, Innovations, and Integration.

The Developmental Model of Loganbill, Hardy and Delworth

The authors (1982) hypothesize three stages of supervisee development: *Stagnation*, *Confusion*, and *Integration*. For each stage they elaborate a description of characteristics, attitude toward the world, attitude toward the self, attitude toward the supervisor and value of the stage. They perceive the counselor as cycling and recycling through the stages at increasingly deeper levels.

Some central characteristics of their model are as follows: stage one, *Stagnation* is characterized by not being aware of one's own deficiency in professional functioning or by an unawareness of the issues of supervision or one's own "stuckness" or stagnation. There is typically a limited and constricted view of the world. Thinking tends to be all or nothing. The student may have a low self-concept and be dependent upon the supervisor, or the student may think he/she is functioning well and regard supervision as unnecessary. In stage two, *Confusion*, primary characteristics are "instability, disorganization, erratic fluctuation, disruption, confusion, and conflict" (Loganbill, Hardy & Delworth, 1982, p. 18). It involves a liberation, an unfreezing of attitudes, emotions or behaviors. There is a realization that something is wrong and a fluctuation between feelings of expertise and feelings of failure and incompetence. Attitudes toward the supervisor often change from positively toned dependency to disappointment and anger, a shift that can be quite uncomfortable for both supervisor and supervisee. This stage is perceived as being very positive as it entails the abandonment of old ways of thinking and behaving, and provides the opportunity for new learning to occur. Stage three, *Integration*, "... is characterized by reorganization, integration, a new cognitive understanding, flexibility, personal security based on awareness of insecurity and an ongoing continual monitoring of the important issues of supervision" (p. 19). There is a more realistic assessment and acceptance of the world as it is and of oneself with shortcomings and undeveloped areas. The supervisee has realistic expectations in terms of supervisory goals, is able to perceive the supervisor more realistically, and is capable of assuming responsibility for the content and process of supervision.

The Supervision Focused Model of Grater

Based on his extensive experience as a psychotherapy teacher and supervisor, Grater (1985) created a four stage model of therapist development with particular application to supervision.

Stage 1: *Developing Basic Skills and Adopting the Therapist Role*. The focus here includes the replacement of social patterns of interacting with therapeutic responses. Trainee anxiety is extensive and an important focus for the supervisor. Specific skills include learning about the nuances of client statements, the use of body language and the pace of an interview.

Stage 2: *Expanding the Range of Therapy Skills and Roles*. Here client assessment takes on a more prominent place. The trainee must learn to assess clients in two ways: in terms of the problem areas and in terms of the expectations for the therapy process. Increased therapist flexibility is an important learning goal here.

Stage 3: *Using the Working Alliance to Understand the Client's*

Habitual Patterns. Here the focus is on recognizing how the client brings habitual and often maladaptive patterns into the therapy. The trainee at this level is taught to recognize these patterns and to respond in a way that produces growth rather than client stagnation. The trainee here must learn about the interactions between client, the problem and techniques.

Stage 4: *Using the Self in Assessment and Intervention.* Building from the first three stages, the therapist here learns to use the self as a powerful tool for both assessment and therapy. For example, the therapist learns to use the experience of being challenged as a source of information and a vehicle for a therapeutic response rather than as a time for self protection. Sensitivity to therapy process issues is a focus of this stage.

The Supervision Focused Model of Hess

After reviewing the major stage theories, Hess (1987) provided a synthesis formulated in four superordinate stages. In Hess's formulation, the professional can recycle through the stages in an ascending spiral fashion. The stages are:

1. *Inception stage:* Central characteristics are role induction, demystification of therapy, skill-definition and setting of boundaries.
2. *Skill development stage:* This entails being increasingly able to adapt the didactic and experiential materials being mastered to the client's particular needs. Other stage characteristics include assuming an apprentice role and a beginning identification with a system of therapy and a philosophy of human nature.
3. *Consolidation stage:* Primarily characterized by integrating the knowledge previously acquired. At this level the therapist, recognized by others for particular talents, realizes that one's professional identity is in part defined by her/his skills. There is refinement of skill and competence and the role of therapist personality is recognized.
4. *Mutuality stage:* The therapist emerges as an autonomous professional who engages in the give and take of peer consultation. The individual is able to create unique solutions to problems. Potential concerns of professionals at this stage are burnout and stagnation.

Hess (1986) has also formulated a three-stage model for supervisor development. The *beginning supervisor* typically lacking formal training in supervision, frequently focuses on the concrete and has a teaching focus and is technique-oriented in his/her supervision as a way of coping with the difficulties experienced. The *exploration stage* supervisor regards supervision as a professional activity which is safeguarded and protected from interruption. There is a shift in focus towards truly assessing and addressing student learning needs, a shift towards informal power, and an attention to the supervision literature. In the third stage, *confirmation of the supervisor's identity*, supervisor and student both experience learning as exciting. Hess is particularly observant of the impact of evaluation in the supervisory relationship.

The Integrated Developmental Model of Stoltenberg and Delworth

The recent model of Stoltenberg and Delworth (1987) is based on the models of Hogan (1964), Stoltenberg (1981) and Loganbill, Hardy and Delworth (1982). They conceptualized four levels of development, three of which are trainee levels (*Level 1, 2, and 3 Trainee*) and one as the *Integrated Counselor*.

> The trainee is described as progressing in terms of three basic structures—self- and other-awareness, motivation, and autonomy—in a continuous manner through the levels. This progression is assumed to proceed in a relatively orderly fashion through various domains of functioning relevant to professional activities in counseling and psychotherapy. (p. 35)

According to their model, there is a structural shift across domains in each stage. The eight domains are:

Intervention skills competence,
Assessment techniques,
Interpersonal assessment,
Client conceptualization,
Individual differences,
Theoretical orientation,
Treatment goals and plans,
Professional ethics.

Even though the authors view the levels as irreversible structural changes, their conceptualization allows for temporary lapses and returns to familiar territory. Movement through the levels is seen as occurring through Piaget's (1972) processes of assimilation and accommodation.

Although these models provide many useful constructs, they are also limited. In order to overcome these limitations, we decided to construct a model that was research-based and covered the entire professional lifespace. We wanted to include the broader sources of influence in both one's professional life and one's personal life that do, in fact, seem to impact development. We wanted to use a qualitative method so that the rich, textured data of interviews would not be lost in our inquiry. We decided to use this strength of qualitative inquiry and let our data serve as hypotheses to be proved or disproved by more precise empirical studies.

In the next chapters, we present the results of our investigation. These chapters begin with a description of the lay helper stage and progress to the last stage, the functioning of a senior professional. Following these detailed descriptive chapters, we have written two additional chapters: one is a summary of the major themes across the career life span, the other examines development versus stagnation. In the appendices, we have a description of our research method and also a section which consists of three transcripts from interviews with highly experienced and respected senior practitioners in our study along with commentary which highlights important developmental themes.

The validity of our work is based on two different levels: the construction of the model by the authors and the individual reactions of the informants. Now the validity of the study rests on the two levels of us as authors and you as the reader. We have attempted to construct an accurate model of therapist/counselor development. Hopefully, it is an accurate generalization across individuals. However, it is impossible to describe each individual's developmental path in detailed accuracy. Therefore, the validity of this study rests partly upon you, the reader, recognizing the description and checking the accuracy for yourself. People differ on so many critical dimensions such as age, experience level, gender, race, work setting, cognitive style, theoretical training, and family of origin. It is not desirable and not possible to negate the impact of these individual difference variables. Taking these factors into account can add depth to the descriptions. Therefore, it is important to consider the following stage model as conceptually and structurally flexible and porous. Finally, we are presenting the stage model as a series of hypotheses to be thoroughly examined and proved or disproved by other qualitative studies and by more precise, controlled quantitative studies.

Table 1 provides an overview of the content in Chapters 2 through 9.

Table 1.

	Stages			
Categories	Conventional	Transition to professional training	Imitation of experts	Conditional autonomy
Definition and time period of stage	Untrained, may be many years	First year of Graduate School	Middle years of Graduate School	Internship, 6 months to 2 years
Central task	Use what one naturally knows	Assimilate information from many sources and apply it in practice	Maintain openness at the meta level while imitating experts at the practical level	Function as a professional
Predominant affect	Sympathy	Enthusiasm and insecurity	Bewilderment, then later calm and temporary security	Variable confidence
Predominant sources of influence	One's own personal life	Sense of being overwhelmed because of many interacting new and old data bases	Multiple including supervisors, clients, theory/research, peers, personal life, social-cultural environment	Multiple including supervisors, clients, theory/research, peers, personal life, social-cultural environment
Role and working style	Sympathetic friend	Uncertain/shifting while struggling to fit practice with theory	Uncertain while developing a rigid mastery of basics	Increased rigidity in professional role and working style

Table 1. Continued

	Stages			
Categories	Conventional	Transition to professional training	Imitation of experts	Conditional autonomy
Conceptual ideas	Common sense	Urgency in learning conceptual ideas and techniques	Intense searching for conceptual ideas and techniques	Refined mastery of conceptual ideas and techniques
Learning process	Experiential	Cognitive processing and introspection	Imitation, introspection, and cognitive processing	Continual imitation with alterations, introspection, cognitive processing
Measures of effectiveness and satisfaction	Usually assumed, often not of concern	Visible client improvement and supervisor reaction	Client feedback and supervisor reaction	More complex view of client feedback and supervisor reactions

	Stages			
Categories	Exploration	Integration	Individuation	Integrity
Definition and time period of stage	New Graduate, 2-5 years	2-5 years	10-30 years	1-10 years
Central task	Explore beyond the known	Developing authenticity	Deeper authenticity	Being oneself and preparing for retirement
Predominant affect	Confidence and anxiety	Satisfaction and hope	Satisfaction and distress	Acceptance

(*continued*)

Table 1. *Continued*

	Stages			
Categories	Exploration	Integration	Individuation	Integrity
Predominant sources of influence	New data bases, i.e. new work setting, self now as professional, multiple other sources	Self as professional elder as new influence, multiple other sources	Experience-based generalizations and accumulated wisdom are becoming primary. Earlier sources of influence are internalized, self as professional elder	Experience-based generalizations and accumulated wisdom are primary. Earlier sources of influence are internalized, self as professional elder
Role and working style	Modifying externally imposed professional style	Role and working style as mix of externally imposed rigidity and internally imposed loosening mode	Increasingly oneself within competent professional boundaries	Being oneself
Conceptual system used	Personal rejection of some earlier mastered conceptual ideas	An emerging personally selected synergistic and eclectic form	Individualized and personalized	Highly individually chosen and integrated
Learning process	Reflection	Personally chosen methods	Personally chosen methods	Personally chosen methods
Measures of effectiveness	Increasingly realistic and internalized criteria	Increasingly realistic and continued internalization of criteria	Realistic and internal	Profoundly internal and realistic

CHAPTER 2

Conventional Stage

Definition of the Stage

The key here is being untrained in counseling/therapy yet engaged in the process of trying to help another person feel better, make decisions, understand self or improve relationships. The individual is most often a helper to others as a friend, family member, colleague at work, neighbor or school classmate. The individual has either no training or training that only marginally affects one's helping behavior.

Three variables—age, training and experience—will modify the overall response at this stage. The person with considerable life experience may respond in ways which combine characteristics of this stage and later stages. The following variables will tend to make for a mixed stage response at this point in one's development: being older rather than younger; having received personal therapy/counseling; being involved with a social movement which promotes freedom/liberation/equality; being personally victimized. Training at the paraprofessional or equivalent level will mean that the person exhibits a combination of characteristics of Stage 1 and later stages. Such an individual may work as a peer counselor in a school, be a summer camp counselor, serve as a volunteer counselor in a crisis unit, function as a dormitory counselor at a college, act as a lay helper in a church or be a person recognized by peers as a proficient natural helper. The individual may be a teacher who tries to help students with personal problems, a physician who works with the personal stressors of patients or an attorney who tries to solve emotionally distressing issues of clients.

Central Task

The central task of the untrained helper is to use what one knows—acquired as part of one's own individual development as a person—to help other people. There is a naturalness, a simplicity and an unexamined quality in the attempt to transfer one's personal methods of coping to the other person. The Conventional Stage helper with some training or considerable life experience may have a wider repertoire to draw from. Predominant are the conventional and ordinary methods used by the individual in finding solutions. These solutions are then suggested to the other person. The methods of transferring one's own approach to life often involves listening, fairly rapid problem identification, specific advice concerning the problem and, then, encouragement to the person to follow this course. For example, when told that the person is thinking of leaving a romantic relationship but is confused and distressed, the Conventional Stage helper may employ a highly directive problem solving approach such as "He isn't worth it; you will be better off without him," or "Stick it out. You will be happy that you did." Conversely, the Conventional Stage helper may just listen.

Predominant Affect

At this stage, individuals who are engaged in helping are curious about human behavior and are very interested in people. Sympathy is the predominant affect. The person wants to help, is sincere, and often works very hard at the process. However, the individual is usually not fully aware of the varied motivational forces propelling the helping response.

Sources of Influence

Six major sources of influence seem to play a significant role in the next stages; theories/research, clients, professional elders (professors/supervisors/mentors/therapists), one's own personal life, peers/colleagues, and social/cultural environment. Influence may come now from a variety of these sources. However, often one's own personal life plays the major role since the untrained person has had little exposure to the other sources of influence. In addition, the influence of one's own personal life tends to be unexamined and often misunderstood. However, there are great variations in exact influence when one departs from the modal lay helper at the Conventional Stage.

The following variables are major sources of influence and alter the quality of the helping response of the lay helper: age, life experience, and training and experience in human services occupations. Individuals who are younger and inexperienced in formal helping relationships are qualitatively different than those who are older and experienced.

Role and Working Style

The predominant role of the lay helper is one of a sympathetic friend. Role requirements include things like "just talking with people," "the idea is to relate problems to a friend" or "the helper gives advice." The helper's job is conceived as listening to the pain and trying to help the person; another definition is that the helper just has to give suggestions for a problem. Others, at the beginning, think that the job is to elicit emotions. Often the role and working style includes a strongly directive style involving self-disclosure, i.e., "This is what I did," suggestions for behavior, i.e., "Try harder next time," and a sympathetic interest in the other.

An aspect of the sympathetic friendship role at this point is that the lay helper usually identifies very strongly with the person's problems and rides along with the client as if on a roller coaster of emotions. This results, at times, in an overidentification with the person and an intense eagerness to solve the problems. Continual strong emotional support is the main ingredient offered by the lay helper. Boundaries between friendship and the role of the lay helper are often unknown or confusing to the beginner. From the perspective of the veteran counselor/therapist there are numerous boundary problems for lay helpers. The combination of the emotional roller coaster and problems with boundaries tends to create problems when the lay helper is exposed to the client's painful experiences. As one beginner said, "I was overwhelmed by the pain of the other person and I couldn't sleep at night." Occasionally the opposite occurs; the beginner is rigid and distant in the role of the lay helper. This may be because the person perceives this as proper for the role; it may also be because the helper is afraid of the demands for too much emotional closeness.

Conceptual Ideas Used

The sympathetic friend role enables the lay helper to have a conceptual system based on common sense and one's personal epistemology of life experience, world view, perceptual and value biases and mode of functioning. As much as this natural approach is helpful, the lay helper can be helpful. As much as this natural approach is limiting or harmful, the influence of the lay helper is benign or harmful.

The lay helper is as structured as her/his personality, and the role of sympathetic friend suggests structure. Since the role is conceived of as natural and simple, moderate structure is easily obtained.

Learning Process

For the lay helper the lack of training tends to protect the individual from knowing about the complexity of the work. If friendship is simple, and helping is like friendship, then this process is simple.

How does one learn this simple process? The learning is through the osmosis of living one's own life as a human being. Through one's own life and the richness of the experiences of personal development, the individual is able to draw ideas and information and then apply this data to helping others. The learning process is, therefore, the natural learning of life through living it and then the application of this data to try to help others.

Measures of Effectiveness and Satisfaction

For the untrained helper, the answers to this question are not complicated. The job mainly entails being a sympathetic friend, and this act of sympathetic friendship is one of the keys to the success of helping. When the emotions of friendship are felt by the lay helper, it means one has probably been successful. Other keys to experiencing oneself as effective include enthusiastic interest in the person's welfare, and the application of one's natural everyday human relation skills. The Conventional Stage helper uses her/his idiosyncratic ways of solving problems and projects these to help the other person. To a degree, what is right for oneself is right for others.

Apart from the notion of friendship, there is usually no clear definition or explanation for change. The untrained helper comes to helping with the assumption that the process works and, if done correctly, may work wonders. Having no clear criteria of success, the individual often does not focus on the success of her/his efforts in helping the other. Most lay helpers are not pessimistic about the sympathetic friendship being of significant value to others.

CHAPTER 3

Transition to Professional Training Stage

Definition of the Stage

This stage is defined by the time limit from the individual's formal decision to enter a graduate training program through the first year of a training program in a counseling or psychotherapy field.

The key element of this stage is the individual's decision to enter a therapy/counseling occupation. Central to the decision is the following question: What motivates the individual to enter this occupation? There are varied and complex reasons for this decision. The therapist/counselor is often aware of a desire to help other people. Other commonly understood motivators include a desire to study psychology and other behavioral sciences, experiencing a knowledge deficit while working in a counseling position and wanting more skills, wanting to be a licensed professional, looking for a substitute for another field such as medicine, liking people and being told that one is a natural helper, and having a religious or philosophical value base for the choice.

Interviews with experienced therapists/counselors reveal that motives are often unconscious and frequently different from what one knew consciously at this point (i.e., a complete understanding of a need to be needed is often missing). Individuals at the Transition Stage to Professional Training are generally not totally aware of the importance of personal conflicts and personal unresolved problems as motivators for entering this line of work. They may know the issues in an amorphous sense, but later be surprised by the depth and specificity of the elements. Some know that personal issues are key motivators for studying therapy/counseling and becoming involved in this occupation (e.g., one individual told us that it was the death of someone very close to her that led her into this kind of work). The entrance into therapy/counseling work because of personal suffering or after a tragedy or crisis may be understood as follows: the catalytic event may serve as a releasing factor which prompts the individual to express himself/herself occupationally in a manner consistent with Super's (1953) ideas that occupational choice is an implementation of one's self-concept and Holland's (1973) concept of personality-occupational environment congruence. Without the latent fit between self-concept and the job of therapist/counselor, the suffering or crisis by itself would not have produced this occupational direction or at least would not be sufficient to sustain the individual in this direction over a long career. Individuals recovering from chemical dependency who become CD counselors but later leave the field may be examples of a poor person-occupation fit. These individuals fit the Early Exit Stage of the Stagnation route of development (see Chapter 11).

Individuals at this stage can be quite different if they vary significantly on the following variables: age, previous counselor training or experience, impactful personal suffering or personal stress and previous professional work experience. For example, the 35-year-old former substance abuse counselor experiences this stage in profoundly different ways than does the 22-year-old new college graduate. The stage description here is more descriptive of the younger, less experienced individual who has suffered from less personal stress. The older, more experienced person will have already confronted—to some degree—many of the issues addressed here.

Central Task

The central task is the assimilation of an extensive amount of new information which the individual is acquiring primarily from graduate classes and then using this information in practicum. To master theory and apply it in practice is difficult. Anxiety about academic performance and performance in practicum usually makes this central task very stressful. One male at this stage summed up the task as, "Could I really pull it off?" A female at this stage who had done volunteer counseling said the big issue was, "How did it feel to be sitting with a person and being the professional responsible for improvement?" Experience as a new graduate student can also be exhilarating and intellectually exciting.

The individual is moving from the known of the lay helper role to the unknown of a future professional role. The loss of old known structure is occurring and, in terms of the therapist/counselor role, the beginning student is trying as quickly as possible to fill the void by learning a series of discrete, highly pragmatic therapy/counseling techniques.

Predominant Affect

Enthusiasm and insecurity are predominant affective expressions. The beginning graduate student feels very excited about learning how to help others yet very insecure about her/his own knowledge of therapy/counseling procedures and one's own ability to succeed.

Sources of Influence

Six data bases constitute significant sources of influence for the individual: theories/research, clients, professional elders (professors/supervisors/mentors/therapists), one's own personal life, one's peers/colleagues, and social/cultural environment. All sources of influence now impact the beginning student. Alone, data from just one of these sources (i.e., a fascinating article, one's first real client, a comment from a classmate about one's personality) can be very intense and stimulating for the individual. The individual's attention quickly moves from one arena to the next. One female informant said that "something grabs you and you run with it for a while." Another called it the "disease of the week phenomena." The more common experience consists of the interaction of information from all of these data bases. This information, sometimes challenging and sometimes supportive to the individual, combines to make the early graduate school days very, very intense and engrossing.

Professors and supervisors have a major impact here. They are most valued for their enthusiastic support and encouragement because beginning graduate students in therapy/counseling fields feel dependent and vulnerable. Looking back at this time, one Individuation Stage female recalled being observed by her supervisor through a one-way mirror while working with a difficult client. The supervisor's positive feedback was very important to the individual who said, "I can still remember how needed that was."

The social/cultural environment is influential because certain issues are extremely salient at the time one enters graduate school. Although the *Zeitgeist* continues to change, the new students tend to get "imprinted" by issues of the day and to be impacted for a long period by this specific social/cultural environment. Examples of salient social/cultural topics for our total sample who entered graduate school between 1950 and 1986 include (1) civil rights, (2) anxiety and meaninglessness, (3) sexism and women's issues, (4) helping skills training for paraprofessionals, (5) *Gestalt* therapy, (6) cognitive theory, (7) Holland's typology, (8) family systems, and (9) alcoholism.

As important as any influence now is the impact of, and especially support from, one's classmates. They are not just anyone—they are very credible because they have been accepted for graduate study and are preparing for professional therapy/counseling work. They are approachable, present, safe, more spontaneous, social equals and have an accurate awareness of issues. Essential questions for feedback from one's classmates are: "How do you see me?", "What are my personal strengths and weaknesses?", and "Do I have the personality to be an excellent therapist/counselor?" The answer to these questions may come informally or formally. The informal end of the continuum consists of social interaction with fellow students; the most formal method is a graduate course, offered by some training programs, which focuses on personal growth. Whether the feedback is very supportive, very critical (which usually does not occur), or mixed, it is of great importance to the individual and is taken very seriously. Admired peers are especially influential.

In one's personal life, the stress of the early graduate school experience is often buffeted by the social support of family and friends. In addition, the lives of significant others and, most of all, oneself are constantly being understood through newly acquired psychological concepts. These psychological concepts provide a lens through which many observations and experiences are viewed. Much of this personal process is strongly internal and introspective in nature.

Concerning the impact of variables such as one's personal life, the beginning student who is young and inexperienced is qualitatively different at this stage than those who are older and experienced. When addressing a draft version description of the younger student with little experience at the Transition Stage, a 40-year-old female beginning student said:

> I don't fit all parts of this stage description, perhaps part of this is a function of being older and already having had two careers which have been rewarding and engrossing for me: teacher and mother. From these I have brought the knowledge that I could work effectively with people, that I could not solve their problems for them without at least equal effort on their part. I think I also have the notion that in any field there are many theories and that I can comfortably pick and choose and combine elements from any or all of them as they seem appropriate and helpful for me. I have also done

extensive reading on the subject. I think this has served to cushion me from many things that you describe in Stage 1 and 2 of the draft copy such as feeling a need to solve all my clients' problems and not understanding my personal issues and their relation to choosing counseling as a career field.

Role and Working Style

The role is confusing because the individual is caught between the elements of her/his sympathetic friend role and the elements—essentially unclear at this point—of the professional role of therapist/counselor. There is great shifting between the old and familiar and the individual's often vague or stereotyped elements of the professional therapist/counselor role. One male said, "I was very motivated to be in the right saddle but didn't know what that saddle felt like." The person with extensive paraprofessional counseling experience is much more clear about role than the young, inexperienced person.

The first clients the individual has are often very important to the person; he/she will devote an enormous amount of energy to these clients. The commitment and positive expectations of the beginning student may compensate for the lack of experience-based ability. Yet, overinvolvement, which often accompanies the commitment of the younger beginner without experience, can also be a reality at this point.

The beginning student is frequently trying out her/his interpretation of the therapist/counselor role with friends and family. This can add a positive dimension to the person's interpersonal relationships; at other times the boundary between roles is inappropriately crossed. One female said, "It was powerful to see how you could get friends to talk while trying out being a counselor." Given the emerging occupational title of therapist/counselor, other people sometimes relate in new and unexpected ways to the person. One female said her mother invited her, the new psychology student, to give advice concerning the mother's relationship to other family members. The daughter/new graduate student was uncomfortable with this request. In essence, the trying out of the role with friends and family is a very important part of this stage. One Transition Stage female said, "What I am learning is helpful, much to the chagrin of my family."

Conceptual Ideas Used

At the Transition Stage, she/he increasingly sees as time goes on—near the end of the first year—that the work is very difficult because there is so much data available to the therapist/counselor. The client's self-report, test results and other information can easily overwhelm the beginning student. A Transition Stage female said, "It is harder to be a counselor than it first appeared." Needing to make judgments about this increasing big data base is a key fact in sensing the complexity of the job. Making sense of all this information is overwhelming. In addition, the job of the therapist/counselor is to try to improve the situation for the individual and that is difficult too. One male said, "There was too much data, too many conflicting ideas, and the techniques learned in class seemed kind of wooden and sometimes made things worse." Often there are theory-practice gulfs being experienced at this time. Usually the difficulty is in translating theory into practice. One Transition Stage female said, "At times I was so busy thinking about the instructions given in class and textbooks, I barely heard the client." Difficulty may come when theory suggests certain practice procedures which the individual has not mastered or theory may explain human behavior in a way which contradicts the individual's natural and personal way of understanding.

At this point, the therapist/counselor gradually and then more intensively begins searching for conceptual systems (other terms include models, methods, schools, approaches, frameworks) that will make sense out of all this data and help the individual to find the right direction. The beginning of this vigilant searching is a key aspect of the Transition Stage. Some absorb a variety of ideas—memorizing them and starting to try them out—without any reflection or ordering the ideas. There is a great urgency to acquire and absorb as much information as possible. They feel there is little time for this and plan to reflect later.

Learning Process

The data and insights come to the individual through a variety of methods—reading, introspection, listening, watching, practicing. Insights from work with clients are often readily sought and reacted to. The learning process at this point is often guided by a heavy concentration on a process of trial and error. There are two strong data bases used for learning. One is the information that the student gets in classes and practicum. Here the learning process is structured and dictated by the rules of schools (i.e., tests). The second process involves intensive psychologizing engaged in by the beginning student. The person applies theoretical constructs to self and significant others. Often a version of "medical student disease" occurs. One male at this stage said, "There was so much self-awareness. Every issue seemed to be mine. It got really intense for me." Since few graduate programs formally process this data, the graduate student is usually left to oneself or with peers to process this data.

Measures of Effectiveness and Satisfaction

The young, inexperienced beginning student asks herself/himself a crucial question which is asked and answered only by the new therapist/counselor in training. The question: "I may be able to do all the academic work, but am I any good at really helping people with personal problems?" The new graduate student with paraprofessional counseling experience often asks a little different question, "Am I going to get any better at doing this?" To answer these questions, the therapist/counselor in the Transition Stage usually looks very strongly for client improvement and acknowledgment of this improvement by the client to the therapist/counselor. This information is sought after very eagerly by the therapist/counselor to validate her/his work. Client feedback is thought of as most valuable in part because the client directly experiences the helping attempts of the beginning student. The beginning student directly experiences—verbally and nonverbally—the client's reactions. Effectiveness is measured by the visible and dramatic improvement of the client because the beginner has high expectations for change in a short period of time. If the client gets better, the therapist/counselor is confident of self. Satisfaction comes from client improvement and is tied directly to it. Indications of appreciation from the client—verbal, notes, gifts—are greatly appreciated and sometimes subtly sought. Lack of improvement and lack of acknowledgment of the helpful ways of the therapist/counselor are stressful for the beginner. Direct client hostility toward the therapist/counselor is experienced as very aversive.

The beginning student feels very vulnerable concerning her/his ability to help people in distress. A combination of lack of experience, lack of confidence, high expectation for the efficacy of therapy/counseling which is expressed through expecting quick client improvement provides for likely disappointment. One Transition Stage male said, "If I don't have success I get disillusioned with myself." Another beginner said that her first client experience was such a disaster that she decided right then to become a researcher. A Transition Stage female said, "I have a tendency to measure my success by the success clients are having, that can get you down."

Many beginners constantly monitor themselves to see how they are doing compared with others in the Transition Stage. This comparison process often occurs naturally in the first practicum course of a training program where the individual and her/his peers are constantly interacting. There is a great deal of anxiety about performance and competence at this phase; the anxiety seems to reduce itself if the therapist/counselor feels like she/he is doing a good job as measured by client acknowledgment of one's helpfulness, by supervisor support or by doing as well as one's classmates. In fact, there is much confusion about the effectiveness factors because there seems to be many equally relevant parts that can be thought of as keys to success.

CHAPTER 4

Imitation of Experts Stage

Definition of the Stage

The modal individual is now in the second or third year of graduate school studying counseling and psychotherapy and can be considered an intermediate student in the field. Others may have completed the Masters degree and are now newly employed in the field.

The answers to the questions are becoming more complex, and the central reason for this is because the individual is seeing human behavior generally in a more complex manner. The intermediate student is beginning to understand individual differences and to differentiate oneself from other people on a whole variety of variables. This process is instrumental in seeing the therapy/counseling process as complex and difficult.

Central Task

The central task and challenge of this stage is to maintain an openness to information and theory at a meta level while also engaging in the "closing off" process of selecting out therapy/counseling theories and techniques to use.

The practitioner at this stage focuses on becoming competent in conducting counseling and therapy like experts using acknowledged conceptual systems (schools, methods, approaches). Since completing this task in actuality takes years of effort, the goal from the person's perspective is to simplify the challenge so that some success is possible. As a necessary shortcut the person often first searches for experts (persons and/or conceptual systems) to model. Modeling can be differentiated along a continuum from imitation, which is mechanical repeating, to identification, which is internalization of the characteristics of the model. At this level the modeling process may best be described as imitation although internalization of attitudes and behaviors certainly occurs. Said a male at this stage, "I wanted to absorb from counselors I observed." The person at this point wants to know how experts act, think, and feel in clinical practice and usually prefers to observe models as the way to acquire this information. A female intermediate student was in therapy both to learn about herself and to learn about being a therapist through observation of her therapist. She described the value of her group therapy as a way to learn to be a therapist. There she could watch two therapists with their own styles working with a variety of other group members. She said it was invaluable as a learning experience.

Interacting closely with a dogmatically oriented senior therapist/counselor (i.e., professor or supervisor) may quicken the modeling process. However, it also impedes the opportunity to maintain an openness to information and theory at a meta level. The individual's epistemological search is, therefore, damaged for the benefit of short-term gains.

Predominant Affect

Initial bewilderment leads to later calm and temporary security if the central task of imitation is mastered. The bewilderment relates to the increasing realization that the simplicity and naturalness of the sympathetic friend role ("use common sense and be a friend") is not enough. The individual is frustrated by her/his inability to grasp all the essentials. The bewilderment can also relate to trying to master many theories or master a variety of other tasks. Yet, being competent at alternatives is not a reality either. For the intermediate student the work seems to be getting increasingly chaotic and complex. The simplicity of sympathetic friendship is gone, the less difficult aspects of the work (i.e., "How do you keep talking for a whole hour?") are not fully mastered and the change process seems quite elaborate and unclear. In addition, client problems requiring therapist/counselor responses other than continual emotional support may still be threatening to the student. This includes specific problems needing specific solutions (e.g., panic attacks, career indecision, assessment of alcoholism, suicidal prevention steps). The individual may be able to identify some of the problem and give some support but then gets lost. A male at this stage said, "I've learned that the basic stuff—active listening, support—suffices at many times and this really helps. But it is also true that there is so much to know about specifics. I have to learn but don't have time!" A lifesaver for the intermediate student is the strong emerging utilization of fairly easily mastered conceptual systems (models, methods, schools, approaches, frameworks) which the student works hard to master and apply to all clients. This utilization may lead to later disillusionment, but now it gives one a sense of calm.

We differentiate between developmental and nondevelopmental methods of reducing complexity at this point. The developmental position has an active, searching, exploratory, trying-out quality. It is part of an overall method, where the goal is to arrive at a congruent/integrated position. The non-developmental position, however, has a defensive, experience-limiting, anxiety-reducing quality. It is not a part of an overall developmental scheme. In the extreme form, we may say its aim is short-term survival. This process is similar to the foreclosure option in identity formation described by Marcia (1966). This shutting off is a conceptual shortcircuiting of the possibly intense bewilderment.

These strategies, whether developmental or nondevelopmental in nature, tend to reduce possibly intense feelings of chaos and incompetence leaving only a milder form of bewilderment. Usually the use of modeling at this stage will provide the student with a direction and structure. Eventually this gives the student a sense of calm and temporary security.

Sources of Influence

As in the past, there are six different sources of influence that the individual is using at this point in therapy/counseling work: theories and research that is read and presented in classes, direct and indirect feedback from clients, feedback and modeling from professional elders (professors/supervisors/mentors/therapists), one's own life experiences (perhaps one's experiences as a therapy/counseling client), one's peers/colleagues, and the social/cultural environment.

Through the process of acquisition, application and validation, the Imitation Stage individual truly learns. This occurs through a complex interaction between information from the six different sources of influence. In contrast to what is generally thought about individuals reading the research and the theories and then directly applying them, it seems that the application of the six data bases is as follows: the individual reads about, is exposed to, or observes a conceptual idea or framework, perhaps from a professor or supervisor, and talks about it with peers. He/she then applies that conceptual idea or framework and the ideas from that viewpoint to clients, one's own life and the lives of one's friends and family. If the conceptual idea or framework makes sense in the application to people's lives, then one becomes more committed to it. This application of the theory and research to peoples' lives is the *key* validation experience. This method is consistent with Howard's (1986) concept of private research as a scientific method used by practitioners. One female at this stage, reacting to this section of the draft paper, said,

> I'm putting together a jigsaw puzzle. First I pick up a piece to see how it fits with another. I turn it around to try and get it to fit. I try lots of different combinations. If a piece fits, I keep it and it becomes a natural part of the puzzle. If it doesn't fit, I keep trying to find a place for it. Eventually, with no place, it gets dropped.

If the theoretical ideas are not validated, they tend to gradually lose acceptance and use by the therapist/counselor. However, if a particular conceptual idea or framework is promulgated within the culture of the graduate program or practitioner agency, the individual will often persist with this approach at this point irrespective of disconfirming personal data.

The student may urgently search for viable models who can be actively imitated. Supervisors are very important because they interact so closely with the student in the work setting, they are viable models in doing the work, and they give academic evaluations of the student's performance. Supervisors have direct, powerful impact when they give feedback to the individual (Rønnestad, 1985). For example, negative evaluations in practicum will have a big effect and may produce a crisis period for the student. She/he may search all alternatives within the field or move away from therapy/counseling work. The movement out of therapy/counseling work may be lateral into research, career advising, teaching, administration or some other role. The negative feedback may aid the student not fit for this kind of work to leave the field. However, many qualified therapists/counselors experience frustration and disappointment at this phase because positive feedback is so important. Feedback about clinical work from all three sources—clients, supervisors, peers—is important. The desire to leave can be counterbalanced with positive client experiences, supervisor support and peer encouragement.

Understanding oneself also continues as a thrust. The person at this stage continues a very intense process of psychologizing about human life. Central in this process is the introspection about self. In an intense and pervasive fashion, the individual at this stage experiences strong emotions and compelling conceptualizations about one's past and present life. There is an intensive and private quality to this work. From this introspective and internal work comes a lava flow of new information which serves to strongly influence the individual's development. The person may ask, "What motivates me to be in this occupation?" Yet, because the individual is so deeply involved in academic survival and socialization into the field, questioning one's motivation seems to take less of a center stage than the desire to get through all the mazes of required experience, academic work and evaluations. It is almost too difficult and painful to ask the harder questions like "Why do I want this?" when the evaluations of others and meeting their requirements seem so central. The verbalized reasons often contain elements of altruism, interest in the behavioral sciences and liking to be with people and help them.

The individual's assessment of her/his graduate program is usually most negative at this stage. The assessment contrasts sharply with the anticipation that accompanied one's entrance into the program and the appreciation that may be felt in the years long after the graduate degree. There may be a reality base for this criticism because graduate programs and individual faculty members are often less than adequate. However, the criticism appears to also have a developmental base. Now, disappointment and anger are usually felt and then expressed—most often to the individual's classmates and friends. The disappointment is directed toward the overall program, the required courses and lack of electives, the faculty members and the politics of academic survival.

The individual, at this point, is intensively focused on understanding and judging, as psychological persons, those in authority (i.e., faculty members and supervisors). These individuals may be judged as inadequate on measures of psychological competence or interpersonal relationship skills. Personal conflicts between these senior members of the profession hold a magnetic type focus for the attention of the individual and her/his classmates. Since the field focuses on such a personal topic—human psychology, it is perhaps not surprising that these newer members of the profession are very interested in how senior members of the profession navigate personal relationships. Often the person at this stage makes extreme judgments; he/she is very disappointed by or very positive about the personal human qualities of professional elders.

Imitation of Experts Stage

The Imitation Stage individual's anger and disappointment seem to have various sources. There is a component of program and people (faculty members and supervisors) inadequacy and mediocrity. An additional factor for some is the emerging contrast between very high expectations before entering the graduate program and an emerging realization that these expectations are very different than reality. Third, the individual must now function as a practitioner in practicum and often feels unable to meet this challenge. In addition, supervisors and faculty members have failed to provide all the ingredients to help the student feel adequate as a practitioner. The student's urgency for more does not seem to be understood or responded to by his/her seniors. These factors lead, for many, to frustration and anger. One female said, "I felt a whole lot of anger about not being prepared." Only in later stages may the individual look back and understand that the intense negative feelings may have been caused in part by the strong demands for practicum performance at this point. Said one more experienced sample subject about criticism at this stage, "The intensity of the anger comes from the next set of challenges. The person must perform at a consistent level and often feels unprepared."

Role and Working Style

The role of the therapist/counselor is expanding, although the actual complexity of the role is not understood until years later. Now the person is embarrassed about early definitions of role that the therapist/counselor is only a sympathetic friend or a "shoulder to weep on." These ideas seem to be naive notions compared with newer ideas suggested in graduate school. Yet, some of the old still seem to fit because empathy and other similar ideas are thought to be appropriate descriptions for the role of the therapist/counselor.

The certainty of the beginning has given way to uncertainty about role. Now, there is uncertainty as well as trial and error. Friendship and skills plus strategies seem to be emerging role components. The individual is asking: If I am not to be a sympathetic friend, what am I to be? What should I do? Should I be more active? Should I give answers? There are many, many questions about role at this point. Yet, a truly intense crisis about role is usually avoided because the intermediate student therapist/counselor does not allow herself/himself to experience disabling complexity. This may be done by sticking with a few ideas/procedures/techniques and foreclosing on any other data.

Conceptual Ideas Used

The individual is increasingly becoming aware of the complexity of human nature and the change process. A female at this stage said, "I see more than I used to and am looking for more parts of the professional role. I'm now trying to find ways to get to the underlying problems and, therefore, long-term solutions rather than a short-lived quick fix of feeling better because of counselor support." The searching for a way to simplify the complexity through the use of conceptual systems, either explicit or implicit, becomes a major task involving vigilance and preoccupation.

Whether a person adopts a particular conceptual system seems to depend on a number of specific factors. A major factor is the conceptual system of professional elders (professors, supervisors, mentors, therapists) interacting with the individual at this stage. The student is very trusting of those who seem to know how to do therapy/counseling and believes that these knowledgeable individuals—such as professors and supervisors—will teach "good things" and the "right way." A second factor concerns the conceptual systems used at the practicum site or work setting where the individual may be working as a practicum student. A third factor is the *Zeitgeist* of the times regarding the popular issues in that location and the ideas thought of as most important. Within the broader *Zeitgeist* there usually is a category of problem areas (e.g., shame, test anxiety, cognitive impairment, codependency, intimacy) or populations of individuals (e.g., depressed adolescents, violent adult males, individuals from other cultures, adult children of alcoholics) that is receiving a great deal of publicity at the time the person is at this stage.

The great attraction of conceptual systems, at a time when the work seems increasingly complex, is that the ideas help the individual make sense of what to do: what to look for, how to evaluate the information received, how to process that information and what steps the therapist/counselor should take next to make the situation better. Conceptual ideas are often easily learned because it is such an intense "teachable moment."

There seem to be four alternative routes regarding the incorporation of a conceptual system:

1. A few individuals never develop one. This we call *laissez faire*. For these individuals, older notions of common sense and one's personal epistemology coexist with a variety of ideas from theory/research, clients, supervisors, peers and one's personal life.

Imitation of Experts Stage

2. Some combine elements and concepts from different conceptual systems.
3. Some choose a predominant conceptual system but also include other systems that for them have a subordinate position. This can become an implicit conceptual system in which the combining is done more intuitively than explicitly.
4. A fourth group focuses on intensively learning one method and excludes all other viewpoints.

Regardless of the route chosen, a conceptual map of some kind is developed. The conceptual map provides answers to three basic questions: What is normal and abnormal human development? What causes normal and abnormal human development? What reduces problematic behavior, emotions, and thinking? The student learns to take the continual flow of complex data from the client and push it into the evolving conceptual funnel.

Examples of 1 and 2: Focus on responsible behavior (Reality); reflect empathic (Rogers/Carkhuff); recognize interlocking triangles (Bowen); teach what normal is (Adult Children of Alcoholics); look for faulty cognition (RET/Cognitive).

The complex data of the phenomenological world of the individual/couple/family/group

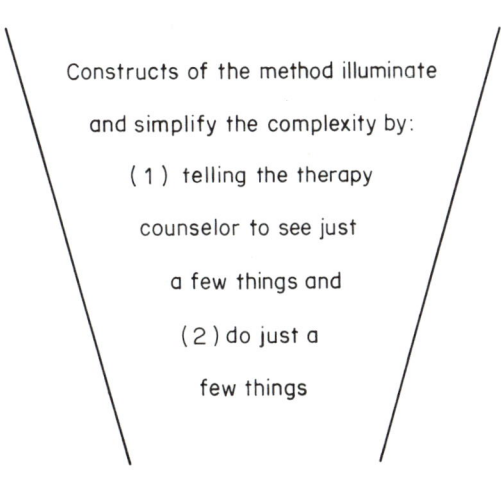

Constructs of the method illuminate and simplify the complexity by:
(1) telling the therapy counselor to see just a few things and
(2) do just a few things

Figure 1. The conceptual funnel

The therapist/counselor rapidly masters some conceptual ideas and approaches counseling with renewed self-confidence. At this point, many client problems are molded to fit into the funnel of this chosen method. One male study subject reflected on earlier substance abuse counselor training and said, "At my drug abuse practicum, I used one way with everyone." The therapist/counselor feels optimistic about the ideas, praises the method's founder(s), and believes the conceptual ideas significantly reduce human suffering.

Complex models are typically avoided because they demand the opposite of what the person desperately needs—a system which can be quickly mastered and gives one confidence to go ahead. Since consumers of workshops are often novices, workshops which focus on new, single ideas (i.e., codependency or shame) tend to be much more successful in terms of enrollment and profit than workshops which focus on complexity or interaction of various concepts (i.e., an integration of behavior, emotions and thinking approaches).

How deeply the individual at the Imitation of Experts Stage enters into the method and becomes a "true believer" (Hoffer, 1951) depends on the environmental press surrounding the individual within the training program, her/his field placement, the approach of a supervisor or faculty member and the student's assessment of that faculty member or supervisor's competence, personal characteristics of the student. One Imitation of Experts male said:

> Early on I was trained in a particular model and when people came in I tried to fit them in. I quickly found out it did not work. I became disenchanted and began to look around. I grasped at another approach and felt more in control. I felt I was doing something here. I was earning my pay.

Even though the model may be fairly simple there is a great deal to learn. The student *does not* first focus on a critique of the efficacy of models. Rather, the focus is on mastery. Therefore, she/he concentrates on practicing. This must come before making judgments about the utility of approaches. One study subject working in a psychiatric unit said, "Patients were my workshop. I would practice theories on them." Another said the lack of focus on critiquing a model is because, "You don't want to shoot it down because you need something to hang onto."

Learning Process

Imitation of international, national, and local experts and admired peers and trying to model their ways is the essential learning method at this point. The concern is not with one's own uniqueness and the expression of this uniqueness. The opposite is more true—the student wants as much as possible to perform like an international expert (i.e., Freud, Rogers, Frankel) or a local expert (i.e., one's supervisor in practicum). There is trust in these experts and a strong desire to learn what they do and to use their methods. Classroom materials used to teach methods can have a major impact if they present easily understood single method approaches applicable to many client problems. The classic *Three Approaches to Psychotherapy* films with Rogers, Perls, and Ellis and edited by Shostrom (1965) are an excellent example of this.

It should be emphasized that the student is usually not passively modeling the complete behavior of any one expert. Rather, the student actively chooses parts of the behavior, appearance, style and viewpoint of various experts to copy. Some individuals use models in a reverse way by rejecting elements of the models' behavior and choosing to operate in another, perhaps opposite, way. Another method is to accept some elements of one model's behavior and to reject elements of another, thereby combining modeled elements in a unique personalized way. People who are clients in therapy/counseling at this point are typically using their own therapist/counselor as a potent model. One Imitation of Experts female said, "I learned more about therapy when I was in therapy."

The age of eclecticism makes the modeling more difficult. When the student is trying to find a model to copy in order to reduce the complexity, the choosing of a model by itself becomes complex. This kind of freedom can bring confusion. Therefore, the search for a solution can become another version of the problem of trying to reduce the complexity.

As previously stated earlier in this section, modeling can be differentiated along a continuum from imitation, which is mechanical repetition, to identification, which is internalization of the characteristics of the model. Identification learning presupposes high intensity and long duration. Modeling one's own therapist/counselor can be a rich experience because the interpersonal encounter provides both imitation and identification components.

Age and experience seem to operate in two ways. Older and more experienced intermediate students may be able to move beyond imitation more quickly. They also seem more able to resist the enculturation of modeling forces when models do not fit with the student's version and standards of competence.

Measures of Effectiveness and Satisfaction

With increased experience, the therapist/counselor is less dependent on constant positive feedback from clients to maintain one's sense of occupational self-esteem. No longer do statements such as the following affect the counselor as they would the beginner: "I'm sorry I can't come to counseling tonight. I have too much on my mind." That message from a client would be especially unsettling to beginning students who typically take those reactions very personally. The intermediate student is better able to judge the meaning of such communication and can deal with it more appropriately. The person is developing a more elaborate way of understanding the change process in therapy/counseling and often developing more realistic expectations as to how much can be accomplished, at what pace, in what amount of time. In the future, small humiliations will often greatly reduce the grandiosity of believing that one can make powerful changes in others' lives. The Imitation of Experts individual is gradually feeling less responsible for clients' emotional health. Yet, this change is slow and fluctuates greatly. One person described the evolution for herself as "Intellectually I know that I am not totally responsible, but emotionally I feel that it is up to me to make the client's life better."

Feedback from clients/supervisors/classmates is still of great importance. For example, the individual may not need to see client change immediately. However, if improvement occurs later than anticipated, the individual at this stage is often distressed, a bit unsure of self and confused about what to do next.

The central attributes of the modeled method dictate the central ingredient of effectiveness factors. It may be so that there is a natural congruence between one's own personality characteristics and ideal self-concept and the demands of the modeled system/approach. The student may choose models that have similarities with perception of self. Consequently, perception of effective factors reflect ideal self-attributes and one's own personality characteristics. There may thus be a strong projective component when the student is determining what constitutes effective factors. For example, one Imitation of Experts person characterized himself as world-travelled and world-wise. Later he cited the necessity of the counselor having varied interest and world sophistication as key elements in success. Another Imitation of Experts subject characterized herself as a good listener and as understanding. She later emphasized these elements in her "good therapist" description.

CHAPTER 5

Conditional Autonomy Stage

Definition of the Stage

The modal individual is a full-time intern at the end of the training program. The individual is under active supervision in an agency, college counseling center, hospital, or similar facility dedicated to training. In addition to the individual there are usually other interns and senior staff members at the facility.

Central Task

The central task is to be able to function at an established, professional level. This is the most intense period of training as a therapy/counseling practitioner. This process entails a concentrated period of socialization/enculturation into the field. One's level of competence is now judged according to three reference groups: experienced practitioners in the field, other interns, and less experienced practicum students. Earlier, experienced practitioners were used as models with the focus on acquiring their expertise through direct observation and indirect means such as interaction at staff meetings. Now the focus is on using the skill level of experienced practitioners as the criteria for judging one's own competence. Interns also actively compare themselves to other interns and expect to function at a higher professional level than practicum students. The intern must demonstrate an expertise equal to the demands and expectations of the training program with the end goal being to receive a graduate degree. This means, in large part, satisfying supervisors.

Predominant Affect

The predominant affect is variable confidence. The individual is at times very confident of oneself and feels highly competent. The confidence is a direct product of increased skills as a result of experience. At other times the person feels much less confident. The lack of confidence seems to come from two sources. One is the internal sense of not being fully able to master the various tasks. Two, there are many individuals and external standards to satisfy. At times the individual is not sure whether he or she is able to meet the expectations of these other people or the agency. For example, a female intern said, "There weren't many times I felt highly competent. I questioned, am I in the right place, is this what I should do?"

Conversely, increased confidence was expressed by three females at this stage who said: "I have gone from being petrified to being comfortable", "Now I'm more self-assured, more firm and less chameleonlike, more assertive and direct without being directive and less afraid. It used to be that I was terrified before sessions", and "I'm less afraid of losing patients than in the past."

The intern expects and demands feedback from her/his supervisors. There is a strong need for confirmation/validation. Although the intern does have increased professional self-confidence compared with earlier stages, he/she is still vulnerable and insecure and therefore actively enlists supervisor reactions to her/his work. If this is not provided, supervision is perceived to be inadequate. Non-confirming supervision experiences are powerful at this level. An individual at the later stages, years removed from the internship, often remembers with distress and anger the negative supervision experiences he/she had as an intern. Others looking back are very positive. One female study subject reflected back and said: "I always got what I needed to do, to do what I needed to do."

Sources of Influence

Professional elders, and especially supervisors, exert influence at this stage. The intern is usually in a subservient position in a power relationship with supervisors. The consequence is that the intern has considerable external dependency. The dependency creates an expectation of supervisor expertise. When this expectancy is not met there is often disappointment.

Reflecting back on her internship a female said, "I wanted to believe that supervisors knew more than I did. It was disappointing to discover that they didn't. It reminded me of an earlier realization that ministers make mistakes." At the same time, the intern has developed a comprehensive experience and theoretical base for professional functioning. Consequently, there is often a great deal of ambivalence about supervisors because the intern wants to be on his or her own and yet still needs to meet the expectations of others. The duality of dependency and professional competency often creates an intense tension and constant self-evaluation during the internship because the day-to-day work involves close work with supervisors who will make assessments of the individual's competence at the senior trainee level.

Although supervisors are the most powerful source of influence at this stage, this influence can be moderated by a number of factors such as the intern's perception of the supervisor's competence, the intern's peer and senior level support system, the intern's age and the intern's experience base.

Working in a setting with other interns provides a second strong source of influence. As in previous stages, peers are an important resource for the individual; they are on the same "wavelength" in terms of experience and status and are usually very trustworthy. These factors make other interns a very strong source of influence.

Supervision of beginning practicum students can also be a powerful source of influence for the intern. One female, reflecting on her internship, said: "It was a concrete realization of what I had learned. It was really valuable. The contrast between them and me helped me see my own style and how far I had come in my development."

Personal life continues as a source of influence for the Conditional Autonomy individual. One common aspect of this is the intern's own psychotherapy/counseling. In addition to using one's own therapist/counselor as a model of how to do the work, the person at this stage is often wrestling with personal issues that have been brought to her/his consciousness during earlier intensive training experiences. The intensive psychological course work, the active discussions with classmates, the stimulation of personal issues brought about by working with clients, and supervision experiences have all been sources that have stimulated personal exploration. For example, one male at this stage said, "Counselor training made me powerfully aware of things I was blissfully unaware of before."

The catalyst for personal psychotherapy is usually the individual's recognition of the impact of personal issues on her/his professional work. For example, one male intern said, "I did not like emotions, and this made it easy for me to develop technique-oriented approaches. But after participating in group therapy, I turned my focus more to the affective." Intern level individuals in our study mentioned the following personal events, as well as many others, as influential: being a parent, living alone, marrying a therapist, having a baby, losing a job.

Sometimes personal life is examined in a circumscribed manner. Some interns are very goal-directed and the examination of personal life is directed, like other elements of the person's life, toward being a good intern and passing the internship hurdle. Since performing professionally is such an important part of the internship, an unincumbered self-examination is often not done at this point.

To the intern, theories and research in the broad academic sense are of diminished interest but specific therapy/counseling issues are of heightened interest. One intern level person summed up the point when she said, "Client issues define what I read about and explore in the literature." If the intern feels very unprepared for a specific client issue (i.e., depression), which he/she must work with as an intern, much energy will go toward reading, discussing, and attending workshops on this topic. A female at this stage said, "I stopped reading textbooks and started reading self-help books. I thought the faculty in my department would die if they found out." The focus is on quickly learning the important material. Accompanying this expenditure of energy may be anger directed toward the training program for not preparing the intern on this topic.

Clients continue to be a very strong source of influence. They are as important as any other source. Their reactions to the intern are very important for the intern's sense of confidence and as a source of learning.

Role and Working Style

At this stage, the Conditional Autonomy individual is still trying to do things the right way and, in fact, is often feeling pressure to do things more right than ever before. The shedding of parts of the conforming professional role will come later. For example, usually it is only later that the person is able to shed the total seriousness that is felt here and use one's natural playfulness and sense of humor in counseling/psychotherapy. The intern usually acts in a conservative, cautious and thorough fashion. Interns can be described in role and working style as serious, strident, urgent and appropriate. Compared with oneself twenty years later, the intern is typically not relaxed, risk-taking and spontaneous. A female reflecting back said, "As an intern I had the idea of this counselor role I had to play. Later it was a revelation when I found out I could be myself." Often the intern is excessively professionally conforming and most able to be autonomous in the sense of using the established professional and conventional knowledge base when working with clients.

The individual at this stage tends to feel she/he should be able to help most clients. The internalized high standards for professional functioning develop a tendency towards excessive and misunderstood responsibility. A female at the Conditional Autonomy stage said, "Every single request for consultation I wanted to do. I wanted to learn things and to prove to the director of training that I could do the job." The intern finds it extremely difficult to terminate or refer a client because of one's own inadequacies. As one male at this stage said, "I thought I could and should help everybody." Even more difficult for the person at this stage is behavior which protects oneself appropriately by, for example, refusing to work with poorly motivated clients. At this stage, the therapist/counselor still easily assumes too much responsibility for client progress. A male intern said, "I do a good job of letting myself feel responsible for everything." There has been some movement since the earlier stages. A male intern said, "Now I'm less intense, less responsible for solutions, trust my intuition more and have better clinical judgment."

It may or may not be difficult for the individual to separate out friendship roles and counselor roles when with friends, acquaintances and family. Sometimes the individual acts as a counselor because of personal wishes or the request of others in one's personal life. The intern may discover that this is a problem area. The discovery often happens when attempts to counsel relatives fail. The intern level individual may be still learning to be supportive and helpful as a friend while reducing and eliminating the interpretations and recommendations of the therapist/counselor role. Two individuals at this stage reflected on this issue when they said, "I found out that I can't counsel relatives, need to dissociate," and, "Being psychologically minded has helped raise issues but I've run into trouble trying to be a therapist to everyone." Another boundary issue is the task of being intensively involved with a client and then severing that professional intimacy on termination. One female intern in the

Conditional Autonomy Stage

sample discussed this, "Termination is difficult for me. Clients don't have much of an idea of the impact they make on my life."

Conceptual Ideas Used

The conceptual system often involves refinement of modeling from the Imitation of Expert Stage and extending beyond it. The individual is often involved in shaping one's own conceptual system; defining, expanding, limiting, changing some of the modeling that has occurred up to this stage.

Individuals at this stage are taking in new ways of conceptualizing client dynamics and methods of change. The intern is gradually more able to differentiate important from unimportant data and to hierarchically order data. Manifestations of this are an increased ability to write shorter case note summaries and greater ease in selecting issues/problems to discuss in supervision. For example, a female intern found, "As I got more confident I realized that I didn't have to remember every detail. The point of notes was not to get everything down but to be able to connect with the client."

One's conceptual system is often stretched by difficult cases. Individuals at this stage mentioned the following client behaviors as difficult for them: intense anger, severe pathology such as schizophrenia and personality disorders, sexual abuse, boredom and apathy, strong depression and suicidal behavior.

Learning Process

A major aspect of the learning process is the continual use of modeling, because it is perceived as an excellent method to remove the mystery of counseling and therapy practice. Modeling is defined broadly by us to include activities such as watching supervisors and professional staff work, hearing how supervisors and professional staff conceptualize cases, the observation of the professional behavior of supervisors and professional staff. Here there is a refined use of modeling. Interns have already gone through several acquisition, application, validation sequences with models and are now actively selecting and rejecting model components. "The extreme trust I had in experienced counselors as people to copy is not so true now because I have seen so many different styles," said one female intern. From supervisors, a male intern said, "I take what I like." A female said as an intern that, "One's own counseling exerts a powerful influence, there's always the, 'What would my therapist do in this situation?' to fall back on." Another female intern said of models, "My God, I don't want to be like that."

Often therapists/counselors in training are frustrated by the lack of opportunities to observe senior practitioners work. One female intern said, "I wanted more opportunities to watch experienced practitioners at work." Another female intern said, "I had very little opportunity to observe experienced practitioners—even after repeated requests of a supervisor. The only model of an experienced person I had was the Gloria films. Supervisors and experienced people were unwilling to demonstrate skills." The lack of models tends to make one's own therapist/counselor important as a source of modeling information.

In the learning process, there is an increased focus on how the intern's personality influences the professional work. A female at this stage said, "Supervisors are important to me both as role models and in helping me identify how my personality influences my work both as a resource and as a hindrance." Active experimentation and reflection form another important learning process. There is a trying things out, accepting them, rejecting them focus. One male intern said, "For me this (active experimentation) applies both to experimenting with myself (i.e., deepening my affective reflections) and with techniques (making my interventions on the spot by acting on hunches)." Methods and techniques that seem to work are reinforced by positive responses or positive movement of clients and used again.

Measures of Effectiveness and Satisfaction

There is a shift away from assessing improvement on the basis of client statements only, towards relying increasingly on more subtle and nuanced ways of assessing change. This is the beginning of a process that continues for many years. For example, a post-intern commented,

> When I was an intern I felt that I was to be in control and powerful. That made me feel responsible. Later it was different. My anxiety went down, I gave up some of the control and I felt less responsible. That helped me see client improvement or lack of improvement as depending on more than me.

The supervisor plays an important role in this broader assessment of client development. Effectiveness is measured externally through good supervisor evaluations. Good evaluations means that the person has been effective and will be certified as having succeeded during the internship. "I felt successful if the supervisor assessed me as doing the appropriate things rather than just feeling successful if the client said he had improved," said one female intern. Critical evaluations are very impactful and can be very stressful.

Compared with earlier stages, the Intern experiences the "buffer effect" of many clients. In the past, the student had a limited number of clients and, therefore, felt pressure to be successful with each one. Now, at this level, the intern is usually busy with many clients, and has less of a need to be successful with each one to feel that he/she is successful.

Interns are very aware of shifts in their way of thinking about success. Here are some examples:

Male intern:	"Since the beginning I saw PhDs who couldn't help people. So, I saw myself as no worse."
Female intern:	"I didn't know what to look for at first. Now, the measure for me is client movement."
Male intern:	"My evaluation of me is tied to my mood. Although I am becoming more accepting, still at times my ego gets hooked because I'm intent on the client succeeding and if not, there is self-doubt. Guess that I'm still hyper more than I would like to be."
Female intern:	"Formerly success was if they liked me, talked a lot, returned. Now it is more if some kind of changes occurred."
Female intern:	"I'm used to being at the top of rating scales. It was hard at first not to be defensive and take it hard. I did some reframing and said I won't be an excellent therapist yet because I am not very experienced."

CHAPTER 6

Exploration Stage

Definition of the Stage

At this point, the modal individual has recently received a graduate degree and then escaped from the external control of the faculty and supervisors of the program. A wide variety of professional and personal experiences have already occurred, and the individual is developing a professional experience base. Yet, many new challenges are currently being experienced and many lie in the future. Full credentialing and licensure may still be years ahead.

Central Task

The central task is exploration beyond what the individual has successfully developed. The exploration is for self by self with self as director. Now, instead of working to be a carbon copy of a master or a composite of masters, the individual must explore beyond imitation. This may involve giving up a comforting dependency and must, of necessity, involve shedding some aspects of what has been learned—perhaps after intense effort and achievement—while continuing to add new assumptions, concepts and techniques. The catalyst, for exploration, is an awareness—developed suddenly or slowly—that the complexities of the work tasks demand new learning. Lack of client success is the key element of this new awareness. The individual is often surprised and very disheartened by this awareness. Implicitly, the individual often believed that the formal training of the past would lead to more of a sense of adequacy than is now being experienced. The end product of this stage is a full readiness for the beginning of an original style.

At this point there is a sense of freedom. For the first time the person is free of external constraints (e.g., practicum, internship, supervisor evaluations, oral and written exams, the ethos of the training program). At this point, there is also a sense of inadequacy which may be surprising. For the first time, the individual can and must decide how to proceed in addressing this awareness of inadequacy. One male at this stage said, "I have a new realization that the therapy model I was taught is inadequate for me. For me, letting go of the internship feels like letting go of those people who knew what to do." Another male at this stage described it this way:

> I didn't anticipate all of this. I was concerned all the time that things wouldn't work if I didn't finish. I used to think that my doubts about me and my despair would go away with the degree. At least on one level I thought this. Now people look at me, call me doctor and want more and expect more. But what am I going after? It is a disorienting process because I don't know anymore now except that there are more expectations. It is great to be done but what do I really want to be? Where do I really want to go? I didn't expect the formal training would lead to feeling adequate until I felt inadequate and then realized how much I expected to know by now. My professional training was over and I lacked so much.

Another male reflected back to this stage and said, "I felt like it was only me going through the disillusionment with what I didn't know. Once I started talking with colleagues, I found that there were others in the same place. Then I didn't feel quite as alone."

This stage is divided into two substages, confirmation and disillusionment. In the confirmation substage the individual works very hard to confirm the validity of one's recently completed graduate training. Confirmation reflects pride in completion, being an official professional, perhaps being called Dr, being a graduate of a well-respected program. After graduating, the individual usually feels proud of the graduate education he/she completed even if, at times, the person was also very critical of it. There is a desire to test out the quality of the program and hopefully defend it. The validity and meaning of one's education is at stake, a very serious issue for the person.

At the disillusionment substage there is more of a focus on disappointments. The graduate training was not in fact as adequate as one hoped. Unfortunately, it seems that there is still more to add and more to discard. A female subject two years beyond graduate school said, "It was unduly optimistic to believe that graduate school fully prepared me. Instead, it provided a basic knowledge and tools for acquiring more knowledge and skill. It has taken a few years to appreciate this gradual shift in my expectations."

During this stage, there occurs a process which may be called "personal anchoring," because the new professional therapist/counselor anchors theoretical/conceptual structures to one's own value base. The therapist/counselor, through reflection, decides for oneself on the important theoretical/conceptual structures. These structures which emerge have a quality of being indisputably true. These structures we call anchors. This process entails making explicit the implicit assumptions of how one understands the professional world. It also influences later theoretical and conceptual choices. Now, exploration involves highly individualized attention to both the personal domain and the theoretical domain.

There often is strong interest in genuinely effective techniques and the theory behind the techniques, an interest which is highly self-directed. The technique and theoretical search involves a thoroughness and a personally based curiosity.

Predominant Affect

Confidence and anxiety are predominant affective reactions. Confidence comes from increased experience and skill in many of the elements of the role, i.e., pacing oneself through an hour interview. Confidence provides the security for exploration beyond the known.

In spite of increased confidence that is a direct result of increased competence, the individual usually at this stage also experiences anxiety. The anxiety comes from realizing that the individual cannot adequately address the complexity of the work tasks. When trying out what one has been taught, clients have not always benefited to the degree one expected and the therapist/counselor must move on and develop more with oneself as director of the search. A female reflecting back to this stage said, "Having less guidance from professors and supervisors was scary." A male said, "People weren't protecting you from taking on too much anymore." The individual also encounters characteristics of the work role that are anxiety provoking. Examples here include being forced to perform tasks that one feels unprepared to do, being unable to do tasks that one was prepared for and wanted to do, and becoming disappointed with colleagues. Said one female at this stage, "Perhaps my greatest reaction was a 'loss of innocence.' I found some coworkers to be an enormous disillusionment and disappointment. Conversely, it was other colleagues who were supportive and important."

Anger, turmoil, disillusionment, uncertainty and anxiety are common affective reactions to this realization. It seemed worse to feel incompetent after finishing graduate school than before. Then it felt normal, after school it feels distressing in part because it is unexpected. The confusion and aloneness now often produces an acute sense of anxious loneliness. One male therapist looked back at this time and said, "There were days when everything I touched turned into horseshit. Whatever made me think I could do it or that it worked, it was a sham, people were paying me to make money off their pain." The anxious loneliness can be reduced through peer support. One female said, "If there weren't good peers around, the feelings would have been much harder to handle."

Sources of Influence

As in past stages, influence seems to relate to six data bases: professional elders (professors/supervisors/mentors/therapists), clients, personal life, peers/colleagues, theories/research, and the social/cultural environment. For the first time since the beginning of graduate school and the Transition to Professional Training Stage, the individual is less directly affected by professional elders. Perhaps the greatest shift is in the dimension of power and control. Professors and supervisors no longer have direct power over the individual and no longer can control what the individual can and must do. Professors can no longer tell the individual to "jump through this hoop and that hoop." This freedom is often welcomed and feels wonderful. But it also leads to another much more surprising response at times—the loneliness and uncertainty of suddenly being in command of one's own work.

The individual will often at this point look for work-place mentors who will offer guidance and support. The new mentor(s) can play a very important role at this point. As opposed to the preceding stage, supervisors do not have a strong impact on the individual. Now the individual usually feels the influence of supervisors less intensely than individuals at earlier stages because the person has built up a base of successful therapy/counseling experiences. The base may be small but at least it is more than the individual had at the practicum/internship level.

As a source of influence, client experiences are of great value. With less of a pull from the formal theory of graduate seminars, the individual is able to listen more fully to clients. By their improvement or lack of improvement, clients provide powerful feedback concerning the utility of many therapy/counseling specifics which the therapist/counselor is invested in and utilizing.

There increasingly is a sense by the individual that people are motivated to become a therapist/counselor for a variety of reasons and that understanding one's own motivations and aspects of that motivation is important for success in the field. The person reflects, like in earlier stages, about her/his motives for entering this work. However, the reflection now may lead to deeper understandings than in the past. Less defensiveness may occur because the individual feels more secure about her/his abilities and less focused on satisfying the multiple evaluations of professors and supervisors who played powerful and often threatening authority roles at the student level. As the individual is increasingly choosing this occupational specialty and increasingly developing a deeper commitment to it, understanding oneself and establishing a personally chosen value base for one's work become an important focus.

Peers and colleagues are an important influence at this time. Perhaps the loss of some professional elders—professors and supervisors—makes peers more valuable than ever. One female commented on this by saying, "Doing cotherapy was very important to me."

Role and Working Style

In the movement from being a beginner to a therapist/counselor at the Exploration Stage there is an increased sense of the complexity of therapy/counseling work. In this complexity the individual continues to recognize the importance of the therapeutic relationship; and although it is not the same relationship as the one that the beginner had, the relationship is still considered crucial. In the context of the relationship there are new developments including a new found ability to abstract from the relationship and watch the interaction between self and the individual client/family/group. In addition to emphasizing the importance of the therapeutic relationship, the person at this stage also adds skills and specific intervention ideas to her/his repertoire. The renewed emphasis on technique acquisition at this high level, compared with earlier points, is characterized by a more autonomous search for useful techniques.

There is a more mature definition of the role such as: "The job is to empower or unblock or enable the client." The person has a better idea of what exactly he/she is doing and how to get from A to B to C for a client. There is more clarity about how and what one is doing and why one is doing it. There is much more purposiveness, playfulness and understanding of the specifics.

The beginner might understand that the therapeutic endeavor is complex and somewhat overwhelming and confusing. Now there is some clarity regarding the specifics of the complexity. The therapist/counselor is more clear about differentiation of responsibilities. The therapist/counselor at this point feels less responsible for clients' welfare in terms of being totally responsible for either success or failure. The therapist/counselor is better able to differentiate her/his professional responsibilities from the personal responsibility that clients have for their lives. The person might say, "I used to think I could do it for the client, but I know now that was a naive idea." The person at this point might look back and see the beginning stage sympathetic friendship and realize that she/he was overinvested in the work. A male at this stage said:

> I was a pretty personal therapist with clients when I started out in the business. They would call me in a time of crisis or need. They had my home phone number. That isn't working anymore because my case load is big and difficult. Now calls are screened and I use an answering machine. I had to change it because I was getting 'fried' and mad at clients and things like that. But it is tough saying no to people in tremendous distress, I feel guilty when I don't respond to demands, exhausted when I do.

Now there is also an increased recognition of one's own personality being expressed in one's work and one's own individuality coming out in a unique way that is expressed differently depending on client needs. For example, one's natural sense of humor usually disappears during the early years of trying to learn how to be a therapist/counselor. Now it may begin to reappear and gradually be integrated in a positive way.

By this point, the individual has benefited greatly from experience. The Exploration Stage therapist/counselor is able to absorb much of the clinical interview compared with the beginner who grasps only some of the data. The Exploration Stage person is much more able to distinguish the important aspects of a situation compared with the newcomer who cannot make discretionary judgments and must use simple rules that do not always work. The person is increasingly using her/his own professional experience to pick out the key variables rather than use research and theory in a rigid manner. The work of Dreyfus and Dreyfus (1986) on the impact of experience on expertise is useful in understanding individuals at this stage.

Conceptual Ideas Used

The person at the Exploration Stage is often reacting to an earlier investment or lack of investment in particular models. Most individuals at an earlier stage develop some attachment to one or more particular conceptual models, a few do not. With each of four possibilities (no conceptual attachment; multiple serial conceptual attachments; a single, intense conceptual attachment; or a predominant conceptual attachment with influence from others), the individual is now reacting to the earlier decision. Exploration Stage individuals who have never had a conceptual framework often feel like they are floating and that they never have had an anchor to push off against or gauge themselves. This working in a void often means that the individual is using a loose patchwork of ideas—perhaps moving and shifting for various reasons—when working with clients.

Another option includes exposure to multiple systems in the past. While in graduate school, one male study subject experienced multiple attachments. He said:

> I had an existential/humanistic teacher and so for awhile I became an existential humanist and then I had a behaviorist and so I became a behaviorist and then I had a person whose orientation was sex therapy and sexual issues and so for awhile that became paramount in my thinking.

At this present stage he is reacting in a complex way to those multiple conceptual attachments.

At this point the individual who earlier became attached to a single conceptual system often faces disillusionment with that approach. Although it will vary across individuals, the following describes possible routes through this disillusionment: Initial disillusionment occurs when gradually the therapist/counselor realizes that the one method is not working as well as expected. This realization most strongly emerges out of the counselor/therapist's own personal data with clients and, specifically, from the realization that all clients are not getting better. A male reflecting back to this stage said, "I went through a stage of being depressed about work, feeling it was too much work trying to fit people to the model. I found out it didn't turn out for clients the way the theory said it was supposed to." Two other examples of disillusionment from our sample: An individual with a math and science undergraduate degree entered a graduate program with a strong research-based empirical approach. After learning the conceptual model, he applied it in an internship to spinal cord injured patients. He said, "Sometimes you feel like you were trying to fight a forest fire with a glass of water." He became overwhelmed by the emotional anguish and pain of these individuals. The conceptual model with its emphasis on precision and rationality seemed unable to impact this pain. The disillusionment he experienced gradually led him later to an industrial consulting position where the fit—his personality, the conceptual model and the needs of the clients—was better.

A second person trained to be a therapist found that she did little good for the poor, disadvantaged clients she was working with. These multiproblem individuals seemed in need of much greater and intense intervention than the conceptual model she had learned as part of the clinical psychology training program. For her, the uncertainty led to a later assessment position where she did not have to feel the impotence of her earlier work.

Disillusionment occurs quickest when the therapist/counselor does not have a homogeneous client population experiencing homogeneous problems for which the one method has been developed. If the therapist/counselor faces a wide array of client concerns, disillusionment sets in more rapidly. This happens because the single approach corresponds with Maslow's idea: "If the only tool you have is a hammer, [you tend] to treat everything as if it were a nail" (cited by Goldfried, 1980, p. 994). The problem is that everything is not a nail!

Generally, the individual at the Exploration Stage is realizing that context-free theory is not adequate. There is an increasing realization that theory alone can not adequately be the guide. One's own professional experience must also become the guide. Gradually theory comes to serve practice rather than the earlier idea of practice serving theory. Disillusionment often relates to the realization of the limits of context-free theory. A male at the Exploration Stage said, "All conceptual models blow a tire after three months. I'm always amazed by the complexity of peoples' minds and their unique problems. This means I need to adjust the conceptual model to the person."

Now in using conceptual models, the person is much better at discerning the critical elements, the situations where principles do not hold, and the essential variables. This new ability serves as a guide during the self-directed exploration process. The individual may feel resentment toward individuals, such as graduate school professors, who earlier seemed to strongly profess theory that now seems inadequate in providing a framework for the work.

Becoming aware of one's growing disillusionment is often alarming. There is often a great urgency to slow it down and a strong tendency at this point to attribute failure to one of two causes: one's own inability as a therapist/counselor or an inadequacy with the earlier conceptual system(s) used. The next step depends on the specific attributions of the perceived failure. At earlier stages the attribution most often concerns one's own inadequacy. The individual is so preoccupied with mastering the method, in part because of external training program/internship demands to master the method, that he/she usually does not question the adequacy of the method as much as adequacy of self. Now, at this stage, attributing failure to one's inability may lead to leaving therapist/counselor work through either a major career switch or by focusing more on administration, teaching, research or similar less direct service routes.

Being beyond the grips of training program professors and supervisors correlates with more of a tendency to attribute failure to other than inadequacy of self. Attributing failure to the conceptual system may cause hostility toward the earlier model and its advocates and motivate the person to find or develop another method. Finding another method often occurs through workshops. Workshops which offer a new and revolutionary method attract many individuals at this point in their development. Other individuals develop their own method. The new method is often built on polarities between the old and the new.

Sometimes, when the causes of perceived failure are unknown, deeper disillusionment may result. Finding the one method inadequate and being unable to discover a solution may lead to deeper disillusionment which is experienced as the "...loss of old signposts and the experience of being lost and alone in a chaotic world" (Widick, Knefelkamp & Parker, 1980, p. 94). At this point, the therapist/counselor experiences a great deal of emotional pain and anguish. Signs of "burning out," futility and exhaustion are present. For some this is an exit point from active occupational involvement with counseling/therapy. Others wait out the disillusionment and keep trying. Work is difficult and not very satisfying. The therapist/counselor may feel defensive about her/his ability and may hide evidence of lack of success from other practitioners. The individual keeps hoping that things can get better and keeps trying.

Disillusionment with a conceptual system is avoided if: (a) the individual continues to work with a narrow client base for whom the approach was developed, or (b) if the individual never got attached to one model. For the rest, some kind of disillusionment is common at this point. It may be disillusionment not so much with a method as detailed above but disillusionment that is more general with the field (e.g., Is this line of work worthwhile?) or with life itself (a form of existential disillusionment). The disillusionment which appears at the Exploration Stage is usually caused in part by unrealistic expectations of client change and unrealistic perceptions of therapist/counselor power and expertise. One study female said, "I think I become more disillusioned when I have expectations that I need to do it all; it is my responsibility or fault if this person isn't getting better."

The evolution of a therapeutic style may occur without a disillusionment base. One female at this stage described her development of a conceptual style. She said, "I've found that I was in a very cognitive behavioral style. If anyone would have asked me if I endorsed this theory while in graduate school or internship, I would have said 'no' resoundingly. I didn't find an orientation via disillusionment but, rather, by evolution and greater insight into what I actually do as a therapist."

Learning Process

The essential learning process is by reflection. It is the major method used by an individual who is taking responsibility for her/his own understanding. The degree of individual self-directed reflection is the key to movement to the Integration Stage versus an alternative pseudodevelopment route of development. The individual had hoped that the graduate training would have been enough. One female looked back and said, "I realized that graduate training had real gaps. There was much I had to cover that was not offered in graduate school. I remember writing letters to the director of the program, pointing out things that should have been addressed." Now, one's dependency on the graduate program must be severed and self-directed reflection must occur so that the shedding of some of the past and the adding in the future can occur. Some of the individual's anger relates to the realization that full competence continues to be elusive. This reflection encompasses many issues including the meaning of the work, inquiry into self, a search for anchors, a search for techniques and a search for theory. Reflection provides answers to questions such as these: What didn't I get from graduate school? May I deviate from the methods and ideologies I was taught? What do I believe in? How can I proceed? How should I proceed? The individual must come to terms through reflection with painfully contradictory data. Pseudodevelopment seems to occur when reflection is avoided or prematurely foreclosed.

Measures of Effectiveness and Satisfaction

There is often confusion about effectiveness. The person has eliminated many factors that previously were considered effectiveness criteria such as being liked by the client. Perhaps few criteria have emerged as viable alternatives. This may be understood as a process where projections are being abandoned.

Externally, the individual is able to articulate a detailed explanation of effectiveness factors. This contrasts sharply with earlier stages. The problem is, however, that the person may not be convinced of her/his own explanation. Quiet desperation, if present, may be rooted in a deep confusion about the critical effectiveness factors.

At the confirmation substage, client improvement is still the major focus of effectiveness measures. Some, however, are increasingly able to use other criteria than straight client feedback in assessing client development. For example, getting paid serves as a measure of effectiveness for some.

At the disillusionment substage, there seems to be a general regression to emphasizing client feedback as the sole criteria of effectiveness. Often, the therapist/counselor feels there is overwhelming evidence that the clients are not improving enough and that he/she does not feel adequately prepared for the task. This may lead to a distorted view of client progress.

There is often a loneliness in this reflective judgment about effectiveness. The inward, independent, private, isolated nature of the judgment helps produce the feeling of loneliness.

At this point, occupational self-esteem can be increased by acquiring social comparison information. The information that peers are struggling, too, tends to increase self-esteem and is immensely reassuring. This information is not acquired by reading journal articles because articles, by their

Exploration Stage

nature, bleach out nonsignificant results or dispiriting ideas. Knowledge generation and progress—not despair—is the content of the journals and books. Talking to other people in moments of trust and respect is the key. This happens, for example, during the break times at workshops and, more intensively, in therapist/counselor peer supervision groups. A female at this stage commented:

> I find my colleagues to be my best resource. I tap people with similar as well as divergent theoretical orientations. We even have a 'when therapy fails' group to help sort out what happens when we're ineffective... we think we're pretty damn good therapists and so far at least there's been no collective judgment to the contrary. We are quite insular in the city where I work, we feel comfortable within this group of cognitive therapists of taking risks and learning about ourselves.

CHAPTER 7

Integration Stage

Definition of the Stage

Individuals in this group have completed graduate training and have been practicing as professional therapists/counselors for a number of years after the graduate degree. This group has had experience in different settings, and the diversity of the postgraduate settings tends to make them less homogeneous than individuals in graduate school where their experience is structured in similar ways. For example, individuals in industrial settings and individuals in correctional settings work in very different environments which impact on the particular constellation of skills and perspectives at this stage.

Central Task

The central task is to develop a professional authenticity. This includes a conceptual system and working style which are genuine for the individual. True personalization is occurring if the individual is building an authentic professional identity. Shedding of past unauthentic expressions of self continues from the last stage. In fact, consolidation is a major element in this process. One male described his consolidation process as "throwing out the clutter."

The individual must do this work now on her/his own and the professional identity must meet the authenticity requirements of being true to the individual in terms of her/his views of human nature and the change process. The role and working style and conceptual system must of necessity enable the individual's personality to be expressed in a natural and productive way. There is no exception to this need for a close fit! The intensity of this self-selection process, the process of consolidation, and the

Integration Stage

more authentic fit of the person and the therapy/counseling style form a unique task at this stage. As a part of the process of building true professional authenticity, the individual has often searched for a compatible work environment. One male at this stage traced his own postdoctoral search through a variety of mental health settings. Finally he found a compatible work environment. In reactions to a draft description of this stage he said, "The work setting has an enormous impact on the individual."

As a byproduct of accepting one's natural style as a major element in one's work there must also be a keen recognition of the limits of this style and a willingness to try to reduce the negative effects of these limits. In reaction to the increased personalization at this stage, a male study subject said, "I hope some psychologists are not themselves with clients, because their selves are not therapeutic. It would be more important to learn to set limits on their personalities than to express them." So the evolution of the style and the increased personalization is a complex process. Hopefully, the increase in becoming more and more oneself is muted by reduction of the therapeutically negative elements of self.

The Integration Stage individual must devote time to create a personally chosen value anchored explanation of the therapeutic change process. The explanation differs in specific elements across different Integration Stage therapists/counselors. However, each individual must be building a personally chosen, multidimensional explanation of the change process that the individual uses as a blueprint to guide her/his work.

Predominant Affect

Satisfaction is a major affective reaction at this stage. Satisfaction seems to be built on experience, credentials, the coming together of a personally unique conceptual system and working style, and financial rewards. Said one female at this stage, "Yes, the money feels real good!" Perhaps the key is the slow but profound change in expectations. By now the individual has learned through experience—often painful experience—that he/she as a practitioner is not as effective and powerful and therefore responsible for client change as was formerly implicitly believed. This is a humbling experience but also ultimately freeing, too. A true sense of satisfaction in the work often correlates with decreased perfectionism and grandiosity. In addition to satisfaction, individuals at this stage use the following similar terms to describe their predominant affect at this time: hopeful, realistic, peaceful, stable, comfortable.

Many at this stage are pleased with their work; it is the pleasure of learning new things, trying new things and having confidence and feeling good about one's ability after many credentialing mazes have been run. The culminating effect of experience means the individual is more competent in many situations. One Integration Stage male expressed this new experience based competence when he said, "I'm more willing to test my ability in tough situations; there is more confidence." A female said, "Nothing completely floors me anymore. In the past I took it to mean there was something wrong with me if things were novel or new."

Although the overall affect seems to be satisfaction or similar emotions, there are other possible affective responses, too. These include disillusionment for some and an emptiness—"Is this all there is?" for others who have finally gotten through all the professional hoops. Also, the work environment and the demands within that environment can, in fact, greatly impact the predominant affect. Said a female at this stage, "Practice is still difficult... because difficult clients are still draining."

Sources of Influence

The six major sources of influence (theories/research, clients, professional elders [professors/supervisors/mentors/therapists], peers/colleagues, one's own personal life, and the social/cultural environment) continue to play a significant role at this stage. An additional component often occurring at this point is the role of being a professor/supervisor/mentor. The act of teaching/supervising/mentoring provides a different perspective on the work and seems to help individuals clarify their own thinking. Now there are seven sources of influence—the six mentioned previously and one's own teaching/supervision/mentoring.

One's personal life is very important. One Integration Stage male said that his wife's active feminism was a major influence in reorienting his approach from cerebral to affective, task to process. Another male at this stage said, "There was a time I had an investment in one approach in part due to training but exposure to clients, other approaches, and my own therapy led me to change."

Individuals at this point seem to be more open in talking about how their own personal life has affected their therapy/counseling work. This may be a function of two factors. One, the person is often less defensive and more open in describing her/his own personal issues and has a better understanding of these personal issues. For example, one female at this stage said quite openly and in a matter of fact way:

> We are drawn to this field to fix ourselves. That is where the energy to be in this field comes from. And we tend to be controlling people without knowing it. Both of these have to be understood before the person can be really effective. In contrast to the past I now think of myself as a coach or midwife for the client who does her/his own work.

Asked if she could have articulated the issue like this in earlier years, she said, "No. I couldn't have done that." Also, previous successes (e.g., graduate school, licensure, clients) tend to free up the individual so there is less defensiveness about personal issues. Two, these individuals have more experiences to draw on. For example, one female at this stage, chronologically older than most at the Integration Stage, said, "I've lived through a lot of hell and a lot of pleasure; I've just lived a long time and that can be useful if you use it well." Another female at this stage, a mother of young adults, said in a matter of fact way, "You learn a lot from your kids just like you learn a lot from your clients." Chronologically younger practitioners just do not have the broad lessons that come with living a number of decades. This life experience gives older practitioners more data for self-disclosure, understanding issues, and interest in particular topics (e.g., a profound loss experience such as divorce). For example, one Integration Stage female said that her divorce was the most difficult experience of her life. She found it forced her to see herself as a separate person and not a daughter or wife in relation to others. She said, "It really shocked me to my core. I had to dab in some dark places and look at things about me." The whole experience, she said, increased her connections with human pain, made her more intellectually curious, and ultimately helped her be a better therapist.

All seven of the areas of influence may have an effect now. In fact, across individuals at this stage there is great variability and interaction in the sources of influence. Research and theory is now acquired much less through formal courses and more through workshops, reading journals and talking with colleagues. The graduate school emphasis on texts and broad academic questions has been replaced by more pragmatic concerns. Yet, the pragmatic concerns have been broadened from recent years when the individual was often searching frantically for very specific techniques to learn and apply immediately. Now there is less urgency and, therefore, more time to examine more broadly.

The "professional elder" role is evolving and the person at this point is being influenced as a function of teaching/supervising/mentoring. In fact, this emerging role is now for the first time, on average, as impactful as being the recipient of wisdom from other wise elders.

Peer and colleague influence is strong for some at this point. For example, one female at this stage said, "To stay alive in this field you need to talk to colleagues. For me, two long-term peer supervision groups have been absolutely essential to continue and grow as a therapist."

Clients, of course, continue as a powerful source of influence. Increasingly, it is not every client but the unusual client who leaves an impression and is instructive for the person.

As a professional elder, one's own therapist/counselor may be very impactful. Earlier one's own therapist and therapy was probably influenced in three ways: as a way to resolve personal pain and increase one's own emotional health; as a way to experience the process of psychotherapy and know it from the inside; as an intense modeling method where the client is a student watching the therapist do the work and learning how to do it. Now one's own therapy is used more often as an ongoing process to maintain emotional health. For example, one female at this stage described her therapy as, "A place where I can listen to my own internal voice. The clearer I can be and less frightened I am of my emotions, the better I am at helping clients value their own experience and listen to themselves."

Role and Working Style

Role and working style are becoming less rigid for the individual. This decreased rigidity has occurred over a number of years. It may have occurred gradually or in a period of intense rigidity reduction followed by long periods of no change. The individual may or may not have been strongly aware of this decreased conformity and increased creativity in style. One female at this stage explained the shift this way:

> I learned all the rules and so I came to a point—after lots of effort—where

I knew the rules very well. Gradually I modified the rules. Then I began to use the rules to let me go where I wanted to go. Lately I haven't been talking so much in terms of rules.

She went on to explain a rule. For example, for her a rule was that she should not see individuals alone when working with a couple. Yet because of the uniqueness of one situation she broke this rule and in terms of outcome it was absolutely the right choice. Reflecting on this she said, "I never could have been so free this way ten years ago."

Reflecting the same loosening of rigidity, another female at this stage said, "I'm more loose than I used to be in my approach to the work. Sure everything must be done ethically and professionally. That's a given. I'm just not so frantic about answers or even questions. Now I really feel there isn't a right way to do it although there is a right process for me." Yet, she also commented on a seemingly contradictory element of the loosening of rigidity and increased use of one's natural personality in role and working style. She said, "It is natural for me to be very self-disclosing. I need to be less impulsive with it and more calculating. I need to keep asking if this would be useful to the client or a narcissistic urge."

Integration Stage individuals trust in themselves much more and are willing to take more risks than less experienced individuals. They possess much more expertise, and they know how to do things. In addition they are more patient, much more flexible, more knowledgeable and perhaps more humble. Also, they are more comfortable with the idea that there are few clear answers. If the sense of ambiguity is too much and too discomforting, the person has often left the field by now and moved on to something that has more structure, closure and right versus wrong answers.

Increased flexibility in role and working style was expressed by a person who described the situation as being like an amusement park. The amusement park itself was very well known by this time, but within the amusement park there was a great deal of flexibility concerning the ride one would choose at a certain point. The choice would vary depending on the ability of the Integration Stage therapist/counselor to assess the situation. This may be an example of the great creativity that is possible within therapy/counseling work. A person may know everything about a variety of procedures but then at a particular point chooses a constellation of behaviors that have not occurred before. Another person, using a music analogy, said:

> If I know my pieces really well I can then play them individually with ease. Played well together there is a unifying and coherent quality that is difficult to achieve but is beautiful when it occurs.

Individuals at this stage uniformly talk about the importance of the relationship and on one level it sounds like the way beginners talk about being a sympathetic friend. It is similar, but it is very different, too. Individuals at this stage use the relationship as both an assessment tool and as an intervention tool. They have, also, usually developed very strong relationship skills. Many are able to develop therapeutic human relationships with individuals of various backgrounds, deficiencies and past dysfunctional human relationships. Individuals at this stage can develop, maintain and terminate positive relationships with these kinds of clients. So, the relationship is primary in both assessment and intervention.

Integration Stage therapist/counselors are also more clear about the exact aspects of the relationship that are important. For example, they know why trust is important with victims of abuse; they know how victims of abuse will express their distrust; they know how to understand these signs of distrust; and they know how to develop trust with these individuals. Whereas the beginner can only offer emotional support, the professional at this point is able to both support and challenge the individual. The professional at this point is able to set limits with the individual. The professional at this point is able to do well with boundary issues, although sometimes the most difficult boundary problems with clients are hard even for an Integration Stage therapist/counselor, i.e., a client diagnosed as having borderline personality disorder.

Quotes from individuals at this stage include the following: "The relationship is the key that allows the rest to happen." "The relationship sets the tone for the rest of the work." "The therapist is a student learning about the client's problems."

The professional at this point is able to be deeply involved with the other person and yet distant enough from the person's problems. The professional is able to decenter and enter in a very direct way into the client's experience of herself/himself while also simultaneously maintaining a therapeutically positive distance. The person has, for the most part, learned how to separate out the therapist role from roles as friend, parent, spouse. One female reflected back to her graduate school years when this was more

Integration Stage

of a problem. Laughing, she said that her daughter gave her useful feedback when she said, "Mother, will you quit being a damn social worker and just be my mother!"

Conceptual Ideas Used

In the development of a conceptual system, the disillusionment of the Exploration Stage is often eventually followed by reemergence and renewed hope. At this point, one possible avenue provides hope for the therapist/counselor, and that is the avenue of a synergistic effect. The addition of parts begins to make a whole that is promising. The parts are:

1. insights learned from work with a variety of clients,
2. trying out various theories and techniques,
3. learning from a variety of supervisors,
4. working in a variety of settings,
5. the modeling provided by one's own personal therapist/counselor,
6. insights gained from personal maturation via experience and introspection,
7. one's experience and assessment of conceptual systems used in the past,
8. the growing emergence of one's unique personality into one's therapy/counseling work.

These factors lead most individuals to describe themselves as eclectic or integrative in their approach by this point in their career. There are exceptions. One female at this stage said:

> The eclectic label wouldn't fit for me. I still try to remain fairly consistent with a psychoanalytic/psychodynamic framework. I discovered that aspects of this theory are basic enough, true enough that they do fit many unique individuals.

Although a therapist/counselor at this stage may follow one theoretical orientation, it seems that even he/she has personalized the system so that it can more readily fit the person's uniqueness.

Professional experience continues to have a profound effect in increasing competence. One male at this stage told how difficult it was in the beginning to do therapy as he labored to identify what technique was most effective for a specific client's problems while the supervisor watched in a neighboring room. But now, with five years of postgraduate school experience, he is able to process options more quickly and can be appropriately spontaneous amidst the complexity of the work.

Most individuals at this point have less need for a single conceptual funnel to push all the data through. They are beyond the point where they need to perceive all client issues in a uniform way because they only have one well-developed solution. The incredibly intense stimuli coming at them from clients can be more easily managed without resorting to a single model or approach that relies on a limited and prescribed set of variables. A therapist/counselor at this point is able to move beyond a single approach and integrate a whole variety of approaches based on a more systematic and accurate differential diagnosis of the client and a better use of conceptual ideas that fit oneself as a therapist/counselor. Often people at this point are more clear than before about how theories both clarify and distort. A male at this stage said, "I'm more likely now to see people I work with as themselves rather than proof of or support for a particular ideology. It has been interesting to realize what I have perceived with a particular belief system versus letting people be themselves." Now the idea is to truly understand the uniqueness of the client and, therefore, fit the theory, technique and approach rather than attempting to fit the client to the preselected conceptual structure.

Perhaps the therapist/counselor has been working to integrate very diverse and contradictory theories. One person at this stage said her chemical dependency counseling training and her Rogerian counseling training were so different in approach and her integration of them was something she was working on.

At this point, the counselor/therapist has some awareness of how the personally integrated approach is an expression and reflection of her/his personality. In innumerable small ways the conceptual system has become personalized and individualized. Accepting and integrating one's unique personality and letting it be expressed in one's work is a key here to increased competence. If one can be oneself and also offer a powerful healing presence, then a magnificent therapeutic effect is possible.

The therapist/counselor has learned to accommodate her/his own personal needs within an ethical, professional approach. Examples of these needs are a need for verbal dominance, a need for emotional distance, a need to keep anger at a minimum, a need for intense affective expression and a need for intellectual understanding. The therapist/counselor has also learned what kind of client problem she/he works with best as a function of her/his (a) personality and needs, and (b) theoretical approach.

The therapist/counselor has by this point developed a theoretical orientation which answers three questions: (a) What is abnormal and normal human development? (b) What causes normal and abnormal human development? (c) How is it changed? The approach to change nearly always considers the three basic client areas of emotions, thinking and behavior and considers these in the therapist/counselor's chosen priority order for change (i.e., it is best to focus on emotions because that will most quickly lead to behavior and thinking changes).

Learning Process

Personal preference in learning becomes more prominent with the decline of graduate school rigidity—lectures, discussions, tests, papers all within time limits. Individuals increasingly use a self-selected method that works for them. The learning process consists of choosing to learn by practice, reading, watching models, reflecting on critical incidents and a variety of other means. One person at this stage described her method as follows: "In learning new areas I find myself returning to my older method of learning: searching for and finding a trusted mentor."

There is also another structure emerging. That is the structure of professional practice in therapy/counseling within the community. For example, standards of community practice and licensing requirements may suggest a learning structure such as group supervision. In fact, within the structure of peer group supervision many individuals find their greatest intellectual stimulation at this stage.

Measures of Effectiveness and Satisfaction

At this point there is a much stronger sense that the kind of improvement one can expect in working with people is smaller than previously thought, may take longer, and is dependent on many external factors (e.g., client motivation) besides the influence and expertise of the (therapist/counselor. All of these factors—the slowness of change, the small degree of the change, and the importance of other factors—take some of the pressure off the Integration Stage individual and also makes her/him less grandiose about her/his own power to cure people. Coming to this point is easy for some, difficult for others. One male at this stage said, "Often there is still a wish that more could have happened and I would have been more effective." In general, the expectations are reduced compared with the past. For one Integration Stage female who expresses this sentiment, the setting seemed to be instrumental in an early shift in expectations. She said, "Because I worked in a setting with very difficult patients, I was humbled early on and learned how difficult it was to change a lifetime of ingrained personality and behavior." An Integration Stage male reflected on the critical shift in responsibility and control that takes pressure off the therapist/counselor when he said, "...I can't control everyone." Said another male at this stage:

> I now don't work real hard at trying to change people. I'm more with them. When I first started out, my job was to make people change, now I don't get so anxious, nervous, invested in that. I'm excited for clients if they change, but don't need that for confirmation of myself. I already feel I'm good at what I do. If I find myself pushing too hard I look at issues of countertransference.

There is more acceptance of small shifts and less reliance on the client acknowledging improvement, although some acknowledgment from clients is very nice and rewarding. One can, in fact, at this point feel good about the work she/he has done and yet have clients not do very well along some dimensions of functioning. This is very different than individuals at the Conventional or Transition to Professional Training Stage. The shift occurs because the therapist/counselor has learned to judge her/his performance apart from whether the client acknowledges improvement.

It seems that there has been a reframing by this stage of the difficulties of the work; the pointing of the finger is now away from oneself and more toward the inherent limitations of the job. The old judgment "I should be able to help this person with this problem but can't so I am inadequate" has given way to a broader view. The individual is now able to feel less responsible for client welfare and success without this becoming an excuse for incompetence.

As opposed to earlier stages, the therapist/counselor is now better able to filter client feedback about improvement through her/his own assessment of the problem. When client feedback is congruent with self-assessment, the person is more accepting of client feedback. There is not the intense need to have direct verbal feedback from clients about how competent one is as a therapist/counselor. Said one female at this stage, "I no longer need the client to like me as I did. Earlier I wasn't aware of my need to be liked and how I could be greatly influenced by this need." Yet, many do find a great deal of satisfaction in getting feedback from former clients, for example, in a short letter or in a referral by a former client. Said one male, "When clients give me feedback about how great I am I tend not to trust it but I do enjoy getting referrals from them. I also make good money at this. So I get a lot out of it. It isn't just altruistic."

These experienced individuals do, in a sense, say the same things that people at the beginning said in terms of motivation for entering this occupation. These are the same kind of "altruistic, wanting to help people" kind of notions, and yet they sound different after the person has been in the field for a long time. These individuals like to see people change for the better, and make a better life for themselves, to become more satisfied with themselves, and feel fewer negative emotions. They do not, however, feel nearly as responsible as beginners do for the change process.

In addition, for Integrated Stage individuals there is satisfaction from doing something well. They feel suited for the work, they do it well and that in itself is satisfying. Commenting on this dimension one person said, "It is human nature to like to do what we do well, at least it is for me."

CHAPTER 8

Individuation Stage

Definition of the Stage

Differing from some current views, Individuation here is conceptualized as a process that involves both a separation and a relatedness. For our informants, relationships with others was a central part of the Individuation process. A more detailed definition of Individuation can be found on pages 100–101.

An individual in this group has attended graduate school and has been practicing as a professional therapist/counselor for a number of years. Developmental events give these counselors/therapists a unique highly heterogeneous/highly homogeneous mix, a combination not found at the earliest stages. The heterogeneity comes from factors such as the following: They have been working as therapists/counselors longer than individuals at earlier stages, and this length of experience has contributed to the differences. Their diverse work settings have tended to make them interested in and involved in very different kinds of activities. Just as important, these individuals have continued to develop individually, and these individual paths of development have taken increasingly unique and separate ways. Having a vision for one's future is a key to being successful at this task. So is having deeply satisfying work. Almost paradoxically the individuals in this group are also like each other. This is especially true in some of their assumptions, procedures, and expectations about the work.

Central Task

The central task is idiosyncratic and highly individualized growth which adds to a deeper authenticity. Strong personalization must occur. Having a vision for one's future is a key to being successful at this task. So is having

Individuation Stage

deeply satisfying work. The self-selected authenticity of the last stage must be continued for future growth, development and uniqueness to occur. The great challenge at this stage is to both "settle down"—to develop a consistent style that is comfortable and used by the individual repeatedly and routinely—and also to continually explore and push oneself at the frontiers of one's own development as a therapist/counselor. These forces of continuity and change, working together produce the strong need for the individual to develop in a very idiosyncratic way, a way that is not in anyway that of a textbook beginner approach.

The task includes moving in an enhancing and positive direction while moving away from the pull of a disintegrating and negative direction. The individual must continue to move toward fuller and more mature development while eluding disintegrating forces of staleness, frustration and disinterest. One force is energy enhancing, the other is energy draining. The energy draining pull is very strong at this stage and this necessitates an intense concentration on development. The individual usually engaged in a consolidation of activities. There is often a turning away from some work options—and it probably is easier to do this than in the past—in order to concentrate on only some of a possible wide range of activities. A male at this stage helps to explain how authenticity means the increased use of one's own professional experience. He said:

> I think that the more you counsel, the more years that you counsel, you find out more ways of what works. So I think with experience, what you end up doing when working with clients is you do, with all your experience, what you know works, what has worked in the past. So you don't stick with some sort of a model which says you have to do this or you have to do that. ... It leaves you with a model that you developed, that fits your personality, and also from your experience, you know that it works. You start out with a theory and you eventually modify it. I suppose basically, when I first started out, if somebody asked me what model, I would probably say that I followed the client-centered model. But now I am more eclectic. I might use some of the things that Albert Ellis uses, I use some of the things that others use. I guess it is based on the experience ... my own experience of what works.

The great seductions at this stage are intellectual apathy and emotional exhaustion; core aspects of the alternate stage of Stagnation (see Chapter 11). The individual must somehow find a way to keep going on the route to development while avoiding the apathy that comes from not continuing to learn and the exhaustion that comes from not protecting and nurturing oneself while avoiding the burning out element of resentment, bitterness, and boredom. Intellectual apathy must be fought through continued intellectual growth in the absence of immediate external rewards (i.e., in graduate school, it was read the material or fail the course. Now an hour reading is not a billable hour as is an hour seeing a client).

Emotional exhaustion is fought by protecting oneself from the emotional demands of the work while also being deeply engaged in the work. One Individuation Stage female commented on this task when she said that the task was "...to continue to be present but not to be used up!" Common elements for therapists/counselors here, but not practiced by beginners, are: Strict time and location boundaries for the work, the regular use of vacations for renewal, and broader definitions of success. A miracle—an immediate transforming cure—is not even a fantasy goal now like it is for beginners. One female at this stage described her strategies to be involved but not used up as including (a) less self-disclosure in her therapy, (b) sufficient charting so that she does not have the client's data swirling around in her head in off hours, and (c) doing the type of therapy where she feels most effective.

Predominant Affect

Predominant affective reactions are satisfaction and distress. Satisfaction comes from living in a work world where the individual feels competent at tasks that are enjoyable. There is often a quiet excitement. The quiet excitement seems to be a byproduct of a deep level of creativity being experienced by the individual in her/his work as a professional therapist/counselor. The creative process with all of its sense of wonder, fear, uncertainty, newness, disappointment and the unknown combines to produce a freshness in one's work. One person at this stage said, "The creativity I'm enjoying with my new project is delightful." The more individual and idiosyncratic nature of this process produces positive feelings which can be summed up as a feeling of satisfaction.

Distress results from an absence of the predominant emotion of satisfaction. It has many roots. One facet is unsettling boredom that comes from routine tasks completed over and over again. Said one Individuation Stage male, "Much of my work with clients involves teaching 'emotional first grade,' that is, going over basic mental health issues. It gets boring." Distress also contains elements of exhaustion, irritation and meaningfulness.

Usually negative emotions are experienced when the individual is compelled one way or another to complete unpleasant, disliked tasks. Distress can result from feeling one has reached a plateau on a central dimension such as competence, motivation or interest in the work. It can result from an unsupportive work environment. Said one Individuation Stage person, "The work environment is a major problem. It is not very supportive."

Sources of Influence

The major sources of influence have continued but also evolved. Clients continue to be an important source of influence and this seems to be most true with clients who have been particularly successful or clients who have been particularly difficult and traumatizing for the therapist/counselor. Clients who are suicidal or have committed suicide, clients who present very difficult personality disorder type problems, clients who do not seem to benefit from the individual's help are sources of influence. In fact, experience with clients has now become *the* epistemological center in the individual's work. This produces what we call experience-based generalizations and Accumulated Wisdom. One male at the Individuation Stage described this evolved process:

> With a new client I think about cases I've had. I think about how they have gone. Themes come in a case and this stimulates a memory in me. The memory is usually in the form of a collection of vignettes, stories and scripts. It isn't fully conscious but new cases do kick off the memory. The memory of how things went before provide a foundation to begin the current case. Interestingly, most of the stories come from the early days of my practice, they are most embedded. Later cases don't stand out as much except if I was proved wrong or something dramatic happened. Then my thinking changes and my memory changes.

At the earliest stages, therapist/counselor defensiveness was high and intimidation was easy. Then, client feedback was eagerly sought and valued in order to reduce feelings of vulnerability and inadequacy. Now, as in the last stage, client feedback is not sought so much to justify oneself. Rather, learning, not protecting oneself, is the essential purpose of client feedback. In addition the more experienced therapist/counselor benefits from positive feedback which may come from former clients. In contrast, the new therapist/counselor has no residue of former clients and must rely on immediate feedback from current clients. The social/cultural environment for the work is important but not as impactful as in the past. Newer themes in the culture are not as powerful as in the past because they are put in a context of cultural continuity and change over a long period of time.

Theories and research are important because continued professional development is extremely important at this stage. It is easy for some individuals at this point to lose track of the explosion of knowledge in the field in part because the individual is not directly reinforced very much for continuing to read professionally. It was so long ago that the person had to read things because there was going to be a test and a grade and the chance of failing. That strong fear factor is gone. All the credentials are possessed and the individual feels secure in her/his work. The need to keep intellectually alive may be more difficult than in the past. This source of influence, whether it is theories and research through reading, workshops, conventions or some other means, is important, but for some people more difficult than in earlier stages.

Ironically, emerging at this point is an increasingly strongly felt belief that there is not much new in the field. One person said, "I've recently stopped going to workshops. They seemed to be geared to 'Freshman English' and to be old stuff. For example, assertiveness training was done long ago under a different label. I'm especially uninterested in workshops on new little techniques."

Major theoretical leaders or acknowledged master counselors/therapists in the field sometimes capture that person's attention in a way that professors/supervisors/mentors/therapists have in the past. The individual may go to one of these people and learn a new approach or a new way of doing things and this may be influential. This may involve travelling to a distant city and a large expenditure of money and time to learn from a theoretical leader or master therapist/counselor. "Around this time I had my encounter with Albert Ellis," said one study subject.

Peers and colleagues, at this point, are a very valuable source of influence and are more influential than in previous times because the "older/wiser" sources of influence (professors/supervisors) from graduate school are now less available and less impactful. One individual at this stage said, "There are 50 therapists where I work. My spouse is a therapist. I get a lot from these people." However, the individuals at this point may feel very isolated if peer/colleague contact is minimal. He/she may, in fact, work alone as a single office practitioner or he/she may have no comparable senior level practitioners nearby. For some, however, just as peers become an essential source of professional feedback, professional isolation may keep one away from this source. For others at the Individuation Stage, peer influence is strong and rich. Said one female, "I rely on my support network of colleagues."

Professional elders (professors/supervisors/mentors/therapists) continue to influence the individual. Personal therapy (individual, marital, family) can also be a powerful source of influence in one's work with one's therapist as the professional elder. Often the influence is not as direct as in former years. The influence of the wise/older primary role model has been internalized for some. Concerning the influence of these primary role models, one individual at this stage talked about John, his supervisor twenty years ago:

> I have running around in my mind words, phrases, quotes that I periodically pull back to...and sometimes I say to myself, how would John handle this situation.

One's own personal life is very influential, and profound events in one's life—i.e., being a parent, being married, getting older, living in a very different culture, suffering a painful loss—provide intensely important information for the individual in terms of her/his counseling/therapy work. Regarding the impact of personal life, one Individuation Stage male said:

> Certainly my experience has been an important factor in my development as a person. My experience of being in the Peace Corps for a few years has taught me... a sense of relativity of this culture. Raising children I think is so important. I got a chance to go back through development with my own children, and to be able to see what it felt like to them.

An Individuation Stage female commented, "I think I used to be more judgmental about marriage and parenting till I tried it myself, it's a humbling experience." Another reflecting on the effect of age on her work said, "I have been consistent in my work because I came into the field after 10 years in another field so I was older and more formed as a person when I started than I think many young therapists are." One person said, "My father-in-law is slowly dying. There is no way to see what that is like unless you directly experience it. To go through that is a transforming experience." Concerning this issue, a female at this stage said:

> When I lost a family member, I suffered a very long severe depression, and then I lost other family members ... in time I became a much better psychologist ... because I had many depressed people, and certainly having been there, I could understand and empathize and know what not to say to them ... all the dumb things people said to me that I resented. Oh ... come on, cheer up and that sort of thing ... that is just awful ... and I don't think others understand the horror of depression ... I could never have read it in a book, I could never have felt it.... I don't know whether it is what I say or do ... I try to figure it out ... but I think it is probably the fact that I am a living, breathing example that you can recover ... because the worst with depression is knowing that it will never end and one might as well be dead and you can't stand it. ... Having been through that amount of loss and be able to be healthy, reasonably happy and occupied ... I think it is the example more than anything else that I portray to people who are very sad. It will pass, but will all the agony? I would say that those traumas certainly increased my ability as a therapist.

Not only is the personal life data by itself rich and meaningful, there is, perhaps more importantly, an increased willingness and increased ability to let this data consciously and deliberately influence the counselor/therapist. The person is better able to integrate it in a scientific, ethical, and professional way.

Last, the act of teaching/supervising/mentoring also continues to provide a rich source of information. Seemingly all of a sudden the individual is now a senior member of the profession and considered an experienced person. In reality he/she does have more experience and is older than most members of the field and this does lead others to look to the person for guidance, expertise, advice and support. This also provides for a sense of identity. One individual at this stage said, "Hey, if they recognize me this way, I must be good at what I do." Yet the redefinition does not happen automatically. One male said, "Suddenly I was seen by others as a leader but I didn't see it that way. I didn't feel that I belonged."

Role and Working Style

The evolving role and working style of the Individuation Stage therapist/counselor includes an increased ability to be present for the client while working and paradoxically an increased ability to be distant from client involvement when not working.

The therapeutic relationship has a deep and central role at this stage. As in the previous stage, the relationship is an assessment and intervention device, but here the individual is able to understand it and use it at an even more expert level. One Individuation Stage individual in our sample suggested that:

> The relationship is understood even more deeply at this point where the therapist's power, attention, expectations and own personality, including short-comings and strengths, can be seen, understood and used in a more direct and clear way than before.

Another stated, "The therapist becomes the instrument rather than just using instruments and interviewing techniques. Skill becomes the use of self." Another said, "I'm infusing my own self into therapy and relying less on techniques."

The idiosyncratic nature of the role is perhaps best realized by understanding that the therapist/counselor at this point may have a difficult time articulating what he or she does in response to the question: "What do you do in therapy/counseling?" The Individuation Stage therapist/counselor may have a difficult time articulating his/her style because of its intensely idiosyncratic and changing nature. As one person in our sample said, "It's embarrassing to have that question asked because I don't exactly know what to say." Of course, the beginner also does not know what to say, but the beginner has not been through all the standard textbook type answers to this question. Now, the therapist/counselor finds short responses to be harder because her/his answer is highly personalized. Of course, there are exceptions in this broadly diverse group. One individual at this stage said, "I have been able to articulate my approach because I have systematized it in a very idiosyncratic way."

These individuals use techniques like in the past, but the techniques are much more personalized and used less in a mechanical manner. Techniques are brought out and used at different times and with different people on the basis of an acute differential diagnostic. Techniques are experimented with, but there is much more use of the self in the techniques than in early years. There is also much more of an understanding of the limitations of techniques.

In describing the role, and in the work itself, the individual is less incumbered by the older need from graduate school training to sound professional and respectable and scientific. Now the need is more to sound like oneself and there is less need to be these other things.

The individual is able to deal with responsibility and boundaries better than in the past. There is even more letting go of over-responsibility for the client to work and succeed because the individual realizes with experience and the seeing of people in distress day after day, week after week, month after month, year after year that there is a need to let go of over-responsibility. The therapist/counselor must share responsibility with the client. However, this does not mean that one is irresponsible or uninvolved. There seems to be a thin line between too much responsibility and too little, and with experience the individual can consistently know and function at an appropriate point on the thin line. The increased regulating of involvement expresses itself in the way the person is able to be totally involved in a therapy/counseling session and when it is over, within two or three minutes, the therapist/counselor is done with that and on to total involvement with another person's world. At the end of the day the individual can be done and move on to other aspects in her/his life. This capacity to be totally involved and then totally uninvolved with intimate, distressing, and important aspects of another person's life is mastered at a higher and more proficient level by these therapists/counselors than by earlier stage individuals. However, since this task is intrinsically difficult, even individuals at this stage struggle with it at times.

Conceptual Ideas Used

As with other aspects of the individual at this stage, the conceptual system has become more idiosyncratic. It is built on:

1. all the previous conceptual system integration that has been done by the individual,
2. influenced greatly by the setting where the individual works (i.e., addictions versus corporate outplacement versus family therapy),
3. the profound personal experiences the person has had,
4. less reliance on abstract theoretical concepts and more use of guiding principles that have evolved from the individual's past experience base. Regarding this, one male said, "I am more confident in trusting my experience versus fitting them into a theoretical model or label. I have more willingness to challenge theory and dogmatic beliefs."

These four forces combine to form a conceptual system for the person which is a unique way of approaching human issues.

Individuation Stage

Even as each approach is unique there are also common guiding principles. There are common therapy/counseling elements such as active involvement by the client and a belief that negative behavior can be relearned. So, there is an idiosyncratic uniqueness to each conceptual system here but also a commonality across the approaches and working style of these individuals.

The conceptual system is inclusive, too, of more and more of the complexity of the situation. At an earlier stage, the individual could not accept some of the complexity because the conceptual system that could be mastered had to be simple. The individual may have used varying degrees of the narrow funnel in the blocking out of information. Said one male at this stage, "Ten years ago I was trying to fit everything into the mold I had learned." Now, at this point, as one person said, an individual is more able to "...have lots of balloons in the air at the same time..." in working with a client. The person can, in an individual way, work now with more things at the same time because he/she can perceive more things at the same time. Perhaps a way of saying this is that the structure of the conceptual system is more porous and it allows more data to enter. The individual is using less rigid categories and this makes for more accurate assessment and treatment. It also makes the chore of making sense out of chaos—complex and often contradictory client data—something that the counselor/therapist can do now much better than in the past.

In short, the person, at this point, is able to fit the conceptual framework and technique to the client, not the other way around. As one Individuation Stage male remarked, "Theoretical orthodoxy become less important than positive outcomes with clients." The person is able to more accurately understand the client and project less from oneself onto the other person. The center of the target—the assessment of the problem—is understood now much better than in the past. The result then is a more creative and sculpted conceptual system for the particular client issue.

Learning Process

The process of individuation is of extreme value in part because it naturally stimulates learning and development. The individual continues to refine and develop her/his unique way of learning. It may mean meeting individually with a colleague for lunch once a week and talking about therapy/counseling cases in a very trusting and open way. It may mean leaving the USA for six months and going to study in Europe with a renowned therapist of some kind. It may mean watching commercial movies or reading novels and looking for the psychological themes. It may mean becoming more of an expert on behavioral genetics as a way to understand the psychological issues of individuals.

The learning process is very self-directed at this point and the learning style is very individual. Both the form of learning and the pace of learning are self-directed. One person described his normal learning pace as full of fits and starts without a steady stream. He said that he is comfortable with this rhythm. Essential for the Individuation Stage counselor/therapist is a self-directed process of learning and development. Without it, alternative stages of Stagnation and Resignation become more of a reality for the person because internalized rigidity can evolve in the absence of intellectual stimulation.

Methods of motivating self are also individual. One Individuation Stage therapist/counselor said:

> At this point I have to fight to stay current with new developments in the field and not fall into a comfortable rut. I think that is a large motivation for my undertaking a huge project—teaching a seminar for professionals. I guess I need this kind of challenge to continue learning.

Measures of Effectiveness and Satisfaction

At the Individuation Stage, the explanation of effectiveness factors is highly idiosyncratic, and authentic to the individual. There is a creativity to the effectiveness factors. The personalized response to the question of effectiveness factors usually has an informal, non-textbook tone.

Acceptance of one's expertise and giftedness is now a given. In a profoundly different way than in the past, much less psychic energy goes into the search for external (clients/supervisors/peers) praise. Now, individuals at this stage can firmly believe as did one female that, "Just because clients are happy with me doesn't mean I've done a whole lot for them." The need for external approval may still occur at transition points such as taking a position in a different agency, experiencing a dramatic and unexpected drop in one's referrals, or having a new director. As one male at this stage said, "I changed jobs four times in six years during this time. That meant I was constantly concerned about the evaluations of supervisors." In times of homeostasis, however, external praise is much less necessary because the therapist/counselor is internally sure of her/his ability. Enough positive experiences (i.e., with clients, licensure, supervisors) have occurred to produce a solid sense of ability.

Coupled with this solid sense of expertise, somewhat paradoxically, is a broadened definition of success and a stronger assertion of self protection. There is a strong sense of what our sample group at this stage called "reality about the work" and "an acceptance of limitations in oneself and others." Success is defined more as "some positive change" not as "a quick and intense transformation." A male at the Individuation Stage said:

> I am more willing to let people be and know it takes time; earlier I was too eager to bring about change... I am more comfortable letting the problem be with the person and not take it on myself.... People have so many problems, counseling is so damn hard. I've scaled down my expectations about change and sometimes expect no changes.

A female at this stage said, "I have a better sense of personal boundaries and blame myself less if things don't work out well. I'm more of a facilitator and less of a fixer. I do a lot more letting go in that way." Another person at this stage reflected back. He said, "I always felt I was responsible for making them change. I've learned over the years that I use my skills to help them make a decision and if they make a decision and choose not to change, its still their responsibility and not mine. Now the criterion is whether I did what was appropriate for that person at that time."

In order to protect oneself in terms of one's capacity to become exhausted and hurt and overused easily, the individual does not extend herself/himself over safe limits. This seems analogous to the veteran older athlete who knows her/his limitations and is much more able to monitor oneself and slow one's self down at important points while also being able to be very proficient. The person can more readily refer clients to other individuals as well as restrict one's time and work in a way that is much more arbitrary than previously true. For example, constantly thinking when off work about ways to reduce a client's depression is the kind of thing beginners occasionally do. Now it is done much less often because it violates the counselor/therapist's time and location boundaries which protect the individual over the long run from emotional exhaustion. But it is not an all or nothing issue. Human lives are involved and the therapist/counselor even now can feel deep distress. One female at this stage said, "Sometimes I can't let go of feelings brought out by child clients getting sent back to parents who probably victimized the kid. At home I get angry about it."

The limits used at this stage—a broader definition of success and only certain times devoted to the work—usually does not reduce the chance for satisfaction. Rather these limits increase the chance for satisfaction over the long haul. It is the long-haul perspective of the Individuation Stage therapist/counselor that leads to these redefinitions of success and satisfaction.

Old themes also remain. There is still a sense, as in previous times, of the tremendous gratification that comes from profoundly helping another person. Being able to work successfully with the most difficult problems is gratifying. As one person said: "Going to sleep I say, 'That's my piece for humanity.'" Supervising newer people in the field is also, at times, immensely gratifying.

CHAPTER 9

Integrity Stage

Definition of the Stage

Individuals in this group have practiced for about 25 to 35 years as postgraduate therapists/counselors and average about age 60 to 70. Equally important is the fact that their working life is approximately 90% complete; the number of years of active work in the field since the beginning are much greater than the years left. Retirement is close.

As with the last group, this group seems to be both homogeneous and heterogeneous. The homogeneity comes from the fact that they have been in this career field and worked within its parameters for a very, very long time and they chronologically are of a similar age. They all use experience now, rather than experts' theories, as a primary base for generalizations and principles. An exception occurs when the individual enters a new arena. Then theory rather than experience-based generalization serve as a guide. The heterogeneity comes from the individuation that has occurred over the years as each person has developed a unique personal style.

Central Task

The central task is to maintain the fullness of one's individuality while also preparing for retirement. This involves a profound acceptance of oneself as a therapist/counselor and a profound endorsement of oneself as a therapist/counselor. Said a male at this stage, "I think I am more myself than I have ever been." There is no unchecked over-evaluation of self; acceptance and endorsement come within a context of a realism and humility about one's strengths and weaknesses and the possibilities and limitations of the career field. Another male at this stage said, "If I can do three out of four things well, I concentrate on those things. I used to work on the one out of four, but not now."

There is a nourishing of what is and what is believed to be true. It means slow growth in new assumptions, techniques, style, with an overall focus not on newness but on the maintenance and the prizing of what has been developed and what has been accepted as true for the individual to this point.

Predominant Affect

The predominant affective expression is acceptance. Acceptance, at its core, contains a profound acceptance of self. Affective elements of this acceptance include serenity, security, humility and confidence. A male at this stage said, "The longer I've been at it the more I've become accepting of my limitations. That is just the way it is. Some things I do well, other things not so well."

Acceptance is a result of the "fruit of one's labor." The individual has fought the good fight and now lives by the results of that fight. The enormous effort that went into building oneself professionally and the many lessons from successful and unsuccessful experience, over thousands of hours of work, have produced an intense acceptance of oneself as a competent professional in this field. The individual knows how to do the job and has done it very well in countless situations. Confidence and, therefore, acceptance come from repeatedly performing well in a variety of situations. This naturally leads the individual to believe that he/she can do the work. Acceptance of oneself is also rooted in the realization that one's work life is drawing to a close and this is not the time to initiate or experiment. Rather the focus is on doing what one has done before and doing it well.

Performance related anxiety is greatly diminished from previous years. A male at this stage said, "Almost never do I feel anxious about my work. I've done everything before and it has turned out all right." From this perspective of reduced anxiety, the 25-year veteran can understand the intensive and pervasive, although often unrecognized, performance anxiety of earlier years. A female at this stage said that it was like driving a car. At the beginning, one is so worried and responsible, later with years of experience it is much easier. One said, "You try things over the years and keep what works for you and since it works, you don't have regret." Twenty-five years later, acceptance has replaced pervasive anxiety. Only now does the individual fully understand the numerous ways anxiety, expressed earlier, is now absent, i.e., the person worries less about the impression he/she gives to others, talks more freely on a wide variety of topics, feels less restrained by established theoretical structures. Together these dimensions lead to the primary affective expression of acceptance.

Regret, different in tone, is present for some. It contains elements of "too soon old and too late smart," the anticipatory grief over the future loss of active professional work as a therapist/counselor, an acknowledgment that aging is taking a toll on the individual, a full realization of the limits of counseling/therapy work, and sadness about missed opportunities over the years.

Sources of Influence

The same sources of influence (theory and research, clients, one's personal life, peers/colleagues, professional elders [professors, supervisors, mentors, therapists], the social/cultural environment) described earlier continue to be present for the individual at this stage. However, their exact impact differs from earlier years.

Clients continue to be a profound source of influence. Diminished anxiety and increased confidence help the individual to be a participant-observer of self and to learn more from clients than ever before. Yet, the focus is different than for the beginner because by now there is a reduced need for positive client feedback. Given less of a need to protect oneself, there is more of a chance to learn and this means that clients can continually teach the individual. A male at this stage said, "Learning is much more meaningful right on the firing line."

The epistemological center stage is now occupied by the individual's experience-based generalization and Accumulated Wisdom. A male at this stage—in his seventies—said, "It is what you learn from your own work that matters." Most often the person has a constellation of freely chosen theoretical ideas that have come out of her/his experience. Personally untested theoretical ideas are used only when the person enters a new area in which he/she does not have experience. Otherwise, experience —gathered over thousands of hours and dozens of years—has provided guidelines for the work. These ideas gather together to form an intuitive autopilot called accumulated wisdom. It is this accumulated wisdom which provides the central source of influence at this time.

It seems that clients who have profound experiences are the important client teachers for the individual at this stage. Another way that clients are teachers at this point is through their referrals. As one Integrity Stage female said: "It's what they say about you when they tell you they are referring a friend or family member that gives you important feedback about your work with them."

Uniformly, counselors/therapists at the Integrity Stage view clients as much stronger than they did in the early years. A male at this stage said, "You develop a sense that most clients can work through their problems. You believe this more and more over the years." Clients are seen as being able to find their own direction although they may also need direction. A female at this stage said, "I used to be afraid I might make a terrible mistake and ruin someone's life forever and now I feel you can't do that, you're not that powerful."

Theoretical ideas seem to have a strong influence for individuals at this point, yet small empirical research studies in the behavioral sciences have very little impact. Major theories of personality, for example, are valued and used. However, this theoretical framework is not just derived from the psychological literature. The Integrity Stage individual just as readily talks about understanding human behavior through anthropology, literature, novels, poetry, religion, and similar fields. It seems that broad, theoretical ideas are important for the individual because they provide a deep intellectual anchor for one's work. It is an anchor that the individual has come to believe is true for her/him. Perhaps it is the strong acceptance by the individual of her/his unique constellation of theoretical ideas and the importance of the theoretical framework as an anchoring point for one's work that makes theory in the broad sense so important at this level. It is not something that the Integrity Stage individual has newly discovered or newly believed. Usually it has been a passionate intellectual marriage (the individual and the theoretical ideas) for many years. The individual has a sense of allegiance, loyalty and trust toward the theoretical framework and this makes the theoretical ideas about human life important for the individual. Perhaps doubting this theory would in some way be doubting the individual's life work. If the individual came to believe that these ideas were totally unfounded, would not the individual be led to look back over the years, composed of thousands of hours of therapy/counseling work, and feel great self-doubt and despair?

In one sense this may be regarded as renewed confirmation. What is at issue now is not confirmation of the validity of one's training as in the Exploration Stage, but the validity of one's professional life.

One's personal life also continues to have a profound effect. An Integrity Stage individual said, "Doing a lot of living was a great help. I remember, in my 30s, I had a client in his 50s who wanted a divorce. I thought why bother at that age. Then, in my 50s, I finally understood when I got a divorce." Individuals who have been close to the Integrity Stage therapist/counselor for many years (i.e., spouse), exert a powerful influence. Life roles, such as being a parent, continued to teach the individual a great deal and one's own aging process is a source of constant information. Tragedies or intense stressors can have an important impact on one's work. Examples here included death of a partner, serious physical illness and divorce.

Same age colleagues are generally no longer a strong source of influence. Contact with them is often much reduced from previous years. This is largely the result of the decreased number of same age colleagues who the individual works with on a regular basis. Factors such as death, retirement and divergent interests and values and the often present isolation of therapeutic/counseling work has led to decreased contact. For a minority, same-age colleagues are a great source of influence because they are trusted veterans whom one can rely on strongly. There is a great sense of camaraderie, the camaraderie of surviving professionally together. With decreased anxiety and increased confidence about oneself, which are key ingredients of the affect of acceptance, the individual is more able than ever to use peers and colleagues as a source of influence and to accept ideas/feedback from these individuals.

Professional elders (professors/supervisors/mentors/therapists) are not present in the individual's life at this time because the individual is not under supervision, is not a student, does not feel the need for a mentor and is probably not a client. The years have removed the individual from these roles. The role of professor/supervisor/mentor/therapist is almost always filled by an older, wiser person and the person at this stage is now the older, wiser person. There are no individuals who are more experienced except for a few people who are probably retired. However, these individuals are still influenced by older, wiser adults through the process of memory and what one research informant called "fantasy mentors." They often recall with great fondness, and sometimes a sense of unhappiness or bitterness, the days with a professor/supervisor/mentor/therapist years ago. It is analogous to the adult who recalls the days of childhood with one's parent. These memories are present with Integrity Stage individuals and seem at times to be very powerful influences. Some individuals seem to be influenced by someone they have never known but whom they have adopted as a mentor, an example of a so-called "fantasy mentor." One individual mentioned that Freud has served this role for him and said that he could think of other "older, wiser" people in this way.

Some Integrity Stage therapists/counselors are actively involved as professional elders. They are professors/supervisors/mentors/therapists for younger members of the field. If they are strongly involved, the influence here seems to be one of revitalization and a reduction of isolation and professional loneliness. Meeting the challenge of educating younger practitioners keeps them charged up and professionally alive. In describing this issue, one Integrity Stage male said, "Yes, absolutely. Supervising interns really did keep me going." Another said, "They get brighter all the time. I feel that I learn as much from the interns as I teach them. They have become my teacher." A third said, "I like to supervise younger ones at a volunteer agency. I like to teach them about things like handling client rejection by going for a good batting average rather than expecting perfection from oneself and also being less afraid of harming clients." The challenge of telling other people about the field and describing the field forces them to continue to develop. Others at the Integrity Stage serve the profession as elders who make important contributions in professional activities such as political or ethical arenas.

Some Integrity Stage individuals are optimistic and positive about the new individuals who are entering the field, others are more discouraged, concerned or bitter about the competence of the new professionals. If there is bitterness, perhaps it relates to their own assessment of the field. On the other hand, perhaps the bitterness helps them let go of being so involved and attached to a field and a line of work that they love but are getting ready to leave. There is a strong need to let go because retirement and one's age are pulling one away from active involvement in the profession.

Role and Working Style

Personality, experience and work setting are central contributors to the individual's way of working. The role one plays now is not dominated by those external "should" and "should-nots" of a "good therapist/counselor," that one learned earlier. Now the external "should" have been internalized and combined with one's own personality. Individuals have now designed their current professional life. Personal preference is now expressed in numerous dimensions such as formality versus informality, self-disclosure versus lack of disclosure, verbal dominance versus verbal silence in the therapy/counseling session. A male at this point said, "I think I was destined to become the type of therapist I am today just by my temperament."

The culture of the work setting is also a major influence on working style. There are external constraints and freedoms such as acceptable decorations for the office, agency rules and choices, and the demands to satisfy a private practitioner's clients' expectations. In considering this issue, one Integrity Stage individual said, "It was impossible to do *Gestalt* work at the VA!"

A major shift has occurred in the power of external pressure versus internal pressure to influence and dictate one's role. At no time during the individual's career has the person felt more of a sense of freedom to be what he/she wants to be in role and working style. The key difference is the strong autonomy this senior individual now has in expressing self in role and working style.

Finding an appropriate level of involvement with clients has been a long-term career issue. The Integrity Stage therapist/counselor is now operating at the most therapeutic and professional level regarding boundary issues. In earlier years, physical boundary problems were mastered (i.e., permitting/not permitting clients to call the individual at home). Mental boundary problems are more difficult. This means the thinking about clients when the therapist/counselor is not at work. The beginner constantly, on and off work, thinks about clients. The thinking about clients while away from work has a different quality than in the past. Now it is a constructive and active process that leads to new knowledge. In the early years, there was more of a quality of defensiveness and anxiety reduction within an obsessive type context. The older veteran has learned how to regulate this so that mental boundary problems have been mastered. A male at this stage said, "When the session is over I can leave it there." Another said, "I don't worry about it, but I do think about it."

Conceptual Ideas Used

The conceptual system is very similar to that of the Individuation Stage. By this point, a therapist or counselor generally uses a conceptual system that is congruent with one's own personality. For one male at this stage it was, "The more years you counsel the more you find ways that work. That leaves you with a model you've developed that fits your personality and is based on what works." The conceptual system permits the personality to be naturally expressed in one's work. It seems that the personality and professional experience are main determinants, rather than secondary, in the choice of a conceptual system. The individual has not moved to a way of conceptualizing based only on research data from studies or books. Like never before, the therapist/counselor now knows, as one person said, that, "Theory is fascinating but humans don't always fit the book." A female at this stage said, "When I was younger I was more dependent on textbooks and instructors. As time went on, I increasingly used my own experiences and hunches and referred back to texts less often." Another said, "Often in a situation I don't know why but I do know what is the right thing to do. I guess it is intuition."

One's present personality, experience-based generalizations, and Accumulated Wisdom have become the dominant factors; within the professional boundaries of acceptable conceptual systems, the individual has created a system that seems to be most compatible with her/his natural personality and one's experience. This process solidifies during the Individuation Stage and continues. It continues because this most personalized conceptual system is highly authentic for the individual; it is based on the individual's most cherished and confirmed beliefs about human growth, development and change. This personalized conceptual system may be used more rigidly at the Integrity Stage than previously. An Integrity Stage male suggested, "Ten years ago I would have been less self-assured about my answers. I don't know if my answers are different but my confidence in them is." Another said, "My answers are right for me."

Personality seems to be a central factor in one's theoretical orientation. For example, the psychodynamically oriented individuals seem to be drawn to affect, philosophical issues, and introspective ways of understanding and improving human life. Behaviorally oriented individuals seem to be drawn much more to rationality and cognition. They tend not to be very philosophical but rather more pragmatic. They tend to be oriented to action more than reflection and learn by doing something and seeing it being done. It is a "goodness of fit" issue for the individual.

Conceptual systems are by now based more on the individual's experience and the generalizations from it than from the abstract theoretical principles of others. A male at this point said, "You have a foundation of experience that allows you to take greater leaps." Stories and illustrations from direct experience have become conceptually central by now. The individual seldom refers to pure theoretical approaches when deciding one's style.

Learning Process

The individual continues to learn in a very idiosyncratic way. It is the way he/she has chosen. At no time in one's life has the method of learning been more personally chosen. Said a male, "I read more broadly than before. I really like reading psychology through literature." Although new things are learned, the learning is not focused on new elements. The person is not strongly compelled to quickly master large pieces of new material, new approaches, new techniques, new strategies. Whereas the Imitation of Experts Stage individual may be strongly drawn to workshops, the older veteran does not feel this intense pull even if the subject matter is described as a new, unexplored area. One Integrity Stage female said:

> By the time a person reaches the end of one's work life, he/she has seen the wheel reinvented so many times, has seen fashions in therapy/counseling change back and forth. Old ideas emerge under new names and it can be frustrating to the senior therapist to see people make a big fuss about something he/she has known about for years. This contributes to cynicism for the person.

Another said, "Student interns one summer were talking about a new idea in a new book. To me, it was an old idea that was worth a chapter not a book."

The learning now seems to be one of reinterpretation, integration and synthesis of what is known plus the data that comes from one own's personal life, one's clients and one's broad reading. There is not the great desire to know and read everything or a desperate need to learn things very fast which is sometimes true for the younger person. Perhaps the lack of urgency now is related to three factors: an absence of inadequate feelings about oneself as a therapist/counselor, a sense that there really is nothing dramatically new, and a realization that retirement is coming soon.

Measures of Effectiveness and Satisfaction

The work may be more satisfying than ever before. The anxiety of earlier years has greatly diminished, i.e., one female Integrity Stage therapist/

counselor said, "The individual is no longer afraid of clients." The individual has a strong sense of competence, knows how to do the work, takes big risks in the therapy/counseling, has greater control over who she/he will see, needs to put little new energy into building and developing, and yet the clients come and they do benefit. The combination of these factors seems to build an intense level of satisfaction at this point. Related to this, one Integrity Stage male said, "Hang in there, it gets better. I enjoy going to work every day doing what I'm doing." In addition, the individual may be savoring the moment and the work because the work future is finite. The end is drawing near. As one Integrity Stage female said:

> With diminishing anxiety, I became less and less afraid of my clients and with that came an ease for me in using my own wide repertoire of skills and procedures. They became more available to me when I needed them. And during those moments it became remarkable to me that someone would have the willingness to share their private world with me and that my work with them would bring very positive results for them. This brought a sense of intense pleasure to me.

There is a strong sense at this point of the redefinition of the effectiveness away from the beginning when a person felt that he/she could control and mold and change clients. There is a sense now that is arrogant. Individuals now uniformly feel less responsible for client change than earlier. A male at this stage said, "My goals have become more modest with the passage of time. I don't expect to effect major personality change but rather give new options and skills." In addition, the individual is not dependent on constant positive client feedback. As one individual said, "I am ever so much more patient now. Things don't just have to happen and I don't insist on evidence. I'm much less intense about cure and so much less self-conscious." Another said, "If a patient goes away angry I can be happy something has happened. ... Beginners would only feel that way if supervisors helped conceptualize it." One male at this stage said, "I am more ready to say someone is doing better even if they aren't doing ideally well. Maybe that means I've discovered something about my own limits. Maybe I'm not going to make a perfectly insightful, perfectly functioning self-fulfilled human being because I'm not that myself." This relates to the fact that Integrity Stage individuals feel more self-confident. The questions of effectiveness and satisfaction have been redefined and probably have been for a number of years. Usually the explanations from the

Individuation Stage are accepted and defended now. It is now very, very acceptable that success comes in small increments. One person at this stage said, "A client once told me that I don't have to help every time. That has helped me over the years." Less improvement has to be shown from the client to therapist/counselor directly in order for the person to feel like he/she is useful or helpful.

Satisfaction comes from understanding at the deepest level what the work entails and what one can get from the work. The work does not provide for all of life's satisfaction; it cannot and it will not. The Integrity Stage therapist/counselor knows best about the boundaries of satisfaction. There may be irritation about a number of topics such as clients who do not really want to work. However, there is a wonderful quality to the work which is very satisfying. Being permitted to enter a person's personal life and to help the person in a profoundly positive way is an important component of work satisfaction.

Convergence and Divergence Across This Stage Model and Other Research

Throughout the last eight chapters, we have presented the results of our investigation. Now we want to briefly compare and contrast this work with other research.

Few stage models describe the therapist/counselor at the nonprofessional level. The present description of the untrained style as often strong on advice giving and directive guidance is similar to descriptions of untrained helping skills. The description of the Predominant Affect—Sympathy—at this level is the same as that of Hill, Charles, and Reed (1981) for the first phase of a counselor training program. The present emphasis on the use of one's own natural, unexamined personal epistemology as the base for functioning has some parallels to the Stagnation Stage of Loganbill, Hardy, and Delworth (1982) as naive and unaware.

In contrast to the lack of work at the nonprofessional level within the stage literature, there is much description of student/trainee development. There are a number of concepts that seem to be consistently described. Ever since an early description in 1936 by Robinson of social work trainees as highly anxious (cited by Gysbers & Rønnestad, 1974), there have been descriptions of trainee anxiety and the impact of this on development (e.g., Stoltenberg & Delworth, 1987). However, in contrast to many descriptions, our research interviews with therapists/counselors at the student level did not reveal excessive anxiety. It was only when we interviewed senior therapists/counselors that we were able to understand the novice to expert change in anxiety level. As a function of this high level of anxiety, most models describe early trainees as highly dependent on supervisors (e.g., Hogan, 1964; Stoltenberg & Delworth, 1987). In the present model, the dependency is thought of as extending beyond supervisors to a number of professional elders—professors, supervisors, one's own therapist/counselor, mentors, and experts.

Specific skill building is often conceptualized as a desired focus at the early student level to combat excessive anxiety (Grater, 1985) with the supervisor being a teacher and model (Fleming, 1953). Early trainee learning through modeling receives convergent support (e.g., Newman & Fuqua, 1988; Rønnestad, 1977). The popularity of systematic training programs (Baker, Daniels, & Greeley, 1990) at the early student level may result from the teachable moment and student developmental need at this level.

The anxiety of the student seen in many conceptualizations (Hill, Charles, & Reed, 1981; Loganbill, Hardy, & Delworth, 1982; Stoltenberg & Delworth, 1987; and the present formulation) seems related to the addition of much new data which breaks down the student's conceptual scheme. This process is described by Loganbill, Hardy, and Delworth (1982), with their stage Confusion. A study by Hale and Stoltenberg cited by Stoltenberg and Delworth (1987) describes beginner anxiety as related to evaluation apprehension and objective self-awareness. An additional emphasis from the present study is in agreement with Dreyfus and Dreyfus (1986). That is, anxiety relates to inexperience in a complex domain. This inexperience leads to being overwhelmed because of a lack of internal, experience-based expertise.

In the present investigation, we found that beginning students older in age and experience progressed through the student stages more rapidly than did young, inexperienced beginning students. This contrasts with the results of the Hill, Charles, and Reed (1981), investigation.

Another major thrust in the developmental conceptualizations at the student level is the concept of increasing autonomy. Hogan (1964) proposed an autonomy-based conflict at a more advanced student level. Related to this conflict is fluctuating motivation (Stoltenberg, 1981) and our term for Predominant Affect at the advanced student level—variable confidence.

Gradually emerging in most conceptualizations is a move toward identity development and an integrated position. The term integrated is in fact used by Hill, Charles and Reed (1981); Loganbill, Hardy, and Delworth (1982), Stoltenberg and Delworth (1987); and the present model. Some conceptualizations consider this integration to occur early, while still in graduate school (Hill, Charles, & Reed, 1981). Others extend it out further (Loganbill, Hardy, & Delworth, 1982). Perhaps the present conceptualization differs most from other models in our emphasis on development being longer and slower. This probably occurred because we studied veteran practitioners as well as students at different training levels.

The veteran practitioners who served as informants helped us understand important elements of development in the years after training. They helped us understand the impact of intense interpersonal relationships in both the personal and professional domains as critical to professional development. Guy (1987) has discussed personal life but many models do not. Also, the veteran practitioners helped us understand the ongoing reflective process as central to long-term development.

Compared with Loganbill, Hardy, and Delworth (1982) and Stoltenberg and Delworth (1987), the present formulation considers the identity development tasks leading to Individuation to be much longer and more complex than they describe. There are many tasks through the stages of Exploration, Integration and Individuation. As described in the next chapter under Themes 8 and 9, it seems that the intensity of development proceeds way beyond training and that the post-training years are of critical importance in the evolution of the professional self. This occurs, it seems to us, because there are so many elements that must be considered in this professional evolution. They include theory/research, the impact of the culture, clients, professional elders, being a professional elder, and one's personal life. In the present study, integrating and individuating these elements is considered to be a long-term process.

CHAPTER 10

Themes in Therapist/Counselor Development

The process of generating the themes started after we had completed the 8-stage model presented in Chapters 2–9. It was initiated by trying to formulate the essence of our findings. The research methodology we used for this process is elaborated in Appendix A. The themes, 20 in number, are arranged within the following categories: Primary Characteristic Themes, Process Descriptor Themes, Source of Influence Themes, and Secondary Characteristic Themes. We will now present these themes.

Primary Characteristic Themes

Theme 1: Professional Development is Growth toward Professional Individuation

The Individuation process involves an increasingly higher order integration of the professional self and personal self. This integration includes a strong consistency between ideology—one's values and theoretical stance—and methods/techniques used by the individual. It includes a movement from an unarticulated, preconceptual, and ideological way of functioning to a model of functioning which is founded on the individual's own integrated, experience-based generalizations or what we call Accumulated Wisdom. Individuation is an expression of deeper and deeper layers of the self.

As a theoretical concept, our definition of Individuation consists of two elements, a self–other differentiated component and a relational component. This is analogous to the work of Grotevant and Cooper (1986) on the individuation of youth in a family context. Their definition includes both the "... qualities of *individuality* and *connectedness*." (p. 89) Our view of Individuation is also compatible with Jung's concept of individuation (Hall & Lindzey, 1970), in that we are describing deeper and deeper layers of the professional self. Unlike some conceptualizations which equate the concept of individuation with separation and autonomy (Lawler, 1990), we have been struck by how the individuation process for our informants was saturated with relationships. Clients, peers, professional elders, family, friends, and supervisees were all impactful. This is consistent with other counselor development work (Skovholt & McCarthy, 1988) and other theoretical conceptualizations (Karpel, 1976; Stierlin et al., 1984). This individuation concept also has some parallels to the work of Loganbill, Hardy, and Delworth, (1982) on professional identity development.

Ideally, the long-term result of the professional Individuation process is an optimal therapeutic self which consists of a unique personal blend of the developed professional and personal selves. Overall, the sources of influence have gone from heavily external to heavily internal over the course of the professional Individuation process. Within an ethical and competent context, the individual freely chooses the framework and form of professional functioning.

Theme 2: An External and Rigidity Orientation in Role, Working Style and Conceptualizing Issues Increases throughout Training then Declines Continuously

There appear to be three distinct periods of the professional Individuation process:

Pretraining: The Conventional Mode

The first period occurs before professional training. During this period, the individual operates as a helper of others according to the known and natural rules which govern the individual's behavior in personal relationships. The professional realm (as a helper of others) and personal realm are quite similar regarding the individual's functioning.

Training: The External and Rigid Mode

The second phase begins with the start of professional training. From this point to the end of training, a gulf widens between professional and personal functioning. Professional functioning is more and more externally driven with the individual increasingly suppressing characteristic personal

External
orientation

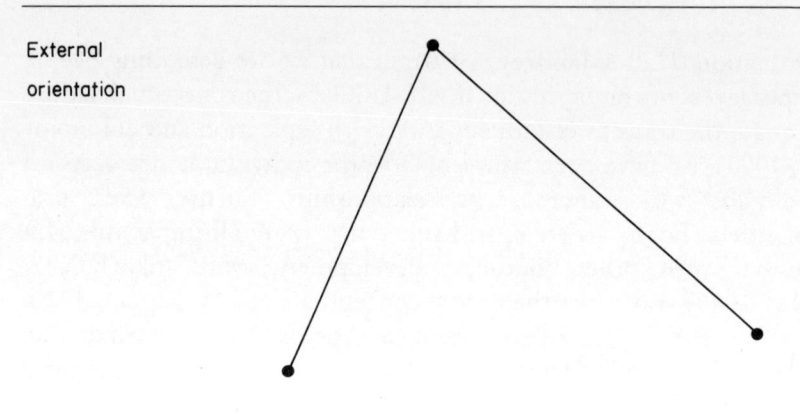

Internal
orientation

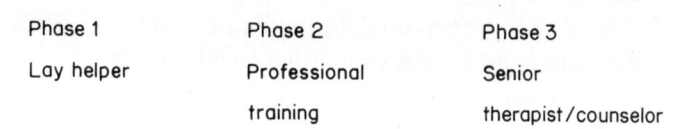

```
Phase 1           Phase 2          Phase 3
Lay helper        Professional     Senior
                  training         therapist/counselor
```

Figure 2. Professional individuation

methods of functioning (e.g., posture, conceptualizing human behavior) for externally imposed, professionally appropriate modes of functioning. This behavior can be described as increasing externally-oriented rigidity. Tracey et al. (1988) found that students exhibited a more rigid response compared with experienced professionals. Usually the beginning and middle periods of training contain the most intense functioning in this mode. For example, one's natural use of humor often follows this gradient. It usually becomes less present during training only to gradually return at a later point. See Lamb et al. (1982) for a description of developmental issues during the internship.

As a function of external regulation in graduate school, mostly in the form of difficult examinations, intense professional socialization, structured internships, and licensing requirements, the individual goes through a long period of learning and demonstration expertise in meeting the approval of the profession's gatekeepers: professors, supervisors, and licensing board members. This is an exhaustive process that commands much of the individual's life energy. Perfectionistic behavior, obsessiveness, and preoccupation characterize many who successfully run this gauntlet. In fact, it is these traits which often enable the individual to be accepted by graduate programs at the beginning of this second phase.

Everyone knows that some people do not succeed in graduate school. This is the catalyst for feeling threatened about meeting the expectations of the professional gatekeepers who hold enormous power over the novice's entrance into the profession. This stressful world—the life of a graduate student—has been described by Guy (1987).

A direct result of this enormous professional pressure is the development of externally imposed rigidity in many areas of professional functioning, such as role/working style, conceptualization of issues, and measurement of success. Generally during training, there is a growing alienation between the pretraining professional self and the developing professional self. This growing gulf is often a focus of intense introspection by the individual.

Post-Training: The Loosening and Internal Mode

A third period begins when training ends. The rite of passage at this point is called commencement, a term used to celebrate an ending. In contrast, it is a commencing, the beginning of third phase work. Although graduation is an abrupt process, the post-training process actually occurs gradually over a number of years. Graduation symbolizes freedom from external control, and this symbolism does serve as a catalyst for the work of this third period which can be described as a loosening and internalizing mode. The work of this phase is a key element in the avoidance of Pseudodevelopment, an alternative stage of development (see Chapter 11) to the normative stage sequence we have described as Exploration–Integration–Individuation–Integrity. The individual moves to the Pseudodevelopment path by continuing in an external and rigid mode. This usually means a strong identification with an acknowledged master or combination of acknowledged masters who are emulated in greater and greater detail and with greater and greater precision. This process, in fact, entails an increased use of the external and rigid mode of the second phase. This means a growing alienation between the authentic personal self and the evolving professional self. The actual third phase of the Professional Individuation process is antithetical to this continuation of the second phase so characteristic of Pseudodevelopment. In the normative third phase, there is convergence between the authentic personal self and the professional self.

Graduation and licensure provide a release from this externally imposed rigidity. Although the individual while in training may be quite hostile toward the gatekeepers, the dreamed release is not always easy. Something desired so much now can be experienced as professional loneliness in a way not experienced before. The demand—to individually decide which elements of the professionally imposed rigidity to shed and which elements of the internal self to express—is often experienced as painful. Backing off of this demand leads to the Pseudodevelopment path; going ahead enables development to continue.

The third period often begins after graduation with a sense of confirmation regarding one's expertise in second phase functioning. The individual wants to feel very positive about one's skills after finishing the training program. However, in time, a period of disquiet often occurs because the externally imposed rigidity seems to be evaporating as the individual is told in subtle ways to begin functioning from a self-direction versus other direction base. This realization can produce a dis-ease and period of crisis. This is one point when the Pseudodevelopment process can be attractive to the individual as an alternative to the self-reliance and introspection which characterizes the Exploration Stage. Although the individual may have strong peer support, external-oriented dependency usually does not produce successful resolution of the identity tasks at this point. The exploration process can be described as a dialectical process involving vacillating between the introspection and extrospection processes, both of which are self-directed.

The Professional Individuation process at this third phase often occurs over a period of 20 to 30 years. At the end of this process, there is some similarity to the beginning of the first period because the professional and personal selves are in close proximity. In another way, the Professional Individuation process at a mature point is radically different than the beginning.

At the most mature stages—Individuation and Integrity, there is an increasing closeness between the professional and personal selves in terms of being authentic at deep levels of the self. Increased authenticity is a major thrust for the individual during this third phase. The push for authenticity may cost the individual because of a need to give up much that has been learned earlier (i.e. a conceptual system that was learned thoroughly in graduate school but that no longer is acceptable because of the internalized need for authenticity).

Ideally the long-term result of the Professional Individuation process is an optimal therapeutic self which consists of a unique personal blend of the developed professional and personal selves. Overall, the sources of influence have gone from heavily external to heavily internal over the course of the Professional Individuation process. There are few external mentors by this time, although internal mentors and constant interaction with others may guide the individual. Within an ethical and competent context, the individual freely chooses the framework and form of professional functioning.

The healthy evolution of the Professional Self permits the therapist/counselor to consistently meet one's own needs within an ethical, competent role. There is more flexibility and more creativity in, for example, applying clinical knowledge to unique client problems. The more integrated professional role means there is a deeper base of identity and more consistency between ideology (values and theories) and procedures (methods and techniques). The use of a conceptual system at this advanced level reflects the powerful impact of the therapist/counselor's personality and cognitive schema more than the impact of empirical outcome research. A byproduct of the Professional Individuation process is a sureness and confidence that comes out of long-term experience and consistent authentic functioning. This produces a greatly reduced sense of anxiety about work performance.

Theme 3: As the Professional Matures, Continuous Professional Reflection Becomes the Central Developmental Process

Professional development leads to Professional Individuation by the essential method of Continuous Professional Reflection. This is a major method of professional development. The individual uses this process in order to grow and develop. Reflection occurs most of all through the processing of interpersonal experiences. These include both professional and personal relationships. The impact of conceptual and theoretical knowledge is typically mediated through interacting with clients as well as senior professionals such as supervisors and professors, as well as admired peers. Reflective experiences are experiences which a person thinks about and which produce learning. They serve as small transformations in the way the individual perceives, conceptualizes, and acts. Elimination of this process helps produce Pseudodevelopment and also brings on professional stagnation. There are three necessary parts of Continuous Professional Reflection: professional and personal experience, connections to other searchers via an open and supportive work environment, and a reflective stance.

Professional and Personal Experience

The process of Continuous Professional Reflection demands an ongoing flow of professional interaction. Some of these interpersonal experiences occur through direct interaction with clients, supervisors, professors, therapists, and peers. In this people-centered business, direct human contact is essential. Some of the interpersonal interaction is more indirect. This occurs when individuals such as supervisors mediate for the individual important theoretical and empirical concepts as well as ethical and professional points of view. It is not only professional relationships which serve in the reflective process. Personal human experiences are also central. These include important personal relationships with family of origin members, one's spouse or significant partner, one's children, personal friends, and important acquaintances. Our senior informants pointed to these intense interpersonal experiences as essential to their development. Another source of data for reflection consists of solitary activities: time spent in activities such as professional reading, movies and television, and personal introspection.

An element of the ongoing flow of professional interaction is direct professional work as a therapist/counselor. At a less direct level, professional experience also occurs. The structure for these relationships may differ greatly across individuals and occurs in such diverse settings as peer supervision, research collaboration, consulting, close colleague friendships, workshop and convention attendance, and editorial board work.

Open, Supportive Work Environment

It is important to have an environment supportive of one's search, an environment where the person is connected to other professional searchers. Such an environment is not dogmatic or rigid but is supportive of professional development and increased competence. Such an environment values high standards of performance and a searching process as opposed to the process of total acceptance of a preordained set of ideological principles. Such an environment supports an exploratory, investigative approach. Such an environment values diversity and has an opening up stance versus a simplification of the complex world, i.e., in working with a client case, such an environment will encourage looking for as many associations on a case as possible versus reinforcing only a narrow, prescriptive theory or method.

Reflective Stance

Paramount in this process is a reflective stance which means that the individual is consciously giving time and energy to processing, alone and with others, impactful experiences. An active, exploratory, searching, and open attitude is of extreme importance. Asking for and receiving feedback is crucial. Benner and Wrubel (1982) describe such a reflective stance when they write about improving clinical knowledge:

> Experience is necessary for moving from one level of expertise to another, but experience is not the equivalent of longevity, seniority, or the simple passage of time. Experience means living through actual situations in such a way that it informs the practitioner's perception and understanding of all subsequent situations. (p. 28)

This helps avoid the loop of continual performance with no feedback and, therefore, no modification.

In the early years when the individual is involved in highly structured professional training, it is important to be able to resist defining self only through the view of others. Later, when the individual is beyond the structure of external control and supervision in graduate school, it is crucial to seek out stimulations and feedback on a continual basis. Stagnation and deterioration can occur for the senior professional who neglects setting up channels for stimulation or feedback or has only confirmatory feedback channels.

Theme 4: Beginning Practitioners Rely on External Expertise, Senior Practitioners Rely on Internal Expertise

In time, experience-based generalizations and Accumulated Wisdom replaces the use of experts' context-free theory and one's own unarticulated, preconceptual ideology as a basis of professional functioning. The demand for external expertise early in development is reflected in these comments by Martin *et al.*, (1989), "As counselor educators, we are constantly being pressured by students to tell them what to 'do' with a particular client." (p. 133)

This theme is compatible with the work of Dreyfus and Dreyfus (1986). In describing the natural, embedded nature of expertise, they quote Pascal in the *Pensées*, published in 1670:

> Mathematical formalizers wish to treat matters of intuition mathematically, and make themselves ridiculous.... The mind...does it tacitly, naturally, and without technical rules. (p. 16)

Our concept of Accumulated Wisdom is also similar to the description of expertise by Glaser and Chi (1988) as entailing a "...rich structure of domain specific knowledge." (p. xxi) Simon describes a related knowledge and experience-based expertise as producing an ability he calls Intuition (Benderly, 1989). As a conclusion of their research contrasting experts and novices, Cummings *et al.*, (1990) state, "...it seems that a combination of experience and training provides counselors with a parsimonious set of deep-level schemata that can be activated consistently to assess in conceptualizing individual clients." (p. 132) Kivlighan and Quigley (1991) describe a similar dimension in group work.

As a prerequisite to operating from Accumulated Wisdom, which is built from experience-based generalizations, the individual must engage in highly disciplined and intensive study of the core body of knowledge in the field. The most impactful theory and research is often mediated through intense interactions with others such as clients, professional elders, and peers/colleagues. From this theory/research base, hundreds of hours of experiences produce useful generalizations which then produce Accumulated Wisdom. This Accumulated Wisdom makes highly competent functioning possible.

Although theoretically not identical, the use of what Benner (1982) labeled "past concrete experiences," Dreyfus and Dreyfus (1986) label "aspect recognition" and "maxims," and we label "experience-based generalizations" and "Accumulated Wisdom" suggests how the senior expert therapist/counselor is able to recognize critical data amidst the complexity of the client's life. For example, knowing how to react swiftly and competently to an initial client problem of relationship loss is dependent on this process. In such a case, the experienced practitioner is able to draw on previous work with others to highlight the most important parts of this problem and then to use these experience-based generalizations and Accumulated Wisdom to intervene in a highly competent way.

Tennis players "react" when expert, and, a surprising amount of the time, so do business managers and experienced doctors and nurses when deeply involved in their professional activities. The expert driver not only knows by feel and familiarity when an action such as slowing is required, but generally knows how to perform the act without evaluating and comparing alternatives. ... Excellent chess players can play at the rate of five to ten seconds or more and even faster without serious degradation in performance. At that speed, they must depend almost entirely on intuition and hardly at all on analysis and comparing alternatives. ... What should stand out [in this formulation] is the progression *from* the analytic behavior of a detached subject, consciously decomposing his [*sic*] environment into recognizable elements, and following abstract rules, *to* involved skilled behavior based on an accumulation of concrete experiences and the unconscious recognition of new situations as similar to whole remembered ones. (Dreyfus & Dreyfus, 1986, pp. 32–33, 35)

Functioning as an expert is dependent on this expertise building process. Intense study along with repetitive practice in a restricted arena as part of Continuous Professional Reflection produces expertise as well as mastery and the ability to function from Accumulated Wisdom. A major difference between the beginner in our sample and the 20-year veteran is the veteran's ability to operate from this expertise base.

Theme 5: Conceptual System and Role-working Style Become Increasingly Congruent with One's Personality and Cognitive Schema

In time the individual gradually sheds elements of the professional role that are incompatible with one's own personality and cognitive schema and adopts elements of the professional role that are congruent with the self. The need for compatibility with the self seems more powerful in choice of professional role, over the many years that Professional Individuation occurs, than the empirical research base or the professional biases of one's graduate training program.

Conceptual system, we concluded, always seemed compatible with the personality and cognitive schema of our senior informants. A number of informants told us of displacing a theoretical approach mastered earlier because it just was not compatible with the person. Sammons and Gravitz (1990) offer support for our results in their study of the impact of former professors on the theoretical orientation of professional psychologists, "Among individuals, theoretical orientations are not very stable over time. The longer the time elapsed since graduate training, the more likely that a change in orientation will occur." (p. 133) Compatibility often was related to whether the emphasis of the approach (e.g., affect, behavior, cognition) matched the personality and cognitive scheme of the therapist/counselor.

Role and working style also seemed to be very compatible with the senior informant as a person. Some individuals were formal, others informal; some very dominant and verbal, others were egalitarian and quiet. The authenticity to self requirement seemed to have been met by these senior informants. Wachowiak, Bauer, and Simono (1979) describe the movement of counseling center psychologists into a variety of work settings within ten years after receiving the doctorate. Perhaps some of this movement correlates with the present compatibility theme.

The learning process is characterized by a movement from the external to internal mode. Also, with experience, learning takes a more heterogeneous form across individuals. Freed from the rigid learning processes used uniformly in formal schooling, the individual is increasingly able to choose how to continue the learning process. Experienced individuals in our sample group varied in preference between such forms as relying on a trusted mentor, using peer group supervision, studying the psychological themes in movies, reading the empirical research, attending workshops, keeping an elaborate journal, or reading religion, history, biography, anthropology, and poetry.

Although sometimes embarrassed to admit this fact, most senior practitioners in our sample did not devote much time to reading empirical journal articles. They do not appear to be directly influenced by data and concepts presented in this format.

Paralleling this increased self-directed preference regarding learning method, the personal use of the Continuous Professional Reflection process takes on a more central role.

Theme 6: There is Movement from Received Knowledge toward Constructed Knowledge

The Internal Expertise of the senior practitioner is guided by an individuated learning method and active knowledge development. The learning process is characterized by a movement from the external to internal mode. With experience, learning method takes a more heterogeneous form across individuals. Freed from the rigid learning processes used uniformly in formal schooling, the individual is increasingly able to choose how to continue the learning process. Experienced individuals in our sample group varied in preference between such forms as relying on a trusted mentor, using peer group supervision, studying the psychological themes in movies, reading the empirical research, attending workshops, keeping an elaborate journal, or reading in areas such as biography, anthropology, and poetry.

Expertise is created differently as the practitioner matures. Belenky *et al.* (1986) in *Women's ways of knowing* provide a model for understanding this evolution in knowledge development. Starting from the Perry (1981) model of cognitive meaning and development, Belenky *et al.* (1986) created seven levels of the ways of knowing. This model seems useful to us as a way of charting the changes in knowledge development for therapists of both genders. They describe an early level, Received Knowledge, as the following:

> While received knowers can be very open to take in what others have to offer, they have little confidence in their own ability to speak. Believing that truth comes from others, they still their own voices to hear the voices of others. (p. 37)

This seems to us descriptive of the knowledge generation method of the new graduate student in a therapy/counseling training program. The senior practitioner operates at a very different knowledge generation level. The highest level of the Belenky *et al.* (1986) model, Constructed Knowledge, seems descriptive:

> All knowledge is constructed, and the knower is an intimate part of the known (p. 137).... To see that all knowledge is a construction and that truth is a matter of the context in which it is embedded is to greatly expand the possibilities of how to think about anything (p. 138).... Theories become not truth but models for approximate experience... (p. 138).

The movement through these levels of knowledge constructions along with the increasing idiosyncratic nature of one's learning style produces profound changes from the life of the novice to the life of the professional elder. For example, at the 1990 Evolution of Psychotherapy conference sponsored by the Milton Friedman Foundation, practitioners of all experience levels were in attendance listening to many theoretical leaders such as Beck, Frankel, Haley, Lazarus, Madanes, Masterson, May, Minuchin, Watzlawick, and Wolpe. In such a rich context new graduate students operating from a position of Received Knowledge would passively accept the speakers' ideas as accurate, truthful and something to be followed. At the Constructed Knowledge position, the speaker ideas would be considered as constructions of the speaker to be rejected or incorporated as part of a much more active knowledge development style. This occurs because the senior practitioner as part of her/his development has a much more elaborate set of personally developed theoretical constructs to balance against the speakers' ideas.

Process Descriptor Themes

Theme 7: Development is Impacted by Multiple Sources Which are Experienced in Both Common and Unique Ways

During the research process, we keep discovering more and more elements that impact development. These elements are: Professional Elders (Supervisors, Professors, Mentors, Therapists, Experts), Peers/Colleagues, Clients, Theories/Research, One's Own Personal Life, the Social/Cultural Environment on the micro level (within the therapy/counseling occupational world) and macro level (the larger society and culture), and Becoming a Professional Elder on One's Own.

They are common because they impact every individual. Yet timing, intensity, and pace dimensions as well as many unique features (i.e., the theoretical approach of a supervisor) produce an incredible uniqueness for the sources of influence.

Theme 8: Optimal Professional Development is a Long, Slow, and Erratic Process

It is not an event and it is not completed during graduate school! The use of Continuous Professional Reflection goes on year after year as the professional base is built, expanded, and individuated. This difficult process occurs for each person as he/she attempts to improve and get better. This normalization of the struggle and the slowness of the development of professional expertise is especially important for the new therapist/counselor to understand. Studying expertise, Glaser says that learning knowledge rich tasks such as medical diagnosis, and presumably therapy/counseling work, takes "hundreds and thousands of hours of learning and experience" (cited by Benderly, 1989, p. 36).

Over the long-term career, the individual developmental process varies greatly. At times the developmental process is continuous. At times it is more of an intense change process, perhaps highlighted by a specific critical incident (Skovholt & McCarthy, 1988), followed by a period of slow change. Stoltenberg and Delworth (1987) describe this process by using the Piagetian concepts of assimilation followed by accommodation. At times it follows a recycling loop in which themes are repeated at increasingly deeper levels. The concept of recycling is compatible with Hess (1987) and Loganbill, Hardy, and Delworth (1982). For example, a theme such as lack of confidence in one's ability may be predominant in the first year of graduate school, then reemerge five years later, and then again 20 years later.

In our stage model (Chapters 2-9), the time period can vary greatly across stages. For example, the Transition to Professional Training Stage lasts for one year whereas the Individuation Stage lasts ten to thirty years. However, the pace of the developmental process can vary greatly across individuals. It is difficult to be specific about the pace because of the impact of so many factors. However, one factor—age when entering graduate school—appears to have a major impact on development. In our sample, older graduate students seemed to go through the early stages (Transition to Professional Training, Imitation of Experts) more quickly than younger graduate students. For example, a new 22-year-old graduate student may identify strongly with a conceptual idea, such as a method to increase self-esteem, while a new 40-year-old graduate student will scan professional and personal experience to support or question the validity of the self-esteem treatment idea. The greater skepticism of the 40-year-old may keep her/him from the later disillusionment and difficult work with reformulation that occurs when limits of the conceptual idea are discovered. The difference in pace based on age at the beginning of graduate school seems to fade with time. Consequently, 20-year veterans of age 42 to 60 do not appear to be as different in professional development as the 22- and 40-year-old beginners. Other factors which often correlate with age—experience in the human services (i.e., earlier career as a teacher), confronting intense personal stress, recovering from a dysfunctional family of origin, and involvement with a cause to promote human development—also seem to increase the pace through the early stages.

Since our sample was only 4% minority, reflecting the therapist/counselor population in Minnesota, we did not attempt to distinguish any racial differences. Both genders were well represented in our sample and our research interviewers. Although the total group was nearly equal in terms of males and females, females predominated in the new graduate school group and males predominated in the senior professional group, which is representative of the population these samples were drawn from. This also seems to be an accurate reflection of the overall shift in the field from predominantly male to predominantly female. Our method of inquiry did not specifically focus on differences in variables such as gender. Using their own experiences, McGowen and Hart (1990) have recently speculated about gender differences in the development of psychologists in the areas of relational focus, distance versus intimacy, and contextual decision-making.

Theme 9: Post-Training Years are Critical for Optimal Development
Most developmental models within the therapy/counseling field are in fact models of student development. Evaluation of graduate school enables investigators to understand changes in training. For example, there is a wealth of supervision oriented studies which consider changes between beginning practicum students and interns on one or more dimensions. The detailed nature of this exploration parallels the intensity of exploration within American psychology which focuses on the most readily available sample base—students. This is expressed by the saying that "American psychology is the psychology of the college sophomore."

In a parallel fashion, graduate students in therapy and counseling are available for research studies by faculty and by students completing a thesis. Trainee development also holds intrinsic interest for graduate students who are looking for a thesis topic. Also, the sample pool is readily available compared with other groups. The result is that, "...little is known about the postgraduate counselor. ...Such studies are necessary for a complete understanding of counselor development across the professional life span" (Borders, 1989, p. 21). Hogan's (1964) often cited work is an example of an incomplete stage model. After three graduate student stages, one enters the fourth stage: Master Psychologist. This stage covers all the years from graduation to retirement. We are reminded of the Freudian psychosexual stages, with the last stage—Genital—covering everything from adolescence to senior adulthood.

Senior members of our sample group helped us understand that therapist/counselor development continues and evolves long after school and that a focus on trainee changes without the larger vision can easily lead to erroneous conclusions and implications. For example, we only understood the profound reduction in pervasive anxiety from the Transition to Professional Training Stage to the Integrity Stage after interviews with senior practitioners. They freely described this major shift in their lives. The beginning informants, perhaps because of minimization and the lack of a contrast effect, were not able to help us understand this dimension.

Even within the postgraduate years, a period of decades, there are major shifts in many dimensions. For example, there is the increased involvement of oneself as a professional elder which serves as a personal source of influence; there is an increased shedding of unauthentic elements of the self during the increased internal orientation of the postgraduate years; there is increased use of experience-based generalizations and Accumulated Wisdom to guide practice. In fact, it may be that the critical factor in professional development is the shift from the external focus of pleasing professional gatekeepers to an internal focus which involves the forming of one's own unique professional self and the avoidance of stagnation and pseudodevelopment. This occurs long after formal training is complete.

Theme 10: As the Professional Develops, there is a Decline of Pervasive Anxiety

The Professional Individuation and Accumulated Wisdom processes are essential in the replacement of pervasive anxiety with quiet comfort and confidence. There is a great reduction in angst between the novice and the senior practitioner levels. The anxiety of the beginner has been discussed by many authors ever since Robinson's description of social work trainees in 1936 (cited by Gysberg and Rønnestad, 1974). Others who discuss the anxiety of the beginner include Dodge (1982), Grater (1985), Loganbill *et al.* (1982) and Stoltenberg and Delworth (1987). Rodolfa, Kraft, and Reilley (1988) found levels of stress differed between practicum students (the highest group), interns (the middle group), and professional staff (the lowest group). In another study, beginners were focused on (1) Learning techniques and meeting client needs, (2) One's role and adequacy as a counselor, (3) Do clients like me? (Littrell, 1978). Senior practitioners do not have these high anxiety concerns.

A crucial factor in the decline of pervasive anxiety is the increase in expertise which results from long periods of experience and training. The increased use of internal expertise by way of experience-based generalizations and Accumulated Wisdom is a key element. Using different terminology, Martin *et al.* (1989) gave support to this idea:

> Experience as counselors gradually equips seasoned practitioners with efficient sets of schemata that they consistently draw on when conceptualizing individual clients and their problems. These schemata probably have tremendous practical advantages in both economy of time and energy *and felt confidence* [emphasis added] for the veteran counselor. (p. 399)

The level of pervasive anxiety has a dramatic effect on the practitioner, and therefore the professional functioning of the individual also differs dramatically in many ways, e.g., needing or not needing direct positive feedback from a client, learning to tolerate ambiguity for a long period of time while working with a client, discovering how to separate self from a client's self. As one greatly respected senior informant said, "In time, you are no longer afraid of your clients."

This gradual reduction in pervasive anxiety, usually related to increased experience, most often continues to decline with time. Accumulated Wisdom is a major factor in the reduction of angst. Often knowledge produces expertise and, therefore, the reduced angst. However, it also increases and decreases in recycling loops. Confidence can be lost for a time during periods of career transition or unusual stress related to work with clients.

Sources of Influence Themes

Theme 11: Interpersonal Encounters are More Influential than Impersonal Data

Intense interpersonal experiences strongly impact professional development. When interviewing our informants and examining the impact of different sources of influence at different levels of professional functioning, strongly human relationships emerged as more important than impersonal data. When asking in the interviews about the impact of theories and research, we thought that theory and research would be perceived as of central importance for subjects' development. However, in the interviews, the subjects kept telling us most about person impact and least about empirical research results.

In the work context, the following people were impactful for our subjects: clients, peers/colleagues, and a group of professional elders (supervisors, professors, one's own therapist/counselor, experts, and mentors). For our informants as a group, person impact in the work context occurred in this order, clients as most impactful, then professional elders, then peers, then being a professional elder for others. Of course, there is a great variety across individuals in their ranking of person impact. In time, being a professional elder can also be very impactful for the individual. Theory and research is often mediated through these individuals, and in this way, both people and theory/research are of importance.

Theme 12: Personal Life is a Central Component of Professional Functioning

The evolution of the Professional Self by way of Continuous Professional Reflection eventually means that personal life becomes more accurately understood and integrated into professional life. This task often takes an enormous amount of time and energy and many years of effort. It is often a very difficult and elusive task to fully integrate themes of the therapist/counselor's personal life into professional practice in a way that is most beneficial to clients and authentic to the individual. The themes often relate to pain involving family of origin, definition of self, or other fundamental issues. Examples include family alcoholism, personal low self-esteem, rejection by spouse in marriage, tragic death of friend, personal victimization, intense cross-culture experience, or similar impactful human experience.

Often these themes are partially unconscious at the time of graduate school admission. (Our graduate school subjects—the novice informants—most often claimed to understand their motivation for entering therapy/counseling work. Senior informants, on the contrary, often said they did not fully understand their occupational motives when a novice.) Later the motivational themes may be expressed in the choice of topic for the M.A. or Ph.D. thesis or the choice of work setting. In time the individual is able to gain perspective on these personal themes, realize how the themes produce energy for therapeutic work and give the individual the double edge of unusual insight and blind spots when functioning professionally. The individual also learns how to use these personal themes to be helpful to clients in a variety of assessment and treatment arenas. However, if the process of Professional Individuation has not occurred through Continuous Professional Reflection, the individual may still be a "wounded healer" who can be harmful to clients in small and large ways.

Events from one's personal life can, if used competently, be extremely illuminating and instructive in one's professional work. Both difficult life experiences and normative life experiences continually impact the professional. Our sample group repeatedly talked about the value they derived from their own loss experiences such as divorce, death, disability, loss of property, and loss of meaning and purpose. These stressful experiences seem to be more instructive than success and achievement experiences because it is these kinds of painful experiences which bring clients to therapist/counselors. Therefore, a personal understanding of emotional pain, loss, and distress seemed of much greater value than success and achievement when understanding clients.

Normative experiences are also of great value. This includes many events such as being a parent, working for a variety of bosses, balancing roles in life, experiencing one's parents' age, being uprooted by a geographic move, going through culture shock, coping with performance failure or experiencing a sudden unexpected process. The personal experience is immensely rich, informative, and motivational for the work of therapy and counseling.

Theme 13: Clients are a Continuous Major Source of Influence and Serve as Primary Teachers

At all levels of experience and education, our sample group reported that clients have a powerful impact on their professional functioning. In so many ways, clients serve as primary teachers. Through their presenting complaints and attempts to solve these complaints, they are constantly providing information about causes and solutions to human distress. The exact expression of both this distress and the attempts to lessen it are of extreme value to a therapist/counselor. In fact, it is the combination of academic and professional work followed by Continuous Professional Reflection which is the key learning experience.

Clients are extremely influential in how they respond to the therapist/counselor. Through the close interpersonal contact between the client and therapist/counselor, the latter is continually receiving feedback on oneself as a person. More specifically, clients continually provide specific feedback regarding the therapist/counselor's intervention attempts. In small ways, clients give valuable feedback regarding the therapist/counselor's attempts to be helpful when using ideas like the following: systematic desensitization, a hypnotic induction, a paradoxical directive, a suggestion of marital therapy for a family with an acting-out child, the use of a career planning inventory, or the hundreds of other similar kinds of therapist/counselor interventions.

A common major crisis for professionals involves a lack of positive client response to the therapist/counselor's use of a major theoretical approach that the therapist/counselor had worked hard to master because of its supposed strong utility. The conceptual approach may be psychodynamic or cognitive or family systems or behavioral or something else. The key element is the lack of client improvement when a supposedly successful therapy/counseling approach is used. This often brings on a searching process for the therapist/counselor regarding the cause of the failure. The quality of this search may impact whether stagnation or development is likely to occur (see Chapter 11).

Theme 14: Newer Members of the Field View Professional Elders and Graduate Training with Strong Affective Reactions

Professional Elders are of extreme importance to newer members of the profession and, therefore, tend to be idealized or devalued. The concept of transference can be used to understand these reactions. The beginner wants to learn from, model after, please, and respect such individuals. Strong admiration is expressed for senior members of the profession who possess behaviors or personal characteristics which are perceived as highly positive, such as intellectual brilliance, strong therapeutic skills, outstanding supervision ability, unusual emotional support for beginners, and the modeling of professional values in personal life. Negative reactions are just as common. Professional elders are devalued if they possess behaviors perceived as highly negative. These include individuals such as an unfair supervisor or a professor who teaches counseling but seems unable to practice it. The student therapist/counselor in time often goes through a transition like the youth who idealizes and devalues the parent—treating the parent as larger than life—only to later, much later in life, see the parent as a person with all the humanness of people in general. Beyond graduate school, professional elders are idealized and devalued less and their humanness—ordinariness, strengths/weaknesses, uniqueness—is understood more clearly.

Most therapists and counselors experience some disillusionment regarding their graduate education and training. The key issue is the gulf between expectations of the program, the university, the faculty, and actual reality. The higher the expectations before training begins, the greater the eventual, though not immediate, disillusionment and its corollaries, disappointment and anger. A major issue is the relatively powerless student role and the constant pressure to perform up to the expectations of the graduate program requirements. After succeeding at meeting the expectations of professors, the individual usually still feels underprepared by the graduate program. Common points for this feeling occur at the beginning of practicum and at graduation. Specific disillusionment issues vary greatly but include academic requirements which seem useless and the lack of enough training in areas which the student views as important. As with professional elders, who ten to twenty years later are often perceived more realistically, one's graduate program also often comes to be viewed more realistically and with more understanding.

Theme 15: External Support is Most Important at the Beginning of One's Career and at Transition Points

In time, support becomes internalized. This means that the advanced professional usually does not need the same kind of external support as the beginner. Common points for strong external support are the beginning of graduate school when professor, advisor, and peer support is desired, at times of practicum and internship when supervisor and peer support is desired, and at the beginning of a new professional position when work supervisor, mentor, and peer support is desired. In the senior years of one's career, external support is often derived through peer relationships and the supervision relationship with younger professionals.

Theme 16: Professional Isolation Becomes an Important Issue with Increased Experience and Age

As time goes on, Professional Elders gradually disappear from one's professional life, and the individual is left with a diminished number of professors, supervisors, therapists, mentors, or experts to lean on, emulate, and learn from. Retirement and death are major reasons for the loss of these individuals.

Professional Elders do continue to be present to the degree that their impact has been internalized, i.e., one member of our sample group often says to himself, "Now how would Ron respond to this?" (Ron was his supervisor 20 years ago in another part of the country.) Another had a place in the office where a picture of Freud could be looked at.

In addition to the loss of Professional Elders, senior practitioners often experience the loss of one's own peer group. Compared with the often intense and continual interaction with numerous classmates in graduate school, an individual 20 years later may live in a much more professionally isolating way. For example, senior practitioners often gravitate to private practice, a setting where there is often less colleague interaction.

Theme 17: Modeling/Imitation is a Powerful and Preferred Early—but not Later—Learning Method

In the first years of professional training, the individual is very eager to absorb by watching experts work and hearing them talk about their work. Experts are defined as writers of major theoretical approaches or techniques for certain problem areas, respected local practitioners, or one's own professors or supervisors. This use of models has a long history in the supervision literature (Rønnestad, 1977). Early in training, the process of learning occurs efficiently through mechanical, repetitive imitation. Therefore, the search for experts to imitate takes on great salience early in one's professional development and modeling is a common early training instructional strategy (Newman & Fuqua, 1988). The strong demand for the "Gloria" films and the growth of this series to nine modeling films (Shostrom, 1965), shown predominantly to audiences of students in training, also supports this finding.

Experienced practitioners have internalized an education via this modeling and have moved beyond the continuum of rote imitation to selective identification. Experienced practitioners are most focused on expanding, clarifying, and elaborating their own style and, therefore, find limited value in watching experts work.

Secondary Characteristic Themes

Theme 18: There is a Movement toward Increased Boundary Clarity and Responsibility Differentiation

At the beginning of professional development, the therapist/counselor typically assumes total responsibility for client improvement and uses directly expressed client satisfaction as the predominant criteria for judging success. In time, the perception of responsibility changes. Increasingly, she/he feels responsible to behave professionally; that is, in such a way that the client is given an opportunity to change if the client decides to do so. However, assuming total responsibility means being responsible to an excessive and unnecessary degree.

After extensive experience, the individual had an increased ability to (precisely) regulate professional involvement within and across three domains of the self: the private self, the personal self, and the professional self, i.e., the art of self-disclosure is practiced with more expertise by the experienced practitioner. There is also an increased ability to use physical, mental, and emotional boundaries within these three domains. For example, with time, one is more able to regulate, in a productive way, the emotional involvement that is given to clients outside of sessions.

By mid-career, there is a noticeable shift in the protection of self. By this time, protection of self is a high priority activity and is expressed by behavior such as strict time limits for work and increased willingness to refer clients. The development of these boundaries is a critical skill and allows the individual to be involved but not depleted by the multiple accounts of human suffering that are repeatedly heard by the average practitioner.

Theme 19: For the Practitioner there is a Realignment from a Narcissistic Position to a Therapeutic Position

With time and the normative variety of experiences with clients that at times produce only limited success, the therapist must develop a posture of realism to replace a previous, articulated or unarticulated, position of idealism. Idealism must be saturated with a reality-based optimism to prevent the burnout elements of discouragement from emerging.

An important component of the change from idealism to realism is a therapist/counselor movement from a narcissistic position to a therapeutic position. The narcissistic position often involves a partially understood attraction to the therapist/counselor role because of an assumption that the role is powerful; one has power to help people, to cure, to lessen dis-ease and anxiety, and, therefore, acting as a therapist/counselor and helping others can increase one's own self-esteem and competence. For a discussion of motivation to become a therapist/counselor, see Guy (1987).

The therapeutic position involves less performance anxiety and a less grandiose sense of self as a curative agent. The shift involves a realignment from a position of therapist/counselor power to client power. Giving up this controlling stance, which is rooted in the professional's desire to feel powerful while experiencing a lack of professional confidence, paradoxically allows the therapist/counselor to be more effective. The shift is reflected in the belief of the beginner that he/she must measure every word because the wrong word can be very destructive. The long-term veteran reacts differently in part because of the realization that he/she is not that powerful. This change in understanding is reflected in the words of an Individuation Stage male who said, "Psychotherapy is what the therapist does while the client is getting better." Also, there is a shift from assessing effectiveness by use of client, supervisor, and peer evaluations to more internalized, professionally-based criteria. For example, a respected senior practitioner in our sample described his work as highly competent even if a client may finish therapy feeling angry. A novice could never conceptualize things this way. This shift in one's assessment of self is suggested in less of a tendency to project one's own professional and personal strengths as the *key* effectiveness factors (e.g., being of a certain age or having certain personal experiences with human distress such as alcoholism).

A factor which helps this process is the "series of humiliations" which happen to practitioners over time. These occur when the best work of the therapist/counselor does not produce desired client outcomes. An analogy is that at times the patient dies even when a physician's performance is excellent. An important part of this shift is the clarity that comes in time that enables the individual to accurately distinguish between normative failure and excessive failure. The beginner most often believes that he/she is responsible for any and all failures that occur in work with clients.

Theme 20: Extensive Experience with Suffering Produces Heightened Tolerance and Acceptance of Human Variability

Through direct work with suffering people, greater understanding develops of the human variability in deciding, coping, and resolving both difficult and sample issues. Equally important the personal life of the therapist/counselor is instructive. Through the process of living one's life as an adult, a variety of experiences, including personal disappointments and choices, helps to make the individual become less judgmental of others.

Summary

Little has been written which describes the detailed structure of normative practitioner development over the thirty years of an average career. The themes presented here suggest that development involves a movement from reliance on external authority to reliance on internal authority and that this process occurs through the individual's interaction with multiple sources of influence over a long period of time. Although development during graduate school has been most extensively studied, the most powerful sources of influence occur with equal or greater power long after formal training is complete. In fact, it may be that a central element which distinguishes development from stagnation or impairment is the presence or absence of the practitioner's own ongoing internalized developmental process.

CHAPTER 11

Stagnation versus Professional Development of Therapists and Counselors[1]

This chapter addresses the issues of optimal development versus stagnation and pseudodevelopment among therapists and counselors.[1] Stagnation is a superordinate concept, the essential aspects of which are the absence of Continuous Reflective Experiences and the fending off from experiencing anxiety arising from confrontation with challenges and complexities which the therapist/counselor is not able to handle. The concept of Pseudodevelopment connotes apparent development, but, in fact, means any change in professional behavior which results from the process of premature closure. Such behavior is defensively motivated and predominantly repetitive (Rønnestad & Skovholt, 1991). (See Appendix A for a description of the method underlying the model presented in this chapter.)

Description of the Stagnation/Development Model

Stages of Development

This conceptual model is intended to describe factors and processes which impact stagnation or allow the professional to continue development as conceptualized within a stage model of development (Figure 3, 1.0). A variety of models of development such as those of Hess (1987), Loganbill, Hardy and Delworth (1982) or our model described in Chapters 2–9, can in principle be used in this conceptualization.

---

[1] A Norwegian version of this work was published by Rønnestad, M. H., & Skovholt, T. M. (1991). En modell for profesjonell utvikling og stagnasjon hos terapeuter og radgivere. *Tidsskrift for Norsk psykologforening*. (A model of the professional development and stagnation of therapists and counselors. *Journal of the Norwegian Psychological Association*, 28, 555–567.)

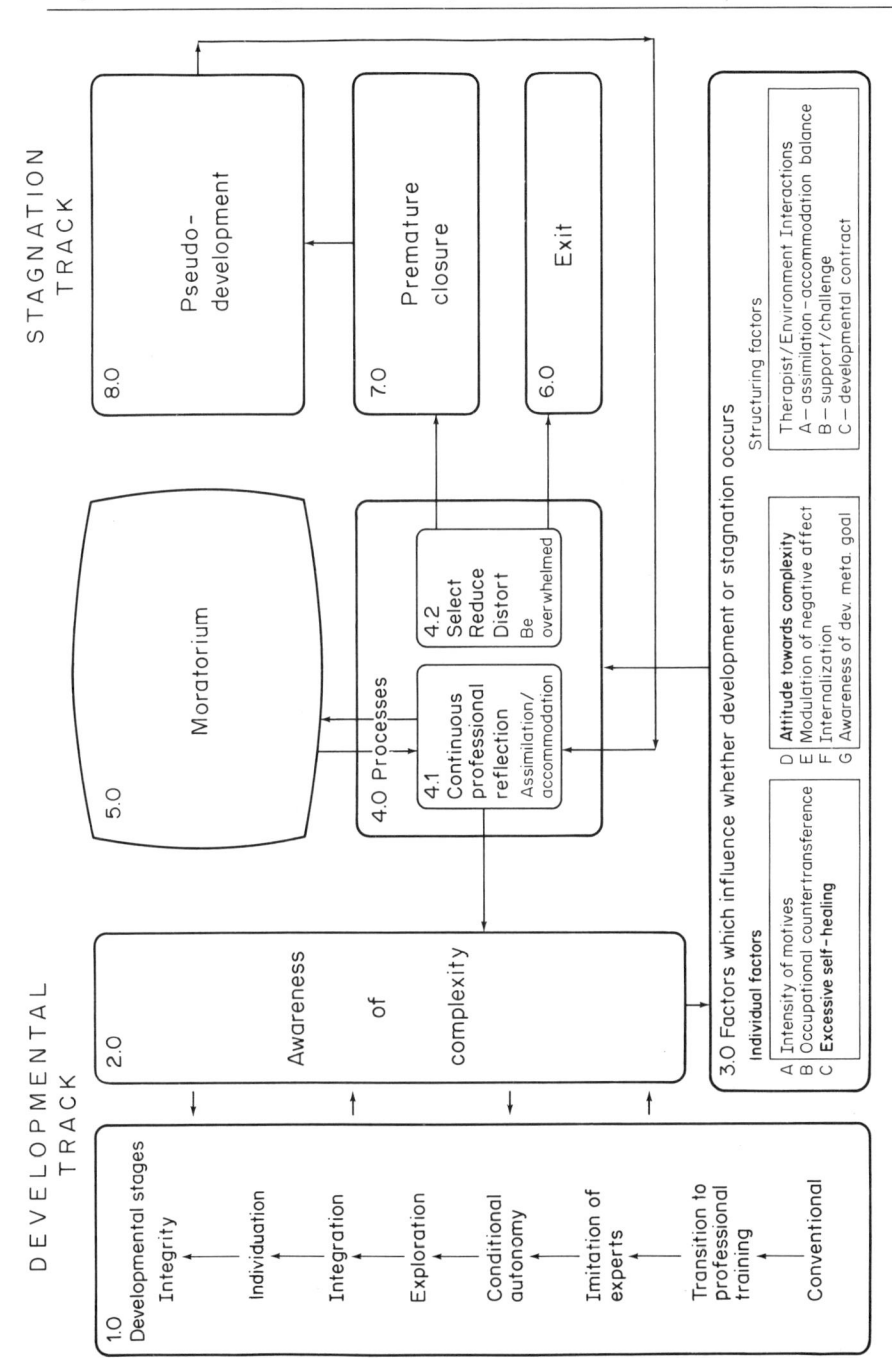

Figure 3. Stagnation/Development Model

Awareness of Complexity as a Prerequisite for Professional Development

Throughout one's career, the practitioner is continually being engaged in, and being the observer of, diverse and extremely complex phenomena and processes. These processes can be understood at many different conceptual levels such as intrapsychic, interpersonal, and systemic. Professional development presupposes an openness and awareness to these phenomena and processes, and presupposes a continual search to arrive at a more profound understanding of them. We use the term *awareness of complexity* in order to contrast this perspective with simplistic and reductionistic notions of truth.

In the stage model of professional development, in Chapters 2–9, we have, at a more specific level, described the different kinds and types of challenges that the individual has to master. For each stage, we have extracted the essential challenge under the category Central Task. Successful mastery of the Central Task is essential for further development.

For example, the novice graduate student is confronted with the task of assimilating an enormous amount of new information and in a preliminary fashion demonstrate how to apply it in practicum. The middle level graduate student assumes the ambitious project of trying to emulate international, national, and local experts while the advanced graduate student, to reconciling the opposing tendencies of independence and dependence, is attempting to function according to realistic criteria for a professional. Throughout graduate school, there are continual challenges relating to assimilating new input and making accommodations in existing cognitive, affective and behavioral structures.

We have found in our research that the new graduate, after a period of seeking to confirm the relevance and value of what she/he learned in graduate school, has to painfully realize that graduate school did not adequately prepare one for all the demands of the work world. The postgraduate professional has to explore beyond the known both in terms of exploring one's personal/professional self and in terms of learning new theories, concepts, and methods/techniques. The seasoned professional confronts her/himself with challenges relating to developing individual and highly personalized ways of functioning professionally. We have called this developing authenticity. Paralleling this, challenges relating to professional burnout need to be handled. The senior therapist/counselor continues the development of the earlier years, but in addition needs to prepare for retirement. According to the present model, challenges such as the ones presented above need to be recognized and handled for development to continue.

Other Factors which Influence whether Development or Stagnation is Likely to Occur

In addition to awareness of complexity, there are several other factors (Figure 3, 3.0) which influence whether the development processes of Continual Professional Reflection (Figure 3, 4.1) or the stagnation processes of selection, reduction, or distortion will occur (Figure 3, 4.2). Some of these are individual factors such as: intensity of motives, occupational countertransference, excessive self-healing, attitude toward complexity, ability to modulate negative affect, degree of internalization, and awareness of a developmental metagoal. Others are structuring factors such as the assimilation/accommodation balance, the support/challenge balance and the use of a developmental contract.

The functional intensity of motives to enter and stay in the profession. The type and intensity of motives of a graduate school applicant in the therapy and counseling fields has a major impact on the individual both as a student and as a postgraduate professional. The motives are critical in determining whether development or pseudodevelopment will occur. We know from numerous sources, including research informants that helped us construct the earlier described stages and themes, that in addition to conscious motives such as "wanting to help people," "wanting to understand people" and "wanting professional status" (Henry, Sims & Spray 1971), there are a variety of motives, generally unconscious, such as: continuing the role of the negotiator in one's family of origin, compensating for loss themes of childhood, expressing a voyeuristic disposition, avoiding isolation and separation anxiety and seeking authority as a compensation for lack of interpersonal power. The therapy/counseling occupational option may also enlist feelings of omnipotence and provide for narcissistic gratifications.

Guy (1987) has provided an overview of "fringe benefits" of professional psychology and related professions, benefits which may motivate entry into the profession. These are independence, financial rewards, variety, recognition and prestige, intellectual stimulation, emotional growth and satisfaction, and personal enrichment and fulfillment. Motives such as these are typically contrasted to dysfunctional motives such as wanting more power and wanting more interpersonal intimacy. We question Guy's idea of functional motives and suggest instead that intensity of motives determines whether or not motives are functional. This perspective presupposes that each human being harbors all motives that we have mentioned (separation anxiety, the need for power, etc.). The structural development of the individual, however, determines the expression, intensity, and degree of awareness of these motives. Awareness of and insight in one's own experiences are prerequisites for being able to empathically connect to what the client is communicating. To have experienced pain gives depth to the therapist/counselor's understanding of clients' suffering. This is consistent with the perspective of the "wounded healer." Repeatedly, our informants told us about the positive impact of painful experiences. The concept of "wounded healer" presupposes a transcendence of one's own pain. The relationship between how functional most lives are and their strength/intensity, can be expressed as a curvilinear function. (See Figure 4.) The relationship between functionality of motives and strength/intensity of motives may thus be best understood as curvilinear.

Occupational countertransference. In our stages and themes, we found that the senior informants generally expressed having gone through a change, usually at a much earlier time, that we have called a movement from a narcissistic to a therapeutic position. These senior informants talked

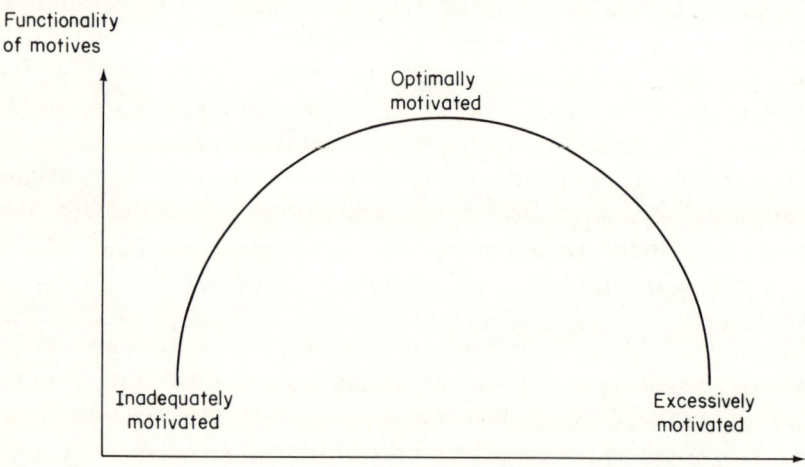

Figure 4. Motive intensity

of humbling client experiences and of feeling less powerful as an agent of change. The data supports in a general way the hypothesis of an omnipotent flavor in the motivation to become a therapist/counselor, but that this motivation is recognized in time and appropriately reduced.

Greenson (1967), has described how disturbed early mother–child interaction may impact the therapist's striving to reestablish contact with a lost love object. If these motives are pervasive and unconscious, the interchange with clients becomes primarily a means to a personal end. The concept of countertransference taps these unconscious processes. The concept of countertransference may be applied not only to understand the interchange between therapist and client, but can be applied to understand the therapist's unconscious career motives.

In classical psychoanalytic theory, the concept of countertransference encompasses the therapist's unconscious conflicting feelings and attitudes, activated in the interchange with the patient. Countertransference was regarded as the therapist's unconscious reactions to the patient's unconscious, a process which threatened the neutral stance of the therapist and thus impeded the therapeutic process. Recent developments within object relations theory (Ogden, 1982) have led to an elaboration and changed perspective. With increased experience with pre-neurotic disturbances, and through recognizing the intensity of the unconscious interchange, theorists and practitioners have come to realize the universality of countertransference. In a controversial and broad formulation, the concept of countertransference has been extended to include all of the practitioner's emotional reactions to the client or patient (Killingmo, 1980). Paralleling this, analysis of the practitioner's countertransference reaction to the patients is seen as a way of contributing to one's understanding of the client. When choosing to become a therapist/counselor, the individual may unconsciously be reacting to a repertoire of images/pictures of the profession. We are suggesting that the countertransference concept can be applied to understand the unconscious reactions, not only to the client, but to the occupational option of being a therapist or counselor.

Excessive self-healing focus. Being a therapist or counselor provides the opportunity for spiritual, intellectual, and emotional growth and may make a person more intuitive, a better risk-taker and a more competent communicator (Guy, 1987; Henry, Sims & Spray, 1971). The self-healing potential in the therapy/counseling professions provides essential rewards for the professional, but also provides an essential danger in an unconscious refocusing toward one's own growth. The sense of satisfaction from helping other people make positive changes, the needs for prestige, authority and autonomy can become excessive. The constant confrontation with peoples' misery and how they cope and accessing the private and personal domains of clients may be focused too much on nourishing one's own relational needs. The existence of these personal benefits is in itself a danger and may motivate a detour away from the normative development route where the well-being of the client is central to the stagnation-centered route where one's own needs are of prime importance.

Attitude toward complexity/challenge. People vary tremendously in their attitudes toward complexities and challenge. At one extreme, some shy away from it; at the other extreme, some actively seek challenges and get enjoyment from battling with what they do not master. This dimension impacts whether or not the individual can tolerate the discomfort and anxiety that accompanies transcending the comfort of the known. The developmental work that focuses on cognitive complexity as a central variable is of importance here (Holloway, 1987) in explaining individual differences.

The ability to tolerate and modulate negative affect. The attitude toward complexity and challenge is greatly influenced by the professional's ability to sustain the experiencing of negative and dysphoric affect, and the ability to modulate different forms of this affect. This introduces a personality variable that should not be overlooked. In the stages and themes descriptions of Chapters 2–10, our informants described emotional reactions which seem to be dominant for individuals throughout their professional life span. Many of these are immediately rewarding and positive, but some can be quite painful. We have learned of the insecurity experienced by the novice student, the bewilderment of the intermediate student, the variable confidence of the advanced student. We have also emphasized the disillusionment of the young professional, distress of the seasoned practitioner, and the regret of the practitioner nearing retirement. Throughout the developmental process, the individual continually has to find her/his way to modulate these affective reactions, the outcome of which depends somewhat upon the flexibility of one's own defense system. In order to understand professional development, it is necessary that we consider this crucial variable. Rigidity in defense system, for example, will necessarily lead to premature closure and, thereby, bring on stagnation.

Internalization. In the stages study described in Chapters 2–9, we have described our most experienced informants as moving towards a highly personalized way of functioning, a movement which can be described as a personal anchoring process. Rønnestad (1985) refers to the process where the therapist/counselor selects out and anchors theoretical and conceptual structures to one's value base. This entails making explicit the implicit premises of how one structures one's conception of the professional world. The process of anchoring involves both an exploration of theory/concepts and of one's own values, beliefs, cognitive and affective processes. The resulting anchors greatly influence subsequent professional identity choices.

By internalization, we mean the gradual attainment of higher levels of internal integration between one's personality, one's value system, one's philosophical base, theoretical and conceptual structures, and methods and techniques. The field of psychotherapy and counseling is unique in the sense that qualities of the *relationship* between therapist/counselor and client(s) generally impact processes and outcome. Working via the relationship highlights the importance of internalization and the genuine and integrated personal side of the professional as these parameters influence level of contact and the quality of interchange with the client.

Awareness of a developmental metagoal. When a person begins the long slow road of professional development, he/she is seldom given a clear picture of the long-term goal. The road is talked about in terms of requirements such as so many practicum hours, a set of courses, a thesis, a licensure test. The person is told about proficiency and allegiance regarding a conceptual system (i.e., family systems), or being knowledgeable regarding a specific problem area/population (i.e., procrastinating college students). In our view, these are all important short-term goals that have been extensively articulated because they are of concern to individuals.

Missing is the long-term, overarching goal. An awareness of the long-term career goal, the articulation of where the person is heading over the 30-40-50-year career, facilitates professional development. On the basis of our interviews with our informants who ranged from new graduate students to Ph.Ds with 30 years of experience, one formulation of this long-term career goal is to become more fully oneself in a highly competent way just as a master artist like Georgia O'Keeffe (Lisle, 1987) in later years expressed an overflowing expression of self in the professional world. Having a clear metagoal facilitates professional development and this long-term individuation process.

Structuring factors

For development to occur, the school milieu of the student or the work milieu of the practitioner needs to be organized in a manner which facilitates development. The physical structures must be suited for relevant professional activities to unfold, the administrative/organizational structures must support and allow professional activities and processes to occur, and the relational/social structures of the work setting must be benevolent to change and development. It is particularly important that the milieu can stimulate innovation and provide the individual with sufficient support and care needed for tolerating complexities and challenges and enduring the often emotionally exhausting nature of therapy work. If one accepts the premise that this kind of professional work entails working via the professional relationship, a primary task for educators and administrators must be to provide the necessary physical, administrative, and relational/social structures to make a positive relationship focus possible. This perspective implies that the school and work milieu must have a focus that encourages and allows for innovation and, equally important, allows for the processing of the emotionally intense experiences that are part of this line of work.

The assimilation/accommodation balance. The developmental milieu must provide the opportunity to balance the processes of assimilation and accommodation (Piaget, 1972), concepts which have previously been applied to understand supervision (Stoltenberg & Delworth, 1987). In graduate training programs and in educational institutions, sufficient time is often allotted for the acquisition and innovative aspects of learning (assimilation), but insufficient time is given to the integrative and consolidating aspects (accommodation). Even though practicum and internships are generally intended to provide for accommodating experiences of applying, adopting and integrating, insufficient time often makes these experiences predominantly assimilative. Interns need structured training time to process the impact of experiences such as intense anxiety, intense mourning, intense hurt, intense anger. The Association for Psychology Internship Centers (APIC) guidelines for doctoral internships require only 25% of the intern's time be spent in direct clinical work (APIC Directory, 1991). This is an expression of the importance of the integrative and consolidative aspects of the internship experience. Unfortunately, as an intern, many students are required to do a high volume of work, and are thus not provided the formal and informal structures for accommodating experiences such as discussion groups and instructional time to think individually or with other interns or professionals.

In most mental health organizations and institutions, this problem is even more dramatic. The problem is not primarily one of balance as resources are generally insufficient for assimilative experiences such as attending workshops, professional conventions, and symposia. The high service press for most mental health service providers generally does not allow enough time to process experiences. In addition, many individuals must, therefore, cope with an "impressional overload" after long-term and excessive containment of negative/dysphoric affect. This kind of work environment encourages repetitive behaviors as elements of the Stagnation Track rather than the "courage to create" (May, 1976) elements of the Developmental Track. Also, the concept of burnout can be applied as contributing to entering the Stagnation Track (Freudenberger, 1974; Maslach, 1982). Burnout results in part from continual unprocessed dysphoric affect which eventually leads to an emotional shutting down.

The support/challenge balance. Normative development entails providing an appropriate balance between the supportive, encouraging and caring dimensions and the challenging, demanding aspects of change. This is a fundamental principle in all human development. This consists of providing the graduate student with an appropriate demand and support progression consistent with her/his competence and self-esteem. It means regulating the content and progression of practicum and internship. It means providing sufficient support, stability and predictability for the student. For the young professional who seeks supervision, it means the supervisor may assist in the selection of appropriate clients and in assisting in the construction of realistic therapeutic/counseling goals. It means helping to make the challenge manageable when the young professional experiences, for example, loss of meaning or confusion in professional work. It means regulating the work-load or modifying the work role for the professional approaching burnout.

Personal life may affect professional life. The in-depth analysis of the narratives of our informants revealed that intense interpersonal experiences had significant impact on professional development. These intense experiences may be in the personal or in the professional domain. Even though the long-term effect of these experiences was generally positive for our informants, provided the individual is able to understand and integrate the experiences; the short-term effect can be overwhelming and crippling, e.g., in periods of mourning after divorce, death of spouse or children, or in periods of anxiety and depression following trauma, disability or intense interpersonal conflict. Support is critical during these crisis periods.

The developmental contract as a structuring tool. At all levels of experience, graduate students and professional practitioners establish either explicit, formal contracts or implicit, informal contracts with their work environment. The informal contracts can be described as implicit psychological contracts (Larsen *et al.*, 1986) between the work environment and the student/professional. The implicit, informal contracts might not be reciprocal, and might easily create misunderstanding and conflicts between the educational/work environment and the individual. The explicit, formal contract (not necessarily in a written form), with mutually agreed upon expectations in terms of process, demands, contributions and goals, will direct and facilitate activities. The structuring function of contracts is particularly useful in highly ambiguous situations such as in supervision of the advanced graduate student, or in the expansion of a professional role in settings with high tension due to unclear boundaries between different professional groups.

Processes/ "The Moment of Truth"

So far, we have emphasized the importance of recognizing the developmental task and of continually maintaining an open and inquisitive stance toward the complex phenomena and processes which unfold in the professional arena. We have also presented some factors which suggest whether development or stagnation is likely to occur. "Moments of truth" are the many instances in one's career where the processes of Continual Professional Reflection allow for changing conceptual, affective or behavioral schemata (i.e., accommodating what has been assimilated), otherwise distortive processes prevail. By distortive processes, we mean distortions of self-concept or distortions such as selections or reductions in perception of a challenge.

A reflective stance is a prerequisite for professional development. The long-term internally directed individuation process, so central in the evolution of a therapist/counselor, involves continually reflecting upon and processing one's experiences. In the Norwegian language, there are two different words for experience: "opplevelse" and "erfaring." The "opplevelse" connotes a here-and-now quality, an immediacy, a lack of processing, while "erfaring" connotes a more integrated, processed experience. Normative development, in our perspective, entails the "erfaring" perspective. This aspect may be portrayed by changing the slogan: "don't just sit there, do something" to "don't just do something, sit there." In the stagnation/development model, we are contrasting the process of Continual Professional Reflection with the process of premature closure, which implies abandoning the reflective stance.

Premature closure and pseudodevelopment

Premature closure means interrupting the reflection process before the assimilation/accommodation work is completed. It is an unconscious, predominantly defensively motivated, distorting process that sets in when the challenge is too great. We use the term pseudodevelopment for any change in professional behavior which results from the process of premature closure. This perspective implies that some changes in professional activity are not development. Frequently, changes in professional activity may be an expression of pseudodevelopment. We have used the term to connote the apparent developmental nature of such changes. The concept of stagnation incorporates both pseudodevelopment and exiting, the alternative of leaving the field altogether.

Moratorium

The moratorium alternative, inspired by Erikson (1968), represents a psychological sanctuary and a temporary retreat. It can be perceived of as a predominantly conscious move into some other non-professional activity such as, for example, volunteer work or a hobby. The common experience of European youth to take time away from school between high school and college to travel is an example of this. It can be perceived of as an essential and necessary aspect of development because the person is providing psychological space in which accommodation occurs. In a similar sense, through the Developmental Track, the practitioner can enter Moratorium for a period of time before reentering a more active learning process.

Illustrations of the Stagnation/Development Model

Graduate students and pseudodevelopment. The qualities of the learning environment and the attitudes of professors and supervisors contribute to the formation of the student's attitude towards learning. We found in our *stages and themes* research a tendency among our student informants toward an external and rigid mode. This may occur because of the high externally imposed demands on students combined with extensive structuring in terms of examinations and licensing requirements. The complexity that the graduate student experiences at this phase of development can be reduced through focusing on one method of therapy or counseling or a series of discrete techniques. The challenge of this phase is to maintain an openness to phenomena and theory at a meta level, while engaging in the apparent "closing" process of learning one or more methods well.

Interacting closely with a dogmatic or discipleship-oriented supervisor/mentor, for example, may facilitate the premature closure process in identity formation so well described by Marcia (1966). Marcia's model of identity formation emphasized the value of crisis and making a committed choice in identity formation. This model, based on Erikson (1956, 1963) was developed to describe general identity development and has been used extensively in this context. For example, Josselson (1990) used the Marcia formulations in a study of women's identity development. However, the concepts also have specific utility in understanding professional development.

A prerequisite for achieving professional identity is having experienced uncertainty and anxiety, and having experienced the discomfort of not feeling competent. We found in the narratives of all our senior informants in our stages and themes study the themes of struggle, uncertainty and hardship. Most of our senior informants told us with confidence and clarity that they considered earlier struggles to be central developmental factors. The uncertainty and hardship of the student role often means that much complexity is experienced. The student may be solidly stuck at a rigid level if the learning environment is strongly dogmatic (i.e., a training program that maintains a strong one dimension only theory or philosophy) where the student is not able to maintain an independent stance.

In interviews with our informants, we discovered four typical orientations regarding the acceptance of a conceptual system at this phase of development. A few individuals never choose one; some choose a predominant conceptual system, but also include other systems that for them have a subordinate position; some focus intensively on learning one method well and exclude all other viewpoints; and some either combine elements and concepts from different conceptual systems or continually change perspective. We have called these orientations: *laissez-faire*, sus-

		Commitment	
		Yes	No
Crisis	Yes	No option here at student level	Suspended judgment or multiple attachments
		(Achieved identity)	(Moratorium)
	No	True believer	Laissez-faire
		(Foreclosed identity)	(Diffused identity)

Figure 5. Theoretical identity at the student level. Identity concepts from Erikson (1956, 1963) and Marcia (1966)

pended judgment, true believer, and multiple attachments. Applying Marcia's (1966) model sheds further light on these alternatives. The model can be summarized in a two-by-two matrix: the therapist/counselor has or has not experienced a crisis along one axis, and either has or has not made a committed choice along the other. This yields four alternatives which Marcia named Diffused identity (no commitment, no crisis), Foreclosed identity (commitment, no crisis), Moratorium identity (crisis, no commitment), and Achieved identity (commitment, crisis).

The *laissez-faire* orientation may in a professional identity sense be similar to Diffused identity. There is a drifting about quality and lack of investment/engagement that is typical for the student. She/he is typically unsure about the appropriateness of the career choice. The student is often defensive, colorless, invisible. Often a personal development and maturation process is necessary to transcend this orientation. For the educational system, the challenge is to enlist engagement. To evoke an identification with a professor, mentor or supervisor or to evoke a belief in one theory or system is both a challenge and an avenue towards growth.

The suspended judgment orientation, the Moratorium alternative in Marcia's (1966) model, is probably the most common orientation at this phase of development. The student is actively engaged and invested in the learning process. The concern is not with the appropriateness of the career choice, but in finding professional training so that one can become competent at therapy tasks. The student, although she/he may be actively engaged in learning systems/schools/methods, needs more time before a genuine commitment to a conceptual approach can be made. More time is especially important. Here the student has made preliminary theoretical commitments while continuing in the searching process. The position may have a developmental or nondevelopmental orientation which is very similar to the one method position in its differentiation between a positive versus stagnant direction.

The "true believer" (Hoffer, 1951) is committed. At the student level, this orientation is equivalent to Marcia's Foreclosed identity. The student has made a committed choice, without having gone through the self-searching process that precedes the Achieved identity position. Foreclosed identity is similar to the concept of premature closure, which occurs when the individual is unable to bear the discomfort of not knowing. Fanatic advocacy of a conceptual or theoretical approach is possibly the best indicator of premature closure. We know, both from clinical practice and from theory, that decisions made in ambivalence, are often vigilantly defended. However, not all true believers are prematurely closed. Some have arrived at their position through extensive contemplation and exploration.

We may differentiate between a developmental and a nondevelopmental true believer one-method position. The developmental position has an active, searching, exploratory, trying-out quality. It is part of an overall developmental position, where the goal is to arrive at a congruent and integrated position. The non-developmental position, however, has a defensive, experience-limiting, anxiety reducing quality. It is not a part of an overall developmental searching process. In the extreme form, we may say its aim is short-term survival. The environmental press, the impact of supervisors, the personality of the individual all contribute to the molding of a true believer, who may be professionally active, but stagnated in the searching process.

The postgraduate professional and pseudodevelopment. The first years after graduation are particularly important in providing many possibilities for entering stagnation. According to our informants, new graduates often first experience a process we have labelled confirmation. By this, we mean they want to confirm the validity and usefulness of their training. The subphase of confirmation is an active, action-oriented phase where the new graduate may be engaged in learning a new professional role. We perceive of this as a positive task because it supports the young practitioner's sense of meaning after several years of intense effort and after much personal sacrifice. The confirming nature of this search may have a stagnant look, but may better be perceived of as accommodation, and, therefore, developmental.

The crucial moment in terms of development/pseudodevelopment is whether the young professional manages to recognize and bear the unavoidable hardships and challenges that set in after some time. There are many different ways confirmation of the validity and adequacy of one's training can give way to a sense of disillusionment. These include difficulties in establishing and regulating professional relationships; difficulties in handling boundary issues, in particular regulating one's own emotional involvement with clients, and handling the intense negative transference reactions of some clients. Clients may drop out of therapy at a rate that one had not expected, or may not improve their functioning to the extent one expected. One might be experiencing different kinds of demands from the work environment that one was not adequately prepared for in graduate school. For some it could be demands to perform in large group settings; for others it may be the emotional drain from constantly being in conflict with other professional groups. It could be an inability to organize and make priorities in one's work; for some it is the negative impact of the absence of rewards, and for many it is the lack of support one received while still a student.

Experiences such as these may lead to the painful realization that one was not adequately prepared in graduate school, or to the more threatening possibility of perhaps not being suited for this kind of professional work. At this point, one becomes intensively aware of new complexities. It, therefore, becomes easy to prematurely close and enter the Stagnant Track. Some typical ways to prematurely close are: limiting or emphasizing only one aspect of one's professional role or choosing to work with one method only, as for example transactional groups, assertiveness training or systematic desensitization. Some prematurely close by working with clients of a certain age only (for example, only with children or only with the aged). Some may choose another form of employment within one's field as for example becoming a researcher, an administrator, or a teacher. At this point, some leave the field altogether (Figure 3, Exit, 6.0).

Not all movements such as those mentioned above are movements into pseudodevelopment. Pseudodevelopment presupposes premature closure, a predominantly defensively motivated, distortive and unconscious process. Movements based on exploratory reflection, which is not predominantly defensive, which is relatively free from distortions and largely conscious, is not pseudo-development, but development. Many enter personal therapy as a client at this point; for some it is reentry but frequently with a motivation different from the common ritualistic flavor of starting therapy or counseling as a student. Some may change the work roles after careful attention to, and clarification of, their interests, values, capacities, and after an assessment of the content and rewards of their professional roles. This perspective of premature closure may be contrasted with "critical incidents." Critical incidents are highly impactful and unique experiences that occur during one's professional career (Skovholt & McCarthy, 1988).

Summary and Concluding Comments

Throughout one's career, the therapist and counselor has to continually be aware of complex phenomena and processes which impact interchange with clients. Professional development presupposes maintaining an openness to, and searching for, a more profound understanding of these phenomena and processes and an awareness of complexity. There are several factors which influence whether or not the individual is able to maintain this openness and search. The main factors are:

1. The intensity of motives to choose and stay in the profession.
2. The dangers of occupational countertransference.
3. An excessive self-healing focus
4. One's attitude toward complexity.
5. The ability to tolerate and modulate negative affect.
6. The degree to which there occurs an internalization process.
7. The awareness of a developmental metagoal.

In addition to the above, there are three practitioner–environment interaction factors: (a) The assimilation–accommodation balance. (b) The support–challenge balance, and (c) The use of the developmental contract as a structuring tool.

The graduate student or professional therapist/counselor will react when confronted with the complexities and challenges of each developmental stage. The challenges of each stage is a crucial moment because the individual may move left into the Developmental Track, move upwards into Moratorium or move right into the Stagnation Track. If the individual is able to use a process we have labelled Continuous Professional Reflection and through this process accommodate what has been assimilated, the individual has two alternatives. One option is to continue in the Developmental Track. The other option is to enter Moratorium, a temporary retreat from development. We define Continuous Professional Reflection as a central developmental process. It consists of three essential aspects: ongoing professional and personal experiences, a searching process with others within an open and supportive environment, and active reflection about one's experiences. If the individual is not able to sufficiently reflect upon her/his experiences, the individual may defensively select out, reduce, change or distort her/his conception of the demands on the self. The most dramatic option at this point is leaving the field altogether. In cases where the individual is either overwhelmed or the anxiety level is too high, often because the professional self is too threatened, the individual will prematurely close and enter the Stagnation Track. This process occurs unconsciously. We define pseudodevelopment as progression that depends on the exclusive use of the work of others to guide the individual in professional identity, conceptual ideas used and role and working style. This precludes facing the anxiety of choosing one's own identity. Pseudodevelopment has occurred when the individual is unconsciously repeating the behavior that originated through the process of premature closure. The essential components of pseudodevelopment are: absence of Continuous Professional Reflection, unconscious distortion of self-concept or the nature of the developmental challenge, an inability to handle the challenges of one's developmental stage, and repetition in ways of thinking, feeling and behaving in the professional domain.

For individuals who are in the Moratorium option or in the pseudodevelopmental part of the Stagnation Track, movement back into the Developmental Track can occur if the individual again can engage in the process of Continuous Professional Reflection at a level where the challenge of complexity can be handled.

This model is a conceptual scheme, and not a method to assess whether development or pseudodevelopment occurs. Even though the model may assist one in understanding some of the factors and processes which impact the graduate student and the professional, we are aware that there are numerous philosophical and methodological problems associated with defining certain behaviors as either developmental or pseudodevelopmental.

The model emphasizes Continuous Professional Reflection as the fundamental developmental process in professional life. It presents important individual factors which impact whether development or stagnation will prevail. It is essential that we continually increase our knowledge of those dynamics which facilitate and arrest development so that measures can be taken to maintain and advance those structures and processes which increase the level of professional functioning. It is through facilitating the development of the professional therapist or counselor that the general professional level of the profession will increase.

APPENDIX A

Research Methodology and Sample Description

Introduction

When beginning this study, we wanted to construct a model of development with a methodology that had the following characteristics:

1. the inquiry covered the entire professional life span;
2. the analysis took into account both personal and professional sources of influence;
3. the model was research-based;
4. the method was qualitative with the use of semi-structured interviews and follow-up feedback from informants;
5. the inquiry generated knowledge pertaining to broad-band parameters (e.g., challenges, emotional reactions, attitudes toward work, influential factors in development, learning method, perceptions of role and working style, conceptual ideas used, and measures of success and satisfaction).

These parameters would then serve as points of entry for data gathering and data analysis.

Methodology

Our methodology was qualitative, a mode of inquiry receiving both commentary and support within the therapy and counseling professions in the United States (Brown, 1989; Goldman, 1982, 1989; Hoshmand, 1989; Howard, 1986; Neimeyer & Resnikoff, 1982; Patton, 1991; Shontz, 1982).

One of the great advantages of this methodology is that it taps into the natural interviewing skills possessed by individuals with training in counseling work. For example, in a qualitative methodology text, Patton (1990) devotes 83 pages to describing interviewing methods in qualitative research. For individuals with intensive counselor training, this chapter, although of high quality, seems to be a summary for beginners. Also, the qualitative research skills of Theoretical Sensitivity (Strauss & Corbin, 1990) parallel what professional therapists and counselors call therapeutic sensitivity. All of the research interviewers in the present study had received this extensive graduate counselor training before beginning the qualitative research work.

Goldman (1989) describes the link between therapy/counseling practitioner skills and the qualitative research approach.

> Most practitioners never do any formal research after the dissertation, and those who ever read published research find it seldom relates in any meaningful way to their work... [qualitative methods] invite us to *search*, to *discover*, to come in with lots of blank paper and an incomplete, and loose, conceptual structure, and to try very hard to develop and continually modify the structure over the entire period of the study... the research has a continuous task of puzzling, developing, and crystallizing ideas all the way through the process. No, these new methods are not for the faint of heart. They demand imagination, courage to face the unknown, flexibility, some creativeness, and a good deal of personal skill in observation, interviewing and self-examination—some of the same skills, in fact, required for effective counseling. (pp. 81–83)

Qualitative methodology fits very well with the approach (i.e., understand the person holistically versus a small reductionistic part), skill development (i.e., depth interviewing versus a quantitative score), and way of understanding (i.e., textured script pieces woven together to form an individual's life story versus comparison of dependent scores after manipulating an independent variable) of individuals who are practicing therapists and counselors. Their way of understanding the human world through intense interactions with suffering people—their clients—is very different than the most rigorous scientific methods that the human service fields have borrowed from the natural sciences. We chose this method in part because it fits so well with the way our informants understand their human world while doing their investigative work as practitioners.

Regarding methodology, we have been influenced by Sprinthall (1975) who provided an early invitation to think about methodology in a different way. Also, impactful has been the emerging methodologies within feminist work. Most notable here is *Women's ways of knowing* (Belenky *et al.* 1986). The qualitative methodology tradition in Europe has also been influential. For example, see Kvale (1986a, 1987) for a review of dialectical and hermeneutical psychology and methods in Scandinavian countries.

During recent decades, qualitative research methodology has increasingly been applied in different investigation domains. Recently, the use of qualitative research methodology has partly emerged from a critique of the positivist research tradition, the philosophy of science on which this tradition is based, its perspective on validity and reliability, and its methodology. Phenomenology is a primary philosophical foundation for qualitative research methodology. For reviews of the "logical positivist/ phenomenology inquiry" paradigm debate, see Hoshmand (1989), Lincoln and Guba (1985) and Patton (1991). The arguments for alternate models to the positivist science can be summarized under three groupings (Hoshmand, 1989): (a) epistemological, (b) conceptual-empirical, and (c) ideological.

The epistemological arguments against reductive-positivist science concern the nature of knowledge, how we know what we know. As Hoshmand pointed out, meaning context impacts interpretations of observation. There are numerous contributors to this perspective. Constructivists have argued for the impact of language on descriptions of social realities. For example, subject–object dualism in inquiry has been severely criticized. As Polkinghorne (1986) has pointed out:

> Humans are conceived as meaning-givers who compose a conceptual scheme of interpretation through which they determine what counts as objects, while at the same time remaining objects themselves very much like other objects in the world. Each side of the doublet is supposed to yield a complete description without reference to the other. (pp. 134–144)

Polkinghorne argues that the fullness of humanness cannot be captured by either position and that the contextual instability of human concepts makes it impossible for the human sciences to become theoretical sciences. Human sciences can at best produce empirical generalizations. Furthermore, the contextual meaning of human concepts not only varies across individuals, but "changes individually as experiences accumulate and as situations change" (p. 144), and furthermore:

> There is enough cross-contextual stability in interpretations to produce

probability expectations, but not enough to fit into explanatory schemes producing deductive laws. (p. 145)

In the study of professional development, it makes intuitive sense that the continual processing of complex interchanges that the therapist/counselor engages in and observes, leads to changes in contextual meaning of concepts. For our inquiry, it, therefore, seems essential to choose a method of investigation which takes this into account.

The conceptual-empirical arguments against reductive experimental methodology concern limitations of its conceptual base. Hoshmand (1989) has formulated the idea that standards of precision by measurement and objectification by operationalism has inappropriately reduced human phenomena to behavioral and biological laws which do not fit with recent conceptual formulations from the study of cognition, physics, and biology. The perspective of active cognition and concepts such as feedforward capacity of the mind, violates reductionistic formulations and are examples of necessary conceptual-empirical revisions.

The *ideological arguments* against the reductive experimental methodology concern how one perceives the nature of human nature. The reductionistic conceptions of human behavior and the deterministic perception of humans portray a different image than that of humanity characterized by self-determination. Hoshmand (1989) also points to the value aspect of inquiry. "How we map social realities may transform the future that we envision" (p. 9).

Abandoning or supplementing the quantitative methodology with a qualitative methodology, with its accompanying shifts in epistemology and conceptual base, necessitates discussion of standards of reliability and validity of this other method.

Qualitative research presupposes a conception of truth that goes beyond the classical positivist empiricist conceptions of truth. Kvale (1987) refers to the three classical criteria of truth within philosophy: *correspondence*, *coherence*, and *pragmatic utility*. The positivist empiricist conception adheres to the correspondence criterion, i.e., degree to which a statement corresponds to some real nature of the world. This conception presupposes subject/object dualism in inquiry and an objective world with unequivocal facts. The coherence criterion, central in rationalist philosophy and in hermeneutical philosophy, "...involves whether a statement is logically coherent, is there an internal logic in the results, do they form good *Gestalt*" (Kvale, 1987, p. 42). One may add here that the search for logical consistency, for example within psychoanalytic concepts, may lead to greater validity on the coherence criterion, without increasing validity on the correspondence criterion. The pragmatic criterion of truth concerns the degree to which a statement has practical consequences, a utility aspect which is so central in pragmatic philosophy.

> Validity of a text interpretation takes place in a dialogue, it is an argumentative discipline, involving a logic of uncertainty and of qualitative probability. It is then illogical to apply a logic of certainty developed for the observation of unequivocal behavioral facts to the interpretation of ambiguous meanings of texts. (Kvale, 1987, pp. 47–48)

In our investigation, we have strongly emphasized the perspective of *validity through dialogue* which will be accounted for in the description of how we collected our data.

Kvale (1983) has outlined aspects of the phenomenological and hermeneutical mode for understanding the qualitative research interview. It centers on the interviewee's life world; it seeks to understand the meaning of phenomena in her/his life world; it is qualitative, descriptive, and specific, presuppositionless; it focuses on certain themes, is open to ambiguities, it changes, is dependent upon the sensitivity of the interviewer, takes place in an interpersonal interaction, and may be a positive experience.

These aspects are similar to the major themes of the qualitative inquiry of Patton (1990): qualitative designs are naturalistic, i.e., there is no manipulation of the research setting; the designs are inductive; one uses a holistic perspective; one uses qualitative data, i.e., detailed, in-depth inquiry, thick descriptions; the inquiry is characterized by personal contact and depends on insight of researcher; there is an attention to dynamic systems, i.e., to process and change; there is a unique case orientation; there is a sensitivity to context, as, for example, social, historical, temporal; the attitude is one of empathic neutrality; and there is design flexibility.

According to Kvale (1983, 1987), one can interpret the interview text at three different levels: the self-understanding level, the common-sense level, and the theoretical level. At the first level, the researcher aims at clarifying how the interviewee understands the meaning of what is communicated. The validation of statements at this level is simply agreement or disagreement by the interviewee. At the second level, interpretations go beyond the interviewee's own understanding. A broader, common-sense aspect is added. The validity of statements at this level is contingent upon logical coherence and upon general consensus of common-sense interpretations among readers. At the third level, interpretation is made from relevant theory. The validation process entails assessing if interpretations follow logically from theory. Specific theoretical competence is required both to generate theoretical interpretations and to assess validity of interpretations.

Kvale (1983) has pointed to the continuum between description and interpretation and has outlined six possible phases of interpretation. During phase one, the interviewee describes spontaneously his/her life-world, i.e., what he/she does, feels, and thinks about a theme. Here, and in the subsequent phase, there is no interpretation. During a second phase, the interviewee discovers new relations spontaneously, on the basis of own description. In the third phase, the interviewer condenses and interprets the meaning of the interviewee's descriptions. This, occurring during the interview, enables the interviewee to provide verification or correction of interpretations. At this stage, the interview has the form of a dialogue.

The fourth phase represents a shift, in that at this point the interviewer or another person interprets a completed and transcribed interview. At this phase, the interpretation can be made at the level of self-understanding, at the common-sense level or at the theoretical level. The fifth phase is called a reinterview because the initial interview is analyzed and reinterpreted and forms a base for a new interchange. A possible sixth phase is also suggested; here new insight leads to action.

The hermeneutical circle is a concept used to tap the process of arriving at better interpretations of meaning. The essence of this concept is that both the meaning of parts of the text and global meaning of the text are continually modified through an analysis of both. One arrives at a better understanding of the parts through analysis of the global meaning, and one arrives at a better analysis of the global meaning through analysis of parts. This is a continuous and, in principle, finite back and forth process where one reworks the data shifting emphasis on parts and wholes. The process ends when one has arrived at a coherent, part-whole unity, free of contradictions (Kvale, 1983).

Our Specific Method

Inductive analysis (Patton, 1990) served as our overall focus. Our specific method of inquiry was a modified version of what has been labeled the "constant comparative method of analysis" (Glaser & Strauss, 1967, pp. 101–116) or Grounded Theory Methodology (Strauss & Corbin, 1990). This involves a continual reexamination and modification of the data. Grounded Theory is inductively derived from studying the phenomenon it represents which is discovered, developed, and refined. This research study was conducted over five years (1986–1990) and consisted of five phases.

Phase 1

We began with our own written work on the topic (Rønnestad, 1976, 1977, 1982, 1983, 1985; Skovholt, 1985), our own work as supervisors and teachers in graduate programs, our own work as practitioners, and the literature on professional development, e.g., literature on stages of development, supervision, occupational burnout. From this base, we developed a 23-item questionnaire (included in this appendix) that was refined through a series of pilot interviews. We also used this base to create eight categories for structuring the flow of data. They are Definition of the Stage, Central Task, Predominant Affect, Sources of Influence, Role and Working Style, Conceptual Ideas Used, Learning Process, and Measure of Effectiveness and Satisfaction.

Phase 2

This was the initial data gathering phase in the study. One to one-and-a-half hour individual interviews with therapists/counselors as informants served as the first data gathering method. Here we were guided by Kvale (1983, 1986a, 1986b, 1987), the Norwegian methodologist, and Patton (1990), regarding use and validity in the interview method of data collection.

We interviewed a group of 100 therapists/counselors who were divided by education and experience into five groups from the first year of graduate school to 40 years beyond graduate school. This use of education and experience in therapy/counseling as the developmental level variables is similar to the conceptualizations of Dreyfus and Dreyfus (1986) in their work on expertise.

In studying professional development, this kind of cross-sectional design contains both strengths and limitations. There is the possibility of cohort differences confounding stage differences. However, according to a leading developmental researcher (James Rest, personal communication, 28 March 1991), there is a legitimate place for cross-sectional design in studies of development. Most criticisms of cross-sectional designs have occurred within the framework of quantitative methods (e.g., Ellis, 1991). Our methodology was quantitative and contained two elements that made it a modified cross-sectional design: (a) 60 of our 100 informants were again interviewed two years after the first interview; (b) informants provided information regarding their own development at earlier education and experience points. Despite these qualifications, a longitudinal study over 30 years would have been advantageous as compared with the current design.

The total sample consisted of 50 females and 50 males, 96 whites and four minorities with a mean age of 42.4, standard deviation of 12.4, and a range in age from 24 to 71. (Although the ethnic diversity may reflect the professional population in Minnesota, it does limit the usefulness of the study.) These individuals had graduate training in 34 different universities and had been in 47 different programs in these universities. The sample group had received Master's degrees from 29 different universities and within these 29 universities had been in 37 different graduate programs. At the doctoral level, this sample group had received doctorates from 26 different universities and been in 37 different graduate programs in these 26 universities. Since the sample group was interviewed within the Twin Cities area of Minneapolis and St Paul, the large university in that area, the University of Minnesota, was the modal university for training at both the Master's and doctoral levels. Individuals in the sample received training within different graduate programs at this university.

The sample group consisted of 23 individuals who had a doctorate in counseling psychology or a very closely related field, 21 individuals who had a doctorate in clinical psychology and 17 who had a doctorate in a closely related field such as school psychology and human development. Fifty-six of the hundred-person sample were licensed at the doctoral level and this included almost all of those individuals who were eligible, that is the postdoctoral psychologists. Ten individuals were Diplomates of the American Board of Professional Psychology, the highest credential in the field. Five were in clinical psychology, three in counseling, and two in school. These 100 individuals had had practicum, internship, and current work experience in a wide variety of settings such as agencies, hospitals, academics, industrial settings in a variety of states and cities in the United States.

The five groups in the sample can be described as follows: Group A con-

Appendix A   Research Methodology and Sample Description

sists of 20 individuals who were interviewed during the first year of their graduate program in either counseling or clinical psychology at one of four different graduate programs, at two different universities. Reflecting the general gender and racial composition of members in these programs, there were 16 females and 4 males. Eighteen of these individuals were Caucasian, two were minorities. Seventeen were US citizens and three non-US citizens. The average age was 32 with a standard deviation of 7 and a range of 24 to 47. Individuals at the lower end of the age range often were coming to graduate school immediately after a bachelor's degree whereas people at the upper range often had had extensive employment in one or more occupations. These individuals had a wide variety of experience in human services, often as volunteers or paraprofessionals in a human service capacity of some kind.

Group B consisted of 20 advanced doctoral students who had had at least four years of graduate school. Some of these individuals were in their doctoral internship at the time of the interview; some had already finished the internship and were working on the dissertation. All of these individuals were doctoral students at the University of Minnesota in one of two different departments and one of three separate programs in these departments. All of these individuals were in counseling or clinical psychology. There were 13 females and seven males. Nineteen were white; one was a minority. All were American citizens and the average age was 33 with a standard deviation of 4.2 and ranged from age 26 to 44. These individuals had had a wide variety of pre-professional experiences and, in addition, had also had a variety of practicum and internship experiences.

Group C, as with Groups D and E, were chosen from the membership of the Minnesota Psychological Association. Members of this group of individuals had received the doctorate and had had approximately five years of post-doctoral experience. The group was chosen based on a number of factors such as being active as a practitioner, being accessible for the interviews, i.e., living within the greater Twin Cities metropolitan area, willingness to conduct the interview, accessibility in terms of being able to be contacted. Also, there was a general attempt, as in Groups D and E, to find some balance across the group in terms of degrees, training program, and work setting. This group consisted of eleven females and nine males. All these individuals were Caucasian and all were US citizens. The average age was 37 with a standard deviation of 6.1 ranging from 31 to 61. This group of 20 had received Master's degrees from 11 different universities and doctorates from one of eight universities, with the

University of Minnesota being the predominant graduate university. Nine of these individuals identified themselves as counseling psychologists, eight as clinical psychologists, and three as other. Their current work setting was varied across the group and included settings such as hospitals, public and private agencies, colleges and universities, and private practice.

Group D consists of 20 individuals who had their doctorate and approximately 15 years of post-doctoral experience. They were chosen from membership in the Minnesota Psychological Association and lived in the greater Minneapolis–St Paul area. Group D reflects a changed gender balance in the sample with a predominance of males. This seems to be true generally in the field, that is, in the entering group of people within the therapy/counseling field in recent years there are many more females than males, whereas in the most senior levels, especially at the higher levels of education, there are more males than females. In Group D, there were fourteen males and four females. Nineteen were Caucasian and one was a minority. All these individuals were US citizens. This group was chosen like Group C through trying to find balance between factors cited above. The average age was 47 with a standard deviation of 8.8 and a range of 38–71. These individuals had received Master's degrees from ten different universities and doctorates from 12 different universities with the University of Minnesota being the predominant university. Eight of these individuals identified themselves as counseling psychologists, seven as clinical, five as other. Eighteen were licensed at the doctoral level and one was a Diplomate in counseling. They currently work in the greater Minneapolis–St Paul area. These settings included private and public agencies, private practice (which was more predominant than with Group C), and colleges and universities. In their previous experiences, these individuals had worked in a variety of settings.

Group E numbered 20, were chosen from membership in the Minnesota Psychological Association, and lived in the greater Minneapolis–St Paul area. All of these individuals had the doctoral degree and approximately 25 years of post-doctoral experience. There were six females and 14 males. All 20 were white. All were US citizens. Average age was 62, standard deviation was 6.4, and the range was 50 to 70. They, as a group, received a Master's degree from eight different universities, and doctorates from one of ten different universities with the University of Minnesota being the predominant university. Six of these individuals identified themselves as clinical psychologists, five as counseling psychologists, and nine as other. All 20 were licensed at the doctoral level in the state of

Appendix A   Research Methodology and Sample Description

Minnesota, and nine of them had received the Diplomate from the American Board of Professional Psychology, five in clinical, two in counseling, and two in school. As with Groups C and D, they represented a wide variety of current work settings—private practice, agency, hospital, academic. They tended to be more in private practice than other groups, although some had recently retired and were involved in part-time employment. They had, as a group, a wide variety of post-doctoral experience as well as internships and practicums in many settings.

See Table 2 for a summary of the sample.

In addition to the sample of 100, we also interviewed 20 other individuals. Some of these individuals were interviewed at the beginning pilot phase when we were working on the questionnaire. Others were interviewed to help us derive at the characteristics of people at the Conventional Stage. For this purpose, we interviewed lay helpers. Others were people that we interviewed because they seemed to be knowledgeable informants.

The initial interviews were conducted by a research team of the first author and four doctoral students in counseling psychology at the University of Minnesota (two white males, one white female, and one minority male). Each of the individuals completed one or more pilot interviews. Each interview was audiotaped, lasted $1-1\frac{1}{2}$ hours and was guided by the semi-structured, 23-item questionnaire. (The questionnaire is included at the end of the appendix.) After the 20 interviews in each group were completed, the research team met to discuss the interviews. Using the interview outline as a discussion guide, each debriefing meeting served as an intense cross-case analysis (Patton, 1990). At each debriefing, the focus was on capturing essential concepts, subcategories, and categories for the group interviewed (Strauss & Corbin, 1990). These included what Patton calls sensitizing concepts and indigenous concepts (Patton, 1990) for the group interviewed. The thematic content was then put into the eight categories developed earlier by the two authors in Phase 1. After each debriefing meeting, the first author prepared a written description using these eight categories. Members of the interviewing team and informants were asked to read and assess these preliminary descriptions. Each member of the research team and approximately 25% of the informants (five of 20 in each group and 25 of 100) read and reacted to these descriptions. Based on this feedback, the preliminary descriptions were revised. This was an essential aspect of our modified "constant comparative" and modified Grounded Theory Methodology research process that was used throughout the study (Strauss & Corbin, 1990).

Table 2. Sample at time of initial interview, 1986–87

Ed & Exp	Gender	Race	Age	Programs, Degrees	Employment
Group A, $N=20$ 1st year graduate students	16 F 4 M	18 white 2 minority 3 non-US citizens 17 US citizens	$\bar{X} = 32$ $s = 7.0$ Range = 24–47	4 different graduate programs, 3 counseling psychology, 1 clinical psychology, of 2 different universities	Wide variety of preprofessional experience, & some practicum
Group B, $N=20$ Advanced doctorate students, 4–5 years of graduate school	13 F 7 M	19 white 1 minority All US citizens	$\bar{X} = 33$ $s = 4.2$ Range = 26–44	Doctorate studies in one of 3 doctorates programs (2 counseling, 1 clinical) in 2 different depts, University of MN	Wide variety of practicum-internship experience
Group C, $N=20$ Doctorate + approx. 5 years	11 F 9 M	20 white All US citizens	$\bar{X} = 37$ $s = 6.1$ Range = 31–61	11 different masters' universities, doctorate from one of 5 programs in 3 different depts, University of MN or 7 other universities, 9 counseling, 8 clinical, 3 other	Wide variety of current work settings (hospital, agency, university private practice)
Group D, $N=20$ Doctorate + approx. 15 years	6 F 14 M	19 white 1 minority All US citizens	$\bar{X} = 47$ $s = 8.8$ Range = 38–71	10 different masters' universities, doctorate from one of 3 programs in 2 depts, University of MN or 11 other universities, 8 counseling, 7 clinical, 5 other, 18 licensed at doctorate level, 1 ABPP (counseling)	Wide variety of current work settings (agency, private practice, university)

Group E, N = 20 Doctorate + approx. 25 years	6 F 14 M	20 white All US citizens	$\bar{X} = 62$ $s = 6.4$ Range = 50–70	8 different masters' universities, doctorate in one of 3 programs in 2 different depts, University of MN, 9 other universities, 6 clinical, 5 counseling, 9 others, 20 licensed at doctorate level, 9 ABPP (5 clinical, 2 counseling, 2 school)	Wide variety of current work settings (private practice, agency, hospital, academic). Also, some recent retirement & part-time employment
Total N = 100	50 F 50 M	96 white 4 minority	$\bar{X} = 42.4$ $s = 12.4$ Range = 24–71	34 different degree granting universities, 47 different graduate programs in these universities (Masters 29u, 37p Doctorate 26u, 34p) Doctorate: 23 counseling, 21 clinical, 17 other, 56 licensed at doctorate level, 10 ABPP (5 clinical, 2 counseling, 2 school)	

Other N = 20   Pilot and other interviews of nonsample members

The lay helper stage—Stage 1: Conventional—was constructed differently than the others. Here the insights of the total sample group, a review of the literature on nonprofessional helping, and a small sample ($N = 5$) of lay helpers were used to construct this stage.

Phase 3

As a next step, the senior research assistant listened to 75 of the 100 $1-1\frac{1}{2}$ hour taped interviews. At least half of the interviews in each group were included in this critique. The research assistant listened for congruity between the revised preliminary written descriptions and the content on the tapes. The research assistant also chose quotes that would illuminate theoretical concepts. As a next step, again using modified "constant comparative" and Grounded Theory Methodology, the authors met and completely reviewed and revised the manuscript on the basis of the 30-page critique of the research assistant and by listening to selected interviews.

Phase 4

Next, 60 of the 100 member sample group were individually reinterviewed. Approximately 12 of the 20 in each of the five sample groups were interviewed for a $1-1\frac{1}{2}$ hour period by members of a second research group of the first author, a university staff psychologist (a white female), and three graduate students in counseling psychology (two white females, one white male). Each subject in the second interview responded to the accuracy of one or two of the written stage descriptions and was asked via a short form, "How accurately does this describe you when you were at this stage in terms of education and experience?" (The form used for this interview is included at the end of the appendix.) After the second interview, the first author met with each research interviewer individually for those interviews that the first author did not conduct. This use of informants to help the research process is very much in keeping with "constant comparative"/Grounded Theory Methodology (GTM) (Strauss & Corbin, 1990).

Using several interviewers and the continual collaboration of the two authors may be perceived of as investigator triangulation as formulated by Denzin (1978) and elaborated by Patton (1990). Checking back with our informants may also be understood as triangulation. Patton (1990) wrote:

> Another approach to analytical triangulation is to have those who were

studied review the findings. Evaluators can learn a great deal about the accuracy, fairness, and validity of their data analysis by having the people described in that data analysis react to what is described. (p. 468)

Throughout this process, the authors often met, listened to tapes, discussed and revised the descriptions. Strauss and Corbin (1990) suggest that as researchers "you should be asking questions all along the course of your research project" (p. 59). We attempted to be maximally open to the data presented to us so that we could let concepts, subcategories, and categories emerge or decline. For example, the original differentiation on five levels did not sufficiently account for the variations we observed and we finally ended up with eight stages of therapist/counselor development.

Phase 5

The process of generating the themes started after we had completed the stage model (Chapters 2 – 9) and was initiated by trying to distill the essence of our findings. First, from a 120-page summary of the narrative, we jointly extracted the strongest themes within each of the eight categories (Definition of the Stage, Central Task, Predominant Affect, Source of Influence, Role and Working Style, Conceptual Ideas Used, Learning Process and Measures of Effectiveness and Satisfaction). Themes were not extracted unless we jointly agreed that the data provided clear and consistent evidence for such a decision. After this initial extraction, the themes were ordered according to strength of the support in the 120-page narrative. Again this decision was based on a joint decision by us as researchers. At this point, some themes were dropped. Last, the themes, 20 in number, were arranged within the following categories: Primary Characteristic Themes, Process Descriptor Themes, Source of Influence Themes, and Secondary Characteristic Themes. In line with the strength of qualitative research, we believe that the themes, like the earlier stage descriptions, best serve as hypotheses to be proved or disproved by more precise empirical studies.

Phase 6

The model presented in Chapter 11 is based on data from three different data sources:

(a) The investigation method described above in Phases 1–5.

(b) Data generated through supervision seminars and supervisory experiences in Norway. During the last several years, Helge Rønnestad has conducted a series of workshops on supervision for Norwegian psychologists, psychiatrists and social workers. Theoretical presentations on development and stagnation, and systematic feedback from participants and dialogues with supervisors led to a preliminary presentation on the topic (Rønnestad, 1985). This rotation between presentation and feedback has continued during the last years as well.
(c) The existing literature on professional development. See Rønnestad and Skovholt (in press), for a review article on much of this literature.

The methodology of Chapter 11 may be conceptualized as source tringulation and as methods triangulation, processes which integrate data from several sources and apply different methods of inquiry (Patton, 1990).

Original Questionaire

INTRODUCTION
We are aware that there are many issues we could cover when interviewing counselors and therapists. There are issues of public versus private practice, working with groups versus individuals, questions regarding licensure, referrals, ethics, etc. But what we are exclusively interested in is what goes on in the counseling or therapy session. We are hoping to discover if there are common patterns or phases that counselors and therapists go through over the course of their careers. In answering these questions, please use the way you conceptualize counseling and therapy and the methods you use as a frame of reference.

STRUCTURED QUESTIONS
How does counseling/therapy work? Has your view of it changed over time?

Appendix A   Research Methodology and Sample Description   159

What characteristics describe you now in relation to your counseling or therapy that might not have applied in the past?

Are you or have you ever been strongly invested in a particular model of counseling/therapy? Have you ever become disenchanted with that model? How did you come to that conclusion and what did you do as a result?

TRANSITIONS
Can you recall and describe any major changes that have occurred along the way? What precipitated them? When did they occur?

SOURCES OF INFLUENCE
Theories can be a major source of influence. Which have strongly influenced you? Has this changed over time?

Experience with clients can be a strong influence. Has this been true for you? Can you elaborate?

Do you think of other specific people or groups as playing an important role in your approach? If so, can you describe how they affected you?

Events in your personal life, either positive or negative, can also be a source of influence. Is this true for you? Can you elaborate?

Considering these three separate areas of possible influence—theories and research, experience with clients, events in your personal life—can you rank them in order of importance in affecting your work?

PERSONAL THEORIES OF COUNSELOR DEVELOPMENT
Do you see counseling or therapy becoming more complex or simple for you as you have gained in experience? Can you explain?

Do you see yourself progressing along a continuum (or perhaps more than one)? Can you identify it/them?

Have you ever felt disillusioned with the process of counseling or therapy? What caused this and how did you deal with it?

What kinds of people make the best counselors and therapists? Why?

What causes people to leave the field?

What exactly are the satisfactions you get from your work? Have these changed over time?

MISCELLANEOUS

What effect does working with negative emotions much of the time have on you? How do you relate to these emotions and manage them?

Has comparing your ability to help others versus other counselor/therapists' ability to be helpful been an issue for you? If so, when?

Has your knowledge of counseling or therapy been helpful in resolving your own problems?

What issues do you find difficult or threatening to deal with in the counseling or therapy that you do? Have these changed since you began?

How do you measure your success? Has this always been so?

How do you measure the success of your clients? Has this always been so?

What primarily concerns you in your counseling or therapy—thought, emotion, or behavior? How did you come to this view?

Do you find yourself being fairly structured and organized, or having a less structured and more ambiguous approach in your work? Is this different from the past?

Reinterview Form

Stages of Therapist/Counselor Development
Participant's Feedback Form

Participant's Research No. ____

A. How accurate does the content in the *Definition of Stage* Section describe your development when you were at the _____ Stage?

Circle one below.

       1   2   3   4   5

1	2	3	4	5
It is a very inaccurate description	Part of the description is accurate but most of it is not	The description is about evenly divided between being accurate and inaccurate	Most of the description is accurate but part of it is not	It is a very accurate description

What comments do you have concerning the *Definition of the Stage* description we have written?

B. How accurate does the content in the *Central Task* Section describe your development when you were at the _____ Stage?

Circle one below.

       1   2   3   4   5

1	2	3	4	5
It is a very inaccurate description	Part of the description is accurate but most of it is not	The description is about evenly divided between being accurate and inaccurate	Most of the description is accurate but part of it is not	It is a very accurate description

Appendix A Research Methodology and Sample Description

What comments do you have concerning the *Central Task* description we have written?

C. How accurate does the content in the *Predominant Affect* Section describe your development when you were at the _____ Stage?

Circle one below

1	2	3	4	5
It is a very inaccurate description	Part of the description is accurate but most of it is not	The description is about evenly divided between being accurate and inaccurate	Most of the description is accurate but part of it is not	It is a very accurate description

What comments do you have concerning the *Predominant Affect* description we have written?

D. How accurate does the content in the *Sources of Influence* Section describe your development when you were at the _____ Stage?

Circle one below

1	2	3	4	5
It is a very inaccurate description	Part of the description is accurate but most of it is not	The description is about evenly divided between being accurate and inaccurate	Most of the description is accurate but part of it is not	It is a very accurate description

What comments do you have concerning the *Sources of Influence* description we have written?

E. How accurate does the content in the *Role of Working Style* Section describe your development when you were at the _____ Stage?

Circle one below.

1	2	3	4	5
It is a very inaccurate description	Part of the description is accurate but most of it is not	The description is about evenly divided between being accurate and inaccurate	Most of the description is accurate but part of it is not	It is a very accurate description

What comments do you have concerning the *Role of Working Style* description we have written?

F. How accurate does the content in the *Conceptual System Used* Section describe your development when you were at the _____ Stage?

Circle one below.

1	2	3	4	5
It is a very inaccurate description	Part of the description is accurate but most of it is not	The description is about evenly divided between being accurate and inaccurate	Most of the description is accurate but part of it is not	It is a very accurate description

Appendix A Research Methodology and Sample Description 165

What comments do you have concerning the *Conceptual System Used* description we have written?

G. How accurate does the content in the *Learning Process* Section describe your development when you were at the _____ Stage?

Circle one below.

1	2	3	4	5
It is a very inaccurate description	Part of the description is accurate but most of it is not	The description is about evenly divided between being accurate and inaccurate	Most of the description is accurate but part of it is not	It is a very accurate description

What comments do you have concerning the *Learning Process* description we have written?

H. How accurate does the content in the *Measure of Effectiveness and Satisfaction* Section describe your development when you were at the _____ Stage?

Circle one below.

1	2	3	4	5
It is a very inaccurate description	Part of the description is accurate but most of it is not	The description is about evenly divided between being accurate and inaccurate	Most of the description is accurate but part of it is not	It is a very accurate description

What comments do you have concerning the *Measures of Effectiveness and Satisfaction* description we have written?

APPENDIX B

Themes in Interviews with Three Senior Informants

Introduction

The content in this appendix consists of interviews with three senior informants in our study. All three have twenty to thirty years of experience beyond their graduate training. All three are considered master practitioners in the local Minneapolis–St Paul community and are sought out by younger practitioners for supervision and therapy/counseling.

The interview with Dr S, a clinical psychologist, was conducted by the first author as part of the original 100-interview sample. The authors jointly constructed the themes which accompany this and the other two interviews. The interview with Dr M, a counseling psychologist, was an extra interview. It was conducted jointly by the two authors. The interview with Dr A, a clinical psychologist, done jointly by the two authors, was conducted as an extra interview.

Interview with Dr S   THEME

Dr S is a senior clinical psychologist. She is recognized as a master clinician and a very wise practitioner.

1. How does counseling/therapy work? Has your view of it changed over time?
DR S. My persuasion is that therapy works because we are creatures of symbols and we

need to understand reality before we can handle it effectively. So we need accurate labels for things and that is a form of insight. Then the process is one of recognizing alternatives and options and going through the process of selecting and testing. The change over time for me was one of becoming less rigid. I started with more of the psychoanalytic persuasion but I could feel myself become more and more eclectic and being more and more inclusive in thinking about diagnosis, the process of therapy and the method of therapy. I would try new things even though I would be rather skeptical. But I increasingly have tried things and, like with most things, what works we keep and the rest, hopefully with a breath of kindness, we blow away.

Decreased rigidity over time

Feedback on clinical work as influential

I. How does a person know if something works?

DR S. I label it useful if it furthers a process of those things I said were important to the client. Having some knowledge of origins is useful although I got further and further from the historical perspective of psychoanalysis. So I modified the dredging operations of my earlier days.

I. You have been talking here about becoming less rigid, more and more eclectic and more inclusive. When did that process happen to you?

DR S. It has been a continuing process for me.

I. What characteristics describe you now in relationship to your therapy that might not have applied in the past?

DR S. Well, I am ever so much more patient. Things just don't have to happen. They can be very gradual indeed. In some sense I suppose I don't insist on evidence. I am more willing to make the assumption that as the client encounters various aspects of her/his content, this process makes a difference.

I. Do you think this says something about a therapist's own increased sense of professional security? Is this the meaning of being ever so much more patient, of realizing that things don't have to happen quickly and insisting less on evidence? In other words, with professional self-confidence, you know it makes you know that one does not need those external markers.

The decrease in performance anxiety

DR S. I think that is a very good way of describing it. As a neophyte therapist, I was much too intense about cure and ever so much more self-conscious about what I was up to until I realized it was the interaction between me and my clients that made the difference, not the ideas I was promulgating.

I. When did you discover that?

DR S. Oh, I think that came out of my letting go of a more rigid approach. I notice this is also true of the beginning therapists I have supervised at a volunteer counseling center. They are terribly rigid. I think it relates to the extent to which a person feels comfortable with being a therapeutic instrument. You don't have to have ten rules, you don't have to say certain things, you don't have to get the client to say certain things in order to feel that you're achieving certain things.

I. In time, you didn't have to be the expert and "on" all the time?

DR S. No, the ease I developed and felt in time was very useful. Formerly I felt that if I missed something the process would bog down and evaporate in time. Making, controlling, moulding, getting the client to do X, Y, Z—this is the mindset of newer therapists. It is real arrogance but it *also* contributes to the

The new therapist/ counselor's sense of being powerful

Appendix B Themes in Interviews with Three Senior Informants   169

therapist's worry that one can be harmful. One is concerned about being harmful when one also has a view of oneself as so important to the client's life.

I. With this view, one has to be careful of everything he/she does?

DR S. Yes. Weight the phrases, measure the words. That brings me to another change, this is being more free in form.

I. Have you ever been strongly invested in a particular model of therapy/counseling? Have you ever become disenchanted with this model? If so, how did this change occur?

DR S. Yes, very strongly psychoanalytically oriented. Gradually the rigidity of this style has left me. The psychoanalytic model was effective but only in limited situations. Psychoanalysis still appeals to me. Periodically through the years, when with a client, I would say to myself—"Freud was right. There it is!" Two factors stand out: (1) The demands of the practice—where short-term approaches are useful. (2) The distancing demands of the Freudian tradition which are at odds with my personality. In time, it got easier to add my own thinking and my own way of doing things.

I. Gradually with time, your own personality came through more and more?

DR S. Yes, absolutely.

I. Theories and research can be a source of influence. Has this been true for you?

DR S. Yes, but not the statistical studies as much as work studies from areas such as philosophy.

I. More textured work?

DR S. Yes, not the laboratory studies. That always seemed so far away from me.

The reduced impact in time of small research studies

I. How about experience with clients as a source of influence?

DR S. That has been a big influence. I am a firm believer that clients teach us a great deal.

I. How do they do that?

DR S. It occurs through the way they reinforce the therapist. They will say "yes" or "I hadn't thought of that before." They are so reinforcing! They train us. They also taught me a lot about the whole matter of living and struggles that are probably, in many ways, common to all of us. They taught me about their felt needs and what they wanted. Sometimes this was not always what was best for them. When I wasn't as structured with clients, which I did in time, the client could more easily use the therapy to work out relationship problems. Perhaps, for example, I would end up being "Mother" and, in this context, good work could occur.

Clients as powerful teachers

I. Why didn't you do this earlier?

DR S. Because I was taught to have a very structured role.

I. The theoretical approach dictated your role as what?

Using external expertise to guide practice when a beginner

DR S. Don't get involved, don't encourage people to see you in anything but this blank role.

I. How did this change?

DR S. Gradually, I just changed through client experiences.

Clients as very impactful

I. Were individuals such as professors, supervisors, mentors a big influence for you?

DR S. Not very much. I had one supervisor at the VA who I admired so much and who I wanted to emulate. Later, he changed in a negative way and became more self-absorbed. He disappointed me! He fell from grace!

Imitating professional elders as a source of influence

Appendix B Themes in Interviews with Three Senior Informants

I. In the mentoring literature, there is discussion of painful endings to mentoring relationship. Was that true for you?

DR S. Yes. It was so disappointing! I respected him so much.

I. And that was the best relationship you had with a senior person in the field?

DR S. I learned things from other supervisors but I don't think they influenced me in my new found roles.

I. How about the process of being a supervisor/teacher for younger practitioners? Has that been a source of influence for you?

DR S. That is hard to answer. Some of the things taught in the training programs now seem to be counterproductive to developing good practitioners. All of that gets in the way.

I. Often they want to go into private practice right away. Is that bad?

DR S. Yes, they are raw. Early on you need constant colleague contact and supervision. Early on it is easy to get caught up in a fad and to rigidly apply procedures to everyone coming in.

Overutilization of a single conceptual approach

I. Events in one's personal life can also be a source of influence. Is this true for you?

DR S. Yes, I think it is true, perhaps more in later years and specifically to do with my health problems. The health problems raised many new questions regarding what my clients could expect of me.

One's personal life as a source of influence

I. Has the experience made you better?

DR S. Yes, in that I have worked considerably more with individuals who have physical illnesses. And it certainly was a strong motivation to learn about hypnosis and use it in therapy. I probably have been especially good at helping individuals who have become depressed because of physical illness. These individuals don't really get listened to because people don't want to hear things. They are prone to minimize and "buck you up" and insist upon your strengths and optimism. People demand that the physically ill abandon all of their negative thought. I, on the other hand, encourage it. My physical illness has made me very much more sensitive.

I. The power of your own illness has taught you this?

DR S. Yes, but one of my professors taught me long ago that it was not necessary to have *the* experience to help people with it, i.e., one does not need to be a parent to help parents in child rearing. But, I did find myself being more effective including a willingness to be openly sympathetic—I would say, "I feel really bad for you," "That makes me really sad."

I. Of all the sources of influence we have discussed, what have been the most impactful?

DR S. There is another—peers. It is with peers that I have had the most prolonged and intensive conversations.

Peers as a source of influence

I. All the way along?

DR S. Yes, but perhaps more after I developed a sense of confidence in the world of practice. It was peers who validated things for me. They come to you with their problems or send their kids to you. Those add, in my opinion, great increments of esteem to a therapist. In the same way, clients do the same thing by their referrals of friends and family. They also tell you about what there is about you that makes them feel positive about you.

Professional self-esteem coming from success as a practitioner

I. Does positive feedback like this give one a sense of security that the beginner can never have?

Appendix B Themes in Interviews with Three Senior Informants

DR S. Oh, yes, that's true. That is one of the reasons experience is such an important aspect in the development of the therapist. For me, this kind of feedback from experience was so much more validating than the minimal feedback from supervisors I received! The best I ever got from one supervisor—and remember this was years ago—was "You have a good therapy voice." I did not even take it as much of a compliment but that is the most he gave.

I. Now adding peers as a source of influence, how would you rank these?

DR S. Peers, clients, personal life and the literature, but not much the empirical literature. Then professional elders some but not much being a supervisor. I have enjoyed supervising but don't know that I have learned much from it.

I. Do you see counseling/therapy more complex or simple for you as you have gained experience?

DR S. Both! I don't have to be as self-conscious and, therefore, it is simpler. I also appreciate the complexities more than I have in the past. You see and you hear and you incorporate much more as you go along. One also has less of a necessity to emphasize content and more ability to understand meaning. And, in that way, it becomes complex because what people say and also how they say it suddenly matters.

<small>Incorporating more complexity with experience</small>

I. Is there any continuum along which you have progressed?

DR S. Age has an impact. One becomes a "wise old owl" and it defines you in a certain way.

I. What kind of people make the best counselors and therapists?

DR S. Lovers of people. Individuals who really like people and who feel a personal commitment to justice and equality.

I. What causes people to leave the field?

DR S. They can cut it academically but are not good at it. They are cold fish and really don't like people in the way it is necessary for a practitioner. They are miserable, fearful, uncomfortable.

I. What exactly are the satisfactions you get from the work? Have these changed over time?

DR S. The satisfaction of entering another's private world and helping that person has increased over time because my anxiety about performance has greatly diminished.

I. Do you measure success much differently than before?

DR S. Yes, in a less narrow way. There is less pressure on me.

Qualities of effective therapists/counselors

Interview with Dr M

THEME

Dr M is a well respected counseling psychologist who works as a psychotherapist and an organizational consultant.

I. If you were going to now look at your career and look at critical incidents in your development, what would pop out to you?

DR M. There seems to be a life full of crises (laughs). Probably I would say my father's alcoholism was one of the issues that was a critical one. So was codependency stuff. That was probably pretty important and underlying for me to get into this line of work, I would imagine. Because all along the way I don't think I really made a clear career choice until I was 30, and at that point I had been

Personal life as a motivator for entering therapy/counseling work

Appendix B Themes in Interviews with Three Senior Informants 175

into a number of different things. My father lost the business in a poker game when I was in high school, so in a pique I joined the Air Force, and that was just to get away, that was the geographical cure. And I wound up being selected as a result of all the testing for the Russian language school. And I felt if that's what they want me to do; I compliantly went and then I got a nomination for an appointment to the Naval Academy at Annapolis, and it was kind of the same way. My great-aunt had told me that they were offering this state wide examination for an appointment to the Naval Academy, and I thought, well, why not. So I took it, and I was in Japan as an airman and I got a notification that I had been accepted for the nomination.

I. How did you react to that at the time?

DR M. Well, I completely forgot I had done that, and so I didn't know what they were talking about.

I. You're supposed to be excited and glad.

DR M. Well, they had a program whereby people who were coming out of the enlisted ranks could go through a prep school. So I came back in early January to attend this prep school. I talk about these things, I guess, because I was kind of just drifting along in life; that's kind of a theme for a long time, going to the Naval Academy and even going into the submarines. Well, I did take a class for the submarines. But many of those things kind of just happened to me and I responded to them. It wasn't a sense of clear direction. I was an engineer which is clearly not what my heart's desire was all about. (laughs) When I was in submarines and I was on a nuclear submarine in the latter stages of my

His own drifting along and poor vocational fit as possible motivators for late work as a career counselor career, I saw this tremendous waste of talent and people who were so-so bright and who were still enlisted men or they were mismatched. They were not properly placed, and it struck me as such a misuse of talent.

I. You were really in close quarters there, too. I wonder if that's how you got to know others.

DR M. Yes, but the new submarines are quite large; they're 425 feet long and 30 feet wide including carpeting. Pretty plush stuff compared to the old diesel electrics which were very cramped. But that was one of the things that got me thinking about it, and when I left the Navy, I went into a monastery, and the person that I worked with there at this monastery in Kentucky said: "You really ought to work with people and not be in this cloistered order." And that was one of the things that got me thinking, and then I saw, after I left the monastery, on my way back to North Dakota, I stopped in Detroit and there I saw a counseling psychologist and went through a battery of tests looking at what I would be good at because I was thinking about medical school and other things and at that point one of the careers that came to the fore for me was counseling psychology and not clinical. We had some people who had some pretty severe disabilities even in the Navy. Alcoholism, of course, and the last patrol I was on, someone had a psychotic break. It was clear to me at that point that I wanted to work with people who had some things going for them, that their functioning was relatively good. That was a key. So I applied to only one graduate program in counseling psychology.

I. It seems like you were just drifting along, but

Experiencing counseling as a client before entering the vocation

Appendix B Themes in Interviews with Three Senior Informants

also several people saw some resources that you had and kind of pulled you into something.

DR M. That's true. I think even when I was in the Navy a captain said, "We need people like you in the Navy who can talk to people, who can understand." There was a little period of time there when I really wrestled with that whole notion of a religious vocation, whether I was actually going to do that, and I actually submitted my resignation in February of 1963, but because I was assigned to a nuclear submarine at the time, they didn't let me out until February of 1965. So I tell people I lived my first two years of monastic life in the Navy on a submarine (laughs). Even before that when I was at Syracuse University studying Russian one of the things I found was being in the library and reading Karl Menninger's *Man Against Himself*. It first got me interested in the psychodynamic aspects. I remember thinking then how powerful this was, and I was really impressed with the effect people could have in their lives by virtue of their emotions and their thinking. That was probably the first inkling of a move in that direction, and it was then a little bit later when I was just finishing my first year at the Academy when I got into the more existential stuff and started looking at the ultimate meanings of life. And that search started.

I. You seem to have a real active curiosity, and that you find things, like you find existential literature at the Naval Academy. I wonder if there's an inquiring mind or curiosity, what's the dimension here?

DR M. Well, one thing I would say is just that there was an existential void. Although I was

Successful pre-professional experiences with helping as a motivator for the therapy/counseling career choice

Searching for personal answers as a motivator for the career choice going off in this direction and becoming a career Naval officer, there was something that didn't quite fit with what I thought was really important in my life, and so I started looking around for things that would help me make sense of what could fit, and that's when I first got into reading Thomas Merton and reading some theology, especially monastic works and some philosophy. On my first cruise, I was on a destroyer and one of the people who was on the destroyer with me was a professor of philosophy from Notre Dame. He was a reserve officer, and when I got back from that cruise that fall and school started again, I found a whole set of books on the history of philosophy that this guy sent to me. I really appreciated that!

I. I was wondering if the geographic cure, as you put it, was active here in the Navy far away. I was wondering if the impact of your father's alcoholism was at work here.

DR M. Oh, yes, because to me it seems like he was somehow not looking at that, like life is precious. He was anesthetizing himself. It was amazing to me that he could not see what he was doing to himself and his life and to our family. Yes, these issues couldn't be dealt with geographically. There had to be kind of a self-exploration. I will say, even when I was in the Navy, I found myself affiliating with people who were also what I would call searchers. One of the most remarkable people I ever met in my life was the doctor aboard this nuclear submarine. He was truly remarkable, and while we were in the shipyard, we started talking about these kinds of things. Very talented guy, he was in his thirties at that time, and he was starting to explore some of the same issues I was about

Searching for wholeness in one's personal life

The impact of a mentor during the personal/professional search

the meaning of life. We wound up having this group of people, and we met once or twice a month. I always thought of Jim as being kind of a big brother, but in a sense, he was someone who in some ways was more naive than I was. But that was a powerful group for me. I think it was being attracted to people who I could talk about those things with, inquiring people.

I. How about the transition to graduate school in psychology?

DR M. When I started graduate school, it was a fluke; I mean I applied to graduate school in July. And somebody had just dropped out. I was absolutely at the beginning in counseling.

I. Did you begin graduate school without any undergraduate psychology?

DR M. None at all. I was taking Psych 1 and graduate psychology at the same time (laughs).

I. Obviously it worked out well, but how was it at the time?

DR M. I was terrified at the time in some ways; in other ways, I was so interested in it, and I got a 4.0 average. I was just so intensely involved in it. It really was extremely intense. I was so fascinated, I just couldn't quite find enough about it. The first year, I was on a fellowship and felt kind of isolated; and then they brought me back and I was a T.A. in the Psych department, and that's when I met some other students, people like Linda Smith. Wonderful, wonderful woman. And Ellen Johnson. We had a lot of interesting discussions. I think very early on I got exposed to leaders in the field. Exciting, yes, but sometimes I felt just terror that someone was going to find out I really didn't know...

Peers as a source of influence

Anxiety as a primary emotion at the beginning of graduate school

The intense stimulation in the beginning of graduate school

Peers as a powerful source of influence

I. How did you deal with the terror? What was your kind of internal strategy?

DR M. I think at that point it was trying to make sure by reading and reading, but also connecting with people who I felt really knew their stuff, and there was a real connection with what I saw as the clear authority figures, the people I saw who were the best folks around. There was a group of people that were kind of there that I saw as mentors and competent senior people.

Searching for professional elders as a graduate school survival strategy

I. Were they supervisors and professors who you respected and could identify with as a way to handle the anxiety?

DR M. That was right. I would talk about my concerns when I didn't know what to do. A lot of times they helped me see that I really did have a lot more insight into something. I had been reading quite a bit and it was very different.

The search for competence as a counselor in training

I. So it was reading and connecting with people?

DR M. That's right. I forgot about something. It really even was kind of a revolt. A group of graduate students got together, and we got a group going of graduate students talking about our concerns. I forgot about that.

I. It was enlisting the support of peers.

DR M. Yes, it really was. There were some people who were there who seemed like they were above it all. But there was a real core group who you felt like you could really talk to and share these things with. They were very important.

Peer support as critical

I. Important in terms of...

DR M. Of bouncing ideas off, talking about things you'd read, or talking about your concerns. I remember, I had a suicidal client and I think I probably got more what I call real

Appendix B Themes in Interviews with Three Senior Informants

solid support from my peers, my fellow graduate students, than I could possibly have gotten from people who were supervising me at the time. In that respect, there were clearly no boundaries. I mean I was so ... I had this savior complex.

I. No boundaries in terms of what? Just kind of leaping in to help, doing anything?

DR M. That's right, yes, that was true.

I. I was wondering, you mentioned extra workshops you took. Was that part of the searching process?

DR M. Yes, it was. In many ways it was; I think of it now as being defiant against the way things were supposed to be in the department. In some ways I think it was a way of coping with fear. I think first of all was the feeling of being the complete novice and really not knowing anything. That was one, but when I started working with some clients I saw that the approach I was taught just wasn't sufficient.

I. How did you find out that the approach didn't work?

DR M. It just wasn't sufficient. There were a lot of times that family of origin issues were so pervasive and so important in causing the problem, but not helped by the model I was taught.

I. OK. Going back to an earlier point, is it correct to say that in the beginning there was this tendency to connect with people you admire and then there's a point where you were searching, but more autonomous? Does that make sense?

DR M. Absolutely.

I. You finished everything except the dissertation in 1969 and took a full-time job and then finished your dissertation in 1972 so there was that period where you were ...

Intense desire to help as a new counseling trainee

The attraction of extra workshops and training experiences for the therapy/counseling novice

The searching moves from a dependent to an independent base

DR M. I was an instructor and I was an administrator and I was supervising people in student advising, but I still wound up getting involved in some counseling at that point. And I think that the advising job was really a delaying factor. It was something that probably gave me an excuse to delay finishing my dissertation. But also it was secure. We had just had a child at that time. I always knew there would be a next step. There were several possible routes.

I. Was it an extended moratorium?

DR M. Right, that's what I did. Absolutely. And so actually what happened, I have to laugh at the way things worked out. I was supposed to have a day off to work on my dissertation study, and of course, there never seemed like there was time. I didn't have time to do it. The summer of 1972 my wife said, "Listen, I'm going to take the kids and I'm going to your folks. Call me when you're done." And I did it, I finished it in seven days. (laughs)

I. If you think about the moratorium again, what were your motivations for that?

DR M. It was... first of all, I saw what possibilities there were, and I wasn't sure which direction to really pursue.

I. Was there any sense of not feeling quite ready to have the doctorate?

DR M. Oh, absolutely. I used to say that as a result of going to the Naval Academy, I felt that I was trained and not educated; and in a sense, having gone through graduate school, I still felt like I had been trained but not necessarily educated in a real grounded formation process to help launch me into being a full-fledged psychologist. There were missing parts in the graduate program, and I

A conditional autonomy type moratorium

Delaying the challenge of the exploration stage

started to find some of those things. But in the spring of 1973, after four years of budget cuts for my advising program—every year they cut me 10 percent—I was preparing to teach a course, and I'd just gotten through with the budget and gotten cut again, and I got an ulcer. And I said, This is crazy. I got a call from a medical center, and the director said he needed someone to head the counseling unit. And I did that for five years. It was an opportunity to get some experience, and I started being an internal consultant.

I. Within the medical center?

DR M. Yes. It was probably the seeds of my destruction of a career in the medical center. I found myself being cast in the role of a change agent in an organization that was dedicated to maintaining the status quo. You know they were not about to change. It took a year to change a form. And trying to get people to shift out of their roles to try something new was difficult. So that's when I started looking around and started working at an industrial consulting firm part time.

I. How did you get into the internal change agent role at the medical center? I mean, that was not part of your job.

DR M. There was a highly respected clinical psychologist there. She had some credibility with the powers that be because of her longstanding clinical experience. They were getting letters, complaints from people who felt like they were being treated like numbers, very impersonal. So the medical center developed a program called TIGER, which stood for Training in Individual Group Effectiveness and Resourcefulness. And what we did was to get into an interdisciplinary team building process. There was about a

The search for competence, now self-directed, continues after graduation

Discovering incongruities between the emerging professional self and the work environment

four-week training period on being a consultant. Part of that was an intensive T group experience. This was a very constructive experience. It was an intensive and emotional experience for me. Some of those training people were from Houston. There was a lot of emphasis on choices and responsibility, and that's when I started doing some things in *Gestalt*.

I. T group and *Gestalt* training. What came in what order?

DR M. First T group and then *Gestalt*. A *Gestalt* trainer would come to town once a week, and I joined the training.

I. It seems like there was a shift occurring at this time in your orientation, more like an inward orientation.

DR M. Oh, yes, very much so.

I. Can you recall some of the things you were dealing with?

DR M. At this point I was doing a lot of supervision. I was working with about a dozen graduate students at the time and two or three other psychologists and one guy who was a vocational counselor; he did job search. And I think some of it was interaction with those graduate students from a different perspective. It was a whole new area for terror (laughs) and feelings of uncertainty. It's one thing to be a colleague and talking about this and another thing to be a supervisor and to be in charge.

I. Like a challenge to you.

DR M. Oh, it was that! The thing that was really important was that these doctoral interns were from different training programs around the country.

I. Do you remember at times feeling like you wanted to confirm the value of your training,

One's own counseling and training as a source of influence

The impact of self as professional elder for others

The anxiety of becoming a professional elder for others

Appendix B   Themes in Interviews with Three Senior Informants

that you wanted to feel like this really was important or useful.

DR M. It was trying to convince, especially some of these people who had not been brought up in my tradition, the real value of our approach to assessment and testing. Yes, I think there was a little bit of proselytizing.

I. Changing the topic, I am wondering if you can talk about starting graduate school after some life experience versus right after college.

DR M. It was 1965. I was 30 years old, and I remember a classmate. She was sitting next to me in class, and she was about 21, and there was a guy who was also 21. They were such babes in the woods when it came to looking at some of these things. They could talk about theory, but they didn't have a sense of what life experience was about. And in some ways, I always felt like I didn't have either, mine was so biased by 12 years in the military; it's not really real life either. There were a number of young people like that, and they were just incorporating the material.

I. Is that one of the things that's different about having experience?

DR M. Well, I don't know, but that was for me, I think; probably I was a little bit more skeptical about that, things being that simple. But there were differences between some of these people too.

I. It sounds like there were some similarities between people without experience, a vulnerability, a dependency; and then there are some individual differences too between them. So you were searching and being challenged and stimulated by other students. That kind of started a new phase.

I. Did you get involved in any other activities at the medical center?

Margin notes:

The differential rate of development of the older versus younger graduate student

For the older student, conceptual ideas get tested against the extensive personal data base

DR M. I got into lots of things such as a program in chemical dependency counseling. I started getting into that, and I started getting into things like the cardiac rehab program, the psychological medicine program, working with people in that program. Also biofeedback. Those were some of the things that I was interested in; I wanted to find out about them. There was some overlap with some of the things I was doing in *Gestalt*.

I. Any other impactful people for you at this time?

DR M. There was another person when I was still a graduate student who was very helpful to me. She had a Master's degree in theology; she was just about a year or so younger than I was. She was so bright! She converted to Catholicism, and she really got into the yoga stuff. She met a guy, brilliant young guy. They were married in a Hindu wedding, and he really got into looking at yoga at that point. He got into doing some meditation. They were important in that sense that they got me interested in methods of body relaxation.

I. It seems that other people have been very important to you in terms of your own development. You keep talking about these other people.

DR M. Yes. They're usually people I find fascinating or interesting or something about them. It is like their version of what it takes to make life good.

Defining the qualities of admired peers and professional elders that he sought out

I. How did you get from the medical center to industrial consulting?

DR M. The last two years I knew I wasn't going to be able to stay in the medical center because of my experiences there. I was doing fine, but the more I ran into that bureaucracy, the more I thought, this is crazy. It just does not fit for me. So I started working at a mental health clinic. I worked there for a half day per week, and then someone at the industrial consulting firm asked me to go over and do some work for them. This was in 1977, and I worked at the industrial consulting firm for two or three days per month for a year. At the medical center I began working with in-patients who had little incentive to get better. It was really kind of impossible. There were 120 patients! You couldn't believe it. That's when I said, I do not want to work in just strict clinical psychology with psychopathology. So that helped me make my decision. I could have worked at a big local clinic in administration.

I. What made that attractive to you?

DR M. The thing that made it attractive was the variety of people that you'd see there. You saw just such a broad variety of things, like young people who were facing marital/vocational/adjustment problems; but they weren't psychotic. You saw one once in a while, but psychotic patients were very rare. I was interested in that. And then when the decision came whether to work for a mental health clinic or industrial consulting firm, that was a tough one for me. I thought my internal consulting interests could be developed more in industrial consulting. So I did.

I. How was the transition?

DR M. I worked through Sunday to finish things at the medical center, and during that last week I got a call from the president of the industrial firm. He said, "We had somebody get sick. Could you please come to work tomorrow?" So I went off on a five day stretch. I didn't have 24 hours off. Five days

Searching for an optimal work environment for expression of self

Clients as a source of influence

Clients here too as a source of influence

in a row, each day probably 12 hours; and then as a result of that I wound up having like three major reports to write. And that's what I did starting at that firm. I kept getting overextended. No matter what I was doing, there were always these other things; you could do assessment and you had outplacement counseling and the key part was billable time, billable time. Sometimes we went home after midnight, and we were back at 6:00 in the morning. And I felt like I was caught between doing what people wanted me to do but I didn't want to do and disappointing people I didn't want to disappoint. — Distressed about the lack of an optimal environment fit for the self

I. It seems like this was really a very strenuous situation.

DR M. That wasn't all the time, but it was pretty consistent. And if you were to go there right now, matter of fact, I think you'd find most people are working probably 60 hours a week.

I. But if we were to look at this, you had the medical center where there was the administrative bureaucracy, very severe pathology, the rules of the administration, all the constraints that did seem to facilitate progress. It seemed that it produced almost a loss of meaning; it just was not meaningful in a very basic sense.

DR M. That's right.

I. And then the next phase where you were trying out working with a varied client population in the mental health clinic. That seemed like it was a good time. — The exploration stage self-directed search when elements are added and shed

DR M. It was.

I. But that had a time limit on it.

DR M. That's right.

I. And then it sounded like the industrial

Appendix B Themes in Interviews with Three Senior Informants

consulting firm was a place to use some resources that you hadn't used before.

DR M. That's right. Or hadn't developed the level of competency that I really felt that I wanted to have. Yes, and I was going through the *Gestalt* program the last year at the medical center and the first year at the industrial firm. Of course, that program was very helpful for doing lots of groups and looking at oneself, a time for reflection, a time for being clear about my own values.

I. What I hear is a theme of trying to find optimal environments for development and each environment provided things, but then there are liabilities that forced you then to search for people and places and move on. And that's been a consistent kind of theme. Does that sound right?

DR M. Right.

I. And now, how does this environment, the private practice and consulting firm that you created here, fit for you?

DR M. I started four years ago. It was a scary thing at first, but I was confident that I had some of the skills to survive. I survived. I set up shop here, started doing some individual work and corporate consulting, and gradually I started doing work with school systems, health organizations, hospitals, and clinics. A lot of my clients now tend to be in health care education. There's still quite a bit of variety; some of it is more the individual coaching. When you ask what I do, it's hard for me to say sometimes what I'm doing.

I. Conceptually, you mean?

DR M. Oh, yes. It is all so combined in so many ways.

I. It seemed when listening to your background that this setting is excellent for utilizing all of

Individuation stage recycling to earlier insecurity at a point of transition

your experiences in an integrated way—the medical center, the academic, the research, the mental health clinic, the industrial consulting, the military background—that you can pull from in a setting like this.

DR M. Yes, I think that's true. The other thing I found myself doing though is molding different things I do with my personal way of doing it. I do not use much of a formula any more.

I. Does that just gradually go away?

DR M. Yes, I use some models but I've done some other things that other people would think are wacky, like the technology for creativity program or the empowerment workshop I recently did or the leadership and mastery program.

Conceptual system and role working style become highly individualized and internalized by the individuation stage

I. You seem to have come to a point where your experiences are so rich and you've done so much, that your theoretical structure is unique, almost like it is you.

DR M. More and more.

I. Perhaps because it's your unique version that you don't need to put labels on it so much because you're not having to present it quite that way.

DR M. Except with clients and client companies.

I. Is part of your development process that you have to have new things?

DR M. New things are important. I don't think it's just the newness. It's things that seem to be more consistent with my style, with my values. I have also along the way been in and out of my own therapy. That's been very important to me. And I have been with a very good older therapist who has given me a lot.

Avoiding stagnation

Impact of one's therapist as a professional elder

I. If you look ahead, what are your thoughts for the future?

DR M. Sometimes I think I should go drive a cab or something like that (laughs). I see myself doing more and more the things I want rather than what other people want me to do, and I seem to be getting more and more clear about what those things are and doing things that are exciting and interesting to do or that I think have value to other people as well. And I am getting very much involved with alcoholism in families and the way it affects the members of a family—adult children of alcoholics and codependency. It is really interesting. But now it comes out of more who I am, the early experiences with alcoholism and all the things—professional and personal—since then. The more I do that, the more I feel excited about that process, and I don't think I'll ever retire in that sense.

I. Thank you so much for everything. This has been very exciting.

Depending on the internalization process of the Advanced Professional Stage

Interview with Dr A

Dr A is a senior professional psychologist. He is recognized as a therapist for therapists and is widely respected by his colleagues.

I. What are key parts of professional development?

DR A. The people. There was not another psychologist on the staff in my first job after graduate school. I was the psychologist, there were three social workers, we hired an occupational therapist, and then we had the psychiatrist part time. I got to respect those people and respect their knowledge and tried to find out what they could teach me. I found

THEME

out that psychologists weren't the only people in the mental health field, the only ones who knew anything. I developed a tremendous amount of respect for other mental health professionals, especially in the social work field, the ones who knew something about treatment.

Openness to learning

I. How competent did you feel after graduating and going out into your first job?

DR A. Oh, I was scared. You had to be scared. That's an experience.

I. That state of being scared, what happens to that over the years? Is there a way of talking about that?

DR A. You see, that's why I think it's so important to have that experience as a member of a team; you get a kind of group therapy, you get the experience that you're not alone and that other people are having the same kind of problems, and also get the support for what you're doing and an opportunity to talk about it. The people I worked with were good clinicians who were thinking about people the same way I was, and so we were able to share our successes and our failures and really support each other and, of course, at that clinic we also had a terrible population to deal with. These were chronically ill patients, most of them, a majority of them with very little ego strength.

The importance of interaction with colleagues

I. So defining success really gets to be an issue because these aren't the people who are going to get much better no matter what you do?

DR A. That's right, so your idea of success changes. You go for little gains, you know, the primary goal is to keep people out of the hospital, not to get them well, but to keep them from regressing, keep them in the community somehow and keep them functioning.

Defining success in realistic terms

Appendix B Themes in Interviews with Three Senior Informants

I. We have the idea that people when they finish a graduate program have a real desire to show that the training was worthwhile and that what you learned in school and maybe on internship was valuable. It is confirming the value of your training. Does that ring any bells for you?

DR A. I think you are right. The area in which I got the most confirmation was in my diagnostic skills. I think that's what happens to most clinical psychologists who go into clinics in their first jobs, if they are well trained. They are well trained in diagnostic skills; thats where they get their major confirmation.

Confirmation of the validity of one's training

I. That term sounds right to you, the idea of confirmation of your training, that's something important?

DR A. Absolutely. If nothing else, confirmation to the extent that the person feels that the skills he/she was trained in are needed. Now that's another problem area for many psychologists. For example, if you're only trained in one therapeutic modality, that's pretty narrow. When you go into a clinic and they say, we need you to see this kind of patient and do this and do that, and you're not trained to do that...

I. Then what happens to the new professional?

DR A. I think they get pretty frantic.

I. And you were saying that you really felt scared?

DR A. Yes, sure. We felt like frauds, you know, and we got really angry at the graduate school.

Angry about not being adequately prepared in graduate school

I. Yes, we've noticed this same anger in some of the interviews with people.

DR A. Yes, absolutely. Graduate school faculty have too little contact with the outside world in that sense. I think there is a tremendous parallel between development in the medical field and in the psychology field. The development in medicine went through the same phases. Medicine went through a phase when medical training was separate from practice; they had very little relationship to each other and there were the same kinds of problems.

I. What's the big problem right now?

DR A. What happened, of course, was that practice took over the medical schools. So medical school and practice are almost the same thing in many ways. I bet that's what will happen in psychology and clinical psychology also. Then the split is going to be between the practice field, the professional practice field of psychology and the research field; that split is already building.

I. How did you get through those early years?

DR A. I talked about it and asked for a lot of support and leaned on my wife a lot. Support is really important. As much as possible you should be encouraged to develop new skills and expand yourself and how you understand things.

I. One of the reasons we're asking you is because you have a reputation of being a therapist for therapists and that's a very eminent position. When we talk about your development, we're talking about some important things, and maybe how people deal with being scared would be an example of something important to understand and to describe.

DR A. Yes, I think so.

I. What about clients, what kind of impact do they have for you?

DR A. Early, as I said, the client population was

Inadequacy of graduate training

The processing of experiences with others

The quest for new learning

Learning from clients

Appendix B Themes in Interviews with Three Senior Informants

pretty strange and so you learn to set limited goals, and you're not going to get a lot of support from your clients as such. Clients taught me a lot about dealing with pathology and about dealing with emergencies. I learned a lot but was scared a lot, too. I think an important thing you learn over time as a clinician with experience is to be able to deal with any kind of thing that comes before you.

I. How does that happen?

DR A. Just purely experience.

I. What happens with the experience, do you rely more on your experience, previous experience?

DR A. Sure.

I. How long does it take to really feel comfortable as a clinician? How long before a person really feels that he/she knows what is going on.

DR A. Well, I'd say it is a gradual process. We used to say that it took five years of full-time therapy work to really feel that you know what you're doing. By then you've dealt with most of the things with which you're going to be confronted. There are still things, of course, people are unlimited. :... But, you've dealt with most everything, you feel that you can handle it one way or another, and you also build up your resources. You've dealt with all the major kinds of threats to your feeling of worth and confidence, suicide issues, you've hospitalized people and you've diagnosed people in terms of medication and drugs. With all of the problems you've looked at and confronted, you've hopefully worked with most of the ethical issues, like how, why, and when to see patients and what to do and what not to do with them.

I. I was thinking about the Dreyfus and

The need for much experience to feel competent

Dreyfus (1986) work. These are people who have looked at the impact of experience in different fields, like chess players and taxi cab drivers. They suggest that at the beginning people use theoretical ideas but they don't know about the exceptions or they don't have any experience so they just apply things dogmatically and, of course, it doesn't always work very well. With lots of experience, they don't use other people's theories, they use their own experience. They become more atheoretical in the sense that it isn't atheoretical, it's much more personalized, and their own experience provides the paradigms for what they do in certain situations. I wonder if that's true for you.

DR A. Yes, I think you agree with me as a trainer of clinicians that one of the differences between the good clinicians and the bad clinicians is how much they can give up their rigidity. The ones who can't get beyond their training, their system, and try to fit all the patients to their system rather than fit the system to the patients are the ones who are not the good therapists. That is a big difference. Does that make sense?

I. Yes. Why can't they?

DR A. They're stupid, they weren't ever given permission to, they were too rigidly trained, or their personalities are so rigid that they can't get beyond themselves and their system. Those are the usual explanations.

I. We are trying to find out what therapists are doing when they are confronted with difficulties which they are not adequately prepared to handle. What do therapists do there—how do therapists handle that? These issues are pretty important in terms of how a person develops.

Development includes becoming less rigid

Appendix B Themes in Interviews with Three Senior Informants

DR A. That's why I don't like the idea of people going into private practice right after they graduate; they're too alone. If you go into a private practice clinic setting where there's supervision available, that's different. Too many people just go out and hang up their shingle by themselves or with another person who doesn't know any more than they do. In that situation, there is just not enough support and not enough information available. In our system in the USA, the graduates of most of the schools that I know about need supervision after they graduate. They can go out and do some therapy, but they need continued supervision.

Importance of peers and supervision for the new therapist

I. If a person would go into the private practice by oneself or with somebody else, would the person become more rigid then in the way he/she categorizes or be just too anxious perhaps to be able to open up and expand and think different ways?

DR A. They would certainly be anxious and then it depends on how they handle the anxiety, some of them will handle it quite rigidly and some of them will handle it by just getting out of the field. ... It (anxiety) chases people away. Then, for the wrong reasons, they try teaching, research, or administration; it really hurts them. They often end up in therapy since it is a breakdown of their system.

How the therapist/counselor handles anxiety about professional performance

I. That may be the time when therapists make niches for themselves where they are not exposed to so many threatening experiences.

DR A. Oh, yes, sure. That's the rigidity. If they can find it, sure. A safe way to solve their problem, but it's not necessarily a good way to solve their problem because you can't rely on the niche staying the same for you over time.

Rigidity as a method of reducing anxiety

I. It could be a conceptual rigidity or it could be a niche in terms of only working with certain kinds of people.

DR A. Sure. You may open up an anxiety clinic following rigid ways of treating anxiety such as behavioral techniques and that's all you do. Of course, then you're in a really dangerous position because a narrow population supports you, you just treat one diagnosis.

I. Is there a tendency to make everybody into that diagnosis?

DR A. Yes, that too easily becomes a problem.

I. So support is really important. Is it important to be able to say I don't know what I'm doing?

DR A. Sure.

I. We use the term Pseudodevelopment for when someone is selecting a niche and may be engaged in a lot of activity, may be engaged in a search but it is kind of a repetition, and confirming what one knows already instead of attempting to discover something new. How do you react to this idea?

DR A. That's part of the reason for the fads that we go through. People are looking for something that will give them structure and support. People jump on a new theory bandwagon because they are scared and don't know what they are doing or don't know enough about what they are doing and feel unsure. A system comes along and it looks attractive, it says some of the things that you've learned, and it gives you some new ideas about putting things together so you get yourself retrained as a "such and such" therapist, then you're stuck in another theory that isn't broad enough.

I. To handle everything?

Pseudodevelopment increases confidence for the short term

Appendix B Themes in Interviews with Three Senior Informants

DR A. To handle everything that's going to come through your door.

I. When do you think people are most susceptible to looking and finding and jumping in their career to a tight conceptual system?

DR A. I don't know. I see a lot of young professionals who aren't adequately trained, and I also see a lot of the 40-year-olds who are beginning to question: Where am I? What am I doing? Is this really worthwhile? There are also some who have gone through some kind of trauma.

I. Personal trauma maybe?

DR A. Or they're going through a treatment trauma—somebody committed suicide or they're being sued for something. That kind of trauma.

I. Does it happen at one time in a person's career?

DR A. It doesn't. There are always internal and external threats.

I. Is openness to experiences and an active searching attitude essential?

DR A. Yes, essential all the time.

I. Is the sect movement in therapy really contrary to development?

DR A. Yes, in many ways I think it is.

I. Is it possible that if you take a small therapy group that has its own journals, own membership, and then you just go around that small circle, feeling like you're doing something, you may in fact never really be asking questions to find answers, but rather asking questions to feel better about the fact that you already know it. Is that right?

DR A. In all the systems, the extremes, people are the same. You can get too self-contained in any system.

I. We're trying to speculate on the difference between that and development. When you get self-contained, is that when you get stagnation? And the openness to continue to grow, changing produces development? We are just trying to really work on how to conceptualize the difference between development and stagnation.

DR A. Yes. But, of course, the term that you are trying to define is development. I think some of the people in, say, orthodox analysis, would say as long as they keep questioning within their system, they develop; they rarely step out of the system. *Distinguishing between development and pseudo-development or stagnation*

I. Perhaps a working answer is that it is development if the question is really being asked to find the answer, which may disagree with what you already thought was true, versus you are asking the question in a way that can't come up with an answer that's different than what you already believe is true. If you are staying within the conceptual framework, and the problem that you are confronted with really should have forced you to look other places and you are still staying within that system, then that would be pseudodevelopment. So in a way it's the extent that you fit the patients to the system or the system to the patients. *Defining development versus pseudodevelopment*

DR A. That's the struggle that goes on with us all the time, all of us, I think. That's part of the struggle with long-term versus short-term therapy, the fights that we have in the United States in terms of insurance companies—it's really coming around to who needs what kind of therapy.

I. Whether something is development or not, in terms of choice of conceptual framework, is then whether or not you ask the question: Is this what the client needs? What do you think of this?

DR A. Yes, I agree with that, absolutely. The problem with this again is economic. If you ask that question very seriously, you might not get many patients. If you stick with one theory, if you're stuck with one modality, one way of approaching people, then you might not get many patients. Does this patient really fit what I can do, is this what this patient needs?

I. We are really now talking about an economic barrier to development.

DR A. Yes, that is true.

I. Do you think you could generalize somewhat this way and say that people who are more interested in developing tend to be more generalists. With generalists you get people coming at you from all over the place and then you're more threatened, I guess, in the sense that if you have a narrow conceptualist system, it kind of topples quicker; and some people would be attracted to that process, maybe of being able to get a lot of input and then keep going, and other people would be very threatened and want a narrower range of clients to work with. I don't know if I'm really overstating something, but I guess you would, for example, take work with lots of different kinds of people. And some way your way of working with people can accommodate all these.

DR A. I still refer a lot of people to other kinds of therapy. If someone needs a behavioral approach or some specific technique, I send them to somebody else because I just don't do that.

Economics impact the developmental search

I. We're trying to extract some components of what is ideal development. These are kind of value statements.

DR A. That's right.

I. We would like to hear your reactions to this. We are talking about the ability to learn from experience, which means openness to experiences, openness to varied sources of influence. And also the ability to tolerate ambiguity; and may be the most important in our way of thinking, willingness to reflect on one's experiences—thinking about it and talking to other people. And the ability and willingness to confront, see, and recognize one's own resources and limitations. And also, seeking out new experiences, that means taking on new challenges. And as a consequence of this, to adapt, change, and revise one's thinking.

DR A. Yes, and to use what you learn.

I. Maybe pseudodevelopment would involve really lots of repetition and repeating of old solutions. You've got it down and you just kind of keep doing it, and doing it; somehow fitting people into what you do.

DR A. That's right.

I. Is there something here that is more important than the others?

DR A. No, they have to all go together, they all kind of interact. Looking back at my experience.... These are all the things we have talked about.

I. We have been talking about barriers already, mostly internal barriers. Maybe we can focus on the external barriers, maybe barriers within our profession. Are there barriers within our profession? Are there processes within our profession that prevent development?

Appendix B Themes in Interviews with Three Senior Informants

DR A. One of the places to look on the negative side is to look at the literature on burnout. If you consider burnout as a symptom, one of the ways I conceptualize it is that burnout would be a symptom of stopped development. There are career issues that cause people to burn out, and there are ways in which people are forced to burn out. There are internal things which burn people out in terms of their own dynamics and personality. There are external things that burn people out in terms of the community support system, extended family issues, fights with insurance companies. There are active kinds of things that burn people out, such as people who don't actively take care of themselves physically. All of those things arrest development. The systems that we have within our field often burn people out because so many systems don't give people room for continued learning or basic respect as professionals.

I. What systems?

DR A. The way clinics and hospitals operate, the way the schools operate.

I. Mental health centers may not be nurturing enough to the staff?

DR A. That's right. Nurturing in a variety of ways.

I. Do you think people need a lot of nurturing in different ways or else the burnout will occur?

DR A. They need it; so many systems don't care because of the money. They just hire somebody, work them as hard as they can work them and then if they can't do it any more, they'll fire them and get somebody else. Oh, you'd be interested in this, you could teach it to your students. Somebody came up with

Burnout

External threats to development

the most clever idea, to force people to do short-term therapy. You don't have to talk about short-term and long-term therapy, all you do is require somebody to take three new patients a week. That is all it takes. Isn't that clever, a practitioner can't do any long-term therapy because of all the meetings, paperwork, consultation. So how do you develop within that structure? Something has to go. It is important to look at any system and whether it supports and encourages development. It is vitally important to renew yourself.

How structure can cause burnout

Pacing and protecting oneself

I. This has been very interesting. I see that our time is up. We appreciate that you have given us this opportunity to talk to you. Thank you.

References

Ard, B. N. (1973). Providing clinical supervision for marriage counselors: A model for supervisor and supervisee. *The Family Coordinator*, 22, 91-97.

Association of Psychology Internship Centers (1991). *Directory of internship programs in professional psychology (1991-92)*. Washington, DC.

Baker, S. B., Daniels, T. G., & Greeley, A. T. (1990). Systematic training of graduate level counselors: Narrative and meta-analytic reviews of three major programs. *Counseling Psychologist*, 18, 355-421.

Belenky, M., Clinchy, B., Goldberger, N., & Tarule, J. (1986). *Women's ways of knowing*. New York: Basic Books.

Benderly, B. L. (1989). Everyday intuition. *Psychology Today*, September, 35-40.

Benner, P. (1982). From novice to expert. *American Journal of Nursing*, 82, 402-407.

Benner, P., & Wrubel, J. (1982). Skilled clinical knowledge: The value of perceptual awareness, Part 2. *Journal of Nursing Administration*, 12, 28-33.

Blocher, D. H. (1983). Toward a cognitive developmental approach to counseling supervision. *Counseling Psychologist*, 11(1), 27-34.

Borders, L. D. (1989). A pragmatic agenda for developmental supervision research. *Counselor Education and Supervision*, 29, 16-24.

Borders, L. D., Fong-Beyette, M. L., & Cron, E. A. (1988). In-session cognition of a counseling student: A care study. *Counselor Education and Supervision*, 28, 59-70.

Brown, D. (1989). Logical positivism and/or phenomenology. *Counselor Education and Supervision*, 29, 5-6.

Cross, D. G., & Brown, D. (1983). Counselor supervision as a function of trainee experience: Analysis of specific behaviors. *Counselor Education and Supervision*, 22, 333-341.

Cummings, A. L., Hallberg, E. T., Martin, J., Slemon, A., & Heibert, R. (1990). Implications of counselor conceptualizations for counselor education. *Counselor Education and Supervision*, 30, 120-134.

Denzin, N. K. (1978). *The research act: A theoretical introduction to sociological methods*. New York: McGraw-Hill.

Dodge, J. (1982). Reducing supervisee anxiety. A cognitive behavioral approach. *Counselor Education and Supervision*, 22, 55-60.

Dreyfus, H. L., & Dreyfus, S. E. (1986). *Mind over machine: The power of human intuition and expertise in the era of the computer.* New York: The Free Press.

Ekstein, R., & Wallerstein, R. (1958). *The teaching and learning of psychotherapy.* New York: Basic Books.

Ellis, M. V. (1991). Research in clinical supervision. Revitalizing a scientific agenda. *Counselor Education and Supervision,* 30, 238-251.

Erikson, E. H. (1956). The problem of ego identity. *Journal of the American Psychoanalytic Association,* 4, 56-121.

Erikson, E. H. (1963). *Childhood and Society,* 2nd edn. New York: Norton.

Erikson, E. H. (1968). *Identity, youth and crisis.* New York: Norton.

Flavell, J. H. (1963). *The developmental psychology of Jean Piaget.* New York: Van Nostrand.

Fleming, J. (1953). The role of supervision in psychiatric training. *Bulletin of the Menninger Clinic,* 17, 157-159.

Freudenberger, H. J. (1974). Staff burnout. *Journal of Social Work,* 30, 159-165.

Friedlander, M. L., & Snyder, J. (1983). Trainees' expectation for the supervisory process: Testing a developmental model. *Counselor Education and Supervision,* 22, 342-348.

Friedlander, M. L., & Ward, G. W. (1984). Development and validation of the supervisory styles inventory. *Journal of Counseling Psychology,* 31, 541-557.

Friedman, D., & Kaslow, N. J. (1986). The development of professional identity in psychotherapists: Six stages in the supervision process. In F. W. Kaslow (Ed.), *Supervision and training: Models, dilemmas, and challenges* (pp. 29-49). New York: Haworth.

Gagne, R. M. (1968). Contribution of learning to human development. *Psychological Review,* 75, 177-191.

Gergen, K. J. (1985). The social constructionist movement in modern psychology. *American Psychologist,* 40, 266-275.

Gilligan, C. (1982). *In a different voice: Psychological theory and women's development.* Cambridge, MA: Harvard University Press.

Glaser, R., & Chi, M. T. H. (1988). Overview. In M. T. H. Chi, R. Glaser, & M. J. Farr (Eds), The nature of expertise. Hillsdale, NJ: Erlbaum.

Glaser, G., & Strauss, A. L. (1967). *The discovery of grounded theory: Strategies for qualitative research.* Chicago: Aldine.

Goldfried, M. R. (1980). Toward the delineation of therapeutic change principles. *American Psychologist,* 35, 991-999.

Goldman, L. (1982). Defining non-traditional research. *Counseling Psychologist,* 10(4), 91-93.

Goldman, L. (1989). Moving counseling research into the 21st century. *Counseling Psychologist,* 17, 81-85.

Grater, H. A. (1985). Stages in psychotherapy supervision: From therapy skills to skilled therapist. *Professional Psychology: Research and Practice,* 16, 605-610.

Greenson, M. (1967). *The technique and practice of psychoanalysis.* New York: International Universities Press.

References

Grotevant, H. D., & Cooper, C. R. (1986). Individuation in family relationships. *Human Development, 29*, 82-100.

Guy, J. D. (1987). *The personal life of the psychotherapist.* New York: Wiley.

Gysbers, N. C., & Rønnestad, M. H. (1974). Practicum supervision: Learning theory. In G. F. Farwell, N. R. Gamsky, & P. Mathieu-Coughlan (Eds), *The Counselor's Handbook.* New York: Intext Educational Publishers.

Hall, C. S., & Lindzey, G. (1970). *Theories of personality.* New York: Wiley.

Henry, W. E., Sims, J. H., & Spray, S. L. (1971). *The fifth profession.* San Francisco: Jossey-Bass.

Heppner, P. P., & Handley, P. (1982). The relationship between supervisory behaviors and perceived supervisor expertness, attractiveness, or trustworthiness. *Counselor Education and Supervision, 22,* 37-46.

Heppner, P. P., & Roehlke, H. J. (1984). Differences among supervisees at different levels of training: Implications for a developmental model of supervision. *Journal of Counseling Psychology, 30,* 252-262.

Herroid, D. J. (1989). *A model of the process of becoming a master counselor.* Unpublished doctoral dissertation. Minneapolis, MN: University of Minnesota.

Hess, A. K. (Ed.). (1980). *Psychotherapy supervision: Theory, research and practice.* New York: Wiley.

Hess, A. K. (1986). Growth in supervision: Stages of supervisee and supervisor development. *The Clinical Supervisor, 4,* 51-67.

Hess, A. K. (1987). Psychotherapy supervision: Stages, Buber and a theory of relationship. *Professional Psychology: Theory, Research and Practice, 18,* 251-259.

Hilgard, J. R. (1970). *Personality and hypnosis: A study of imaginative involvement.* Chicago: University of Chicago Press.

Hill, C. E., Charles, D., & Reed, K. G. (1981). A longitudinal analysis of counseling skills during doctoral training in counseling psychology. *Journal of Counseling Psychology, 28,* 428-436.

Hillebrand, E. (1989). Cognitive differences between experts and novices: Implications for group supervision. *Journal of Counseling and Development, 67,* 293-296.

Hoffer, E. (1951). *The true believer.* NY: New American Library.

Hogan, R. A. (1964) Issues and approaches in supervision. *Psychotherapy: Theory, Research and Practice, 1,* 139-141.

Holland, J. L. (1973). *Making a vocational choice: A theory of careers.* Englewood Cliffs, NJ: Prentice-Hall.

Holloway, E. L. (1987). Developmental models of supervision: Is it development? *Professional Psychology: Research and Practice, 18,* 209-216.

Hoshmand, L. L. S. (1989). Alternative research paradigms: A review and teaching proposal. *Counseling Psychologist, 17,* 3-79.

Howard, G. S. (1986). The scientist practitioner in counseling psychology: Toward a deeper integration of theory, research and practice. *Counseling Psychologist, 17,* 61-105.

Jablon, M. (1987). Psychotherapists' perceptions of their professional development and supervision. *Dissertation Abstracts International, 47,* SECB, 4302.

Josselson, R. (1990). *Finding herself.* San Francisco: Jossey-Bass.
Kaplan, B. (1983). A trio of trials. In R. M. Lerner (Ed.), *Developmental psychology: Historical and philosophical perspectives.* Hillsdale, NJ: Erlbaum.
Karpel, M. (1976). Individuation: From fusion to dialogue. *Family Process,* **15**, 65-82.
Killingmo, B. (1980). *Rorschachmetode og psykoterapi.* Oslo: Universitetsforlaget. (*The Rorschach method and psychotherapy.*)
Kivlighan, D. M. & Quigley, S. T. (1991). Dimensions used by experienced and novice young therapists to conceptualize group process. *Journal of Counseling Psychology,* **38**, 415-423.
Kohlberg, L. (1979). *Measuring moral judgment.* Worcester, MA: Clark University Press.
Kvale, S. (1983). The qualitative research interview—a phenomenological and a hermeneutical mode of understanding. *Journal of Phenomenological Psychology,* **17**, 171-189.
Kvale, S. (1986a). Meanings of data and human technology. *Scandinavian Journal of Psychology,* **17**, 171-189.
Kvale, S. (1986b). Psychoanalytic therapy as qualitative research. In P. D. Ashworth, A. Giorgi, & A. J. J. deKoning (Eds), *Qualitative research in psychology* (pp. 155-184). Pittsburgh, PA: Duquesne University Press.
Kvale, S. (1987). Validity in the qualitative research interview. *Methods,* **1**, 33-50.
Lamb, D., Baker, J., Jennings, M., & Yarris, E. (1982). Passages of an internship in professional psychology. *Professional Psychology,* **13**, 661-669.
Lambert, M. J. (1980). Research and the supervisory process. In A. K. Hess (Ed.), *Psychotherapy supervision: Theory, research, and practice* (pp. 423-450). New York: Wiley.
Larsen, E., Marnell, M., Marnell, M., & Ronnestad, M. H. (1986). *Medarbetarsamtal: Et kompendium.* Stockholm, Sweden: Skandinavisk Institutt for Ressursutvikling. (*Employer/employee dialogues: A compendium.* Scandinavian Institute of Resource Development.)
Lawler, A. C. (1990). The healthy self: Variation on a theme. *Journal of Counseling and Development,* **68**, 652-654.
Lerner, R. M. (1986). *Concepts and theories of human development.* New York: Random House.
Levinson, D., Darrow, D., Klein, E., Levinson, M., & McKee, R. (1978). *The seasons of a man's life.* New York: Ballantine Books.
Lincoln, Y. S., & Guba, E. G. (1985). *Naturalistic inquiry.* Newbury Park, CA Sage.
Lisle, L. (1987). *Portrait of an artist: A biography of Georgia O'Keeffe.* Albuquerque, NM: University of New Mexico Press.
Littrell, J. M. (1978). Concepts of beginning counselors. *Counselor Education and Supervision,* 30-36.
Littrell, J. M., Lee-Borden, N., & Lorenz, J. (1979). A developmental framework for counseling supervision. *Counselor Education and Supervision,* **19**, 129-136.

References

Loganbill, C., Hardy, E., & Delworth, U. (1982). Supervision: A conceptual model. *Counseling Psychologist*, 10, 3-42.

Marcia, J. E. (1966). Development and validation of ego identity status. *Journal of Personality and Social Psychology*, 3, 551-558.

Martin, J., Slemon, A. G., Hiebert, B., Hallberg, E. T., & Cummings, A. L. (1989). Conceptualizations of novice and experienced counselors. *Journal of Counseling Psychology*, 36, 395-400.

Maslach, C. (1982). *Burnout: The cost of caring*. Englewood Cliffs, NJ: Prentice-Hall.

May, R. (1976). *The courage to create*. NY: Bantam.

McGowen, K. R., & Hart, L. E. (1990). Still different after all these years: Gender differences in professional identity formation. *Professional Psychology: Research and Practice*, 21, 118-123.

Miars, R. D., Tracey, T. J., Ray, P. B., Cornfeld, J. L., O'Farrell, M., & Gelso, C. J. (1983). Variation in supervision process across trainee experience levels. *Journal of Counseling Psychology*, 30, 403-412.

Neimeyer, G., & Resnikoff, A. (1982). Qualitative strategies in counseling research. *Counseling Psychologist*, 10(4), 75-85.

Newman, J. L., & Fuqua, D. R. (1988). A comparative study of positive and negative modeling in counselor training. *Counselor Education and Supervision*, 28, 121-129.

Ogden, T. H. (1982). *The matrix of the mind: Object relations and the psychoanalytic dialogue*. New York: Jason Aronsen.

Patton, M. J. (1991). Qualitative research on college students: Philosophical and methodological comparisons with the quantitive approach. *Journal of College Student Development*, 32, 389-396.

Patton, M. Q. (1990). *Qualitative evaluation and research methods*. Beverly Hills, CA: Sage.

Patton, S. M. (1986). The training and development of counselors and psychotherapists: Toward a comprehensive developmental model. *Dissertation Abstracts International*, 47, SECB, 3538.

Perry, W. G., Jr. (1981). Cognitive and ethical growth: The making of meaning. In W. Chickering and Associates (Eds), *The modern American college* (pp. 76-116). San Francisco: Jossey-Bass.

Piaget, J. (1972). Intellectual evolution from adolescence to adulthood. *Human Development*, 15, 1-12.

Polkinghorne, D. E. (1986). Conceptual validity in a nontheoretical human science. *Journal of Phenomenological Psychology*, 17(2), 129-149.

Rest, J., Barnett, R., Bebeau, M., Deemer, D., Getz, I., Moon, Y. L., Spickelmier, J., Thomas, S. J., & Volker, J. (1986). *Moral development: Advances in research and theory*. NY: Praeger.

Rodolfa, E. R., Kraft, W. A., & Reilley, R. R. (1988). Stressors of professionals and trainees at APA-approved counseling and VA Medical Center Internship Sites. *Professional Psychology: Research and Practice*, 19, 43-49.

Rønnestad, M. H. (1976). Counselor personality and supervisory styles. *Scandinavian Journal of Psychology,* 17, 56-60.

Rønnestad, M. H. (1977). The effects of modeling, feedback, and experiential methods on counselor empathy. *Counselor Education and Supervision,* March, 194-201.

Rønnestad, M. H. (1982). Om psykoterapiveiledningens malsetting. *Tidsskrift for Norsk Psykologforening,* 19, 542-546. (On the objectives of supervision. *Journal of the Norwegian Psychological Association.*)

Rønnestad, M. H. (1983). Psykoterapiveiledning: Henimot en begrep savklaring. *Tidsskrift for Norsk Psykologforening,* 20, 19-23. (Supervision of psychotherapy: A discussion. *Journal of the Norwegian Psychological Association.* English abstract.)

Rønnestad, M. H. (1985). En utviklingsmodell for veiledning i klinisk psykologisk arbeid. *Tidsskrift for Norsk Psykologforening,* 22, 175-181. (A developmental model of supervision. *Journal of the Norwegian Psychological Association.* English abstract.)

Rønnestad, M. H., & Skovholt, T. M. (1991). En modell for profesjonell utvikling og stagnasjon hos terapeuter og radgivere. *Tidsskrift for Norsk psykologforening.* (A model of the professional development and stagnation of therapists and counselors. *Journal of the Norwegian Psychological Association,* 28, 555-567.)

Rønnestad, M. H., & Skovholt, T. M. (in press). Supervision of beginning vs. advanced graduate students. *Journal of Counseling and Development.*

Sammons, M. T., & Gravitz, M. A. (1990). Theoretical orientations of professional psychologists and their former professors. *Professional Psychology: Research and Practice,* 21, 131-134.

Schneirly, T. C. (1957). The concept of development in comparative psychology. In D. B. Harris (Ed.), *The concept of development.* Minneapolis, MN: University of Minnesota Press.

Shontz, F. C. (1982). To study persons: Reactions to qualitative strategies in counseling research. *Counselling Psychologist,* 10(4), 91-93.

Shostrom, E. L. (Producer.) (1965). *Three approaches to psychotherapy* [film]. Orange, CA: Psychological Films.

Skovholt, T. M. (1985). *Optimal stages of therapist/counselor development: A tentative model.* Unpublished manuscript.

Skovholt, T. M., & McCarthy, P. R. (Eds). (1988). Critical incidents in counselor development. Special issue of the *Journal of Counseling and Development,* 67, 69-135.

Sprinthall, N. A. (1975). Fantasy and reality in research: How to move beyond the unproductive paradox. *Counselor Education and Supervision,* 14, 310-322.

Stierlin, H., Rucker-Embden, I., Wetzel, N., & Wirsching, M. (1984). *The first interview with the family.* New York: Brunner/Mazel.

Stoltenberg, C. (1981). Approaching supervision from a developmental perspective: The counselor complexity model. *Journal of Counseling Psychology,* 28, 59-65.

Stoltenberg, C., & Delworth, U. (1987). *Supervising counselors and therapists: A developmental approach.* San Francisco: Jossey-Bass.

Strauss, A., & Corbin, J. (1990). *Basics of qualitative research: Grounded theory, procedures, and techniques.* Newbury Park, CA: Sage.

Super, D. E. (1953). A theory of vocational development. *American Psychologist,* **8,** 185–190.

Super, D. E. (1980). A life span, life space approach to career development. *Journal of Vocational Behavior,* **16,** 282–298.

Tracey, T. J., Hays, K. A., Malone, J., & Herman, B. (1988). Changes in counselor response as a function of experience. *Journal of Counseling Psychology,* **35,** 119–126.

Vaillant, G. E. (1977). *Adaptation to life.* Boston: Little, Brown.

Wachowiak, D., Bauer, G., & Simono, R. (1979). Passages: Career ladders for college counseling center psychologists. *Professional Psychology,* **10,** 723–731.

Widick, C., Knefelkamp, L., & Parker, C. A. (1980). Student development. In U. Delworth & G. R. Hansen (Eds), *Student services* (pp. 75–1116). San Francisco: Jossey-Bass.

Worthington, E. L. (1984). An empirical investigation of supervision of counselors as they gain experience. *Journal of Counseling Psychology,* **31,** 63–75.

Worthington, E. L., & Roehlke, H. J. (1979). Effective supervision as perceived by beginning counselors in training. *Journal of Counseling Psychology,* **26,** 64–73.

Worthington, E. L., & Stern, A. (1985). The effects of supervisor and supervisee degree level and gender on the supervisory relationship. *Journal of Counseling Psychology,* **32,** 252–262.

Yogev, S. (1982). An eclectic model of supervision: A developmental sequence for beginning psychotherapy students. *Professional Psychology,* **13,** 236–243.

Author Index

Ard, B. N., 6
Association of Psychology Internship Centers, 132

Baker, S. B., 98, 102
Barnett, R., 5
Bauer, G., 110
Bebeau, M., 5
Belenky, M., 11, 145
Benderly, B. L., 108, 112
Benner, P., 5, 107, 108
Blocher, D. H., 6, 8, 9
Borders, L. D., 3, 114
Brown, D., 3, 143

Charles, D., 6, 8, 97, 98, 99
Chi, M. T. H., 108
Clinchy, B., 11, 145
Comfield, J. L., 3
Cooper, C. R., 100
Corbin, J., 144, 149, 153, 156, 157
Cron, E. A., 3
Cross, D. G., 3
Cummings, A. L., 107, 108, 115

Daniels, T. G., 98
Darrow, D., 5
Deemer, D., 5
Delworth, U., 3, 6, 9, 10, 12, 97, 98, 99, 101, 113, 124
Denzin, N. K., 156

Dodge, J., 115
Dreyfus, H. L., 5, 6, 56, 98, 108, 109, 149, 195, 196
Dreyfus, S. E., 5, 6, 56, 98, 108, 109, 149, 195, 196

Ekstein, R., 3
Ellis, M. V., 150
Erikson, E. H., 5, 136

Flavell, J. H., 5
Fleming, J., 6, 7, 98
Fong-Beyette, M. L., 3
Freudenberger, H. J., 133
Friedlander, M. L., 3
Friedman, D., 6
Fuqua, D. R., 98, 121

Gagne, R. M., 4
Gelso, C. J., 3
Gergen, K. J., 145
Getz, I., 5
Gilligan, C., 5
Glaser, R., 108, 149
Goldberger, N., 11, 145
Goldfreid, M. R., 57
Goldman, L., 143, 144
Grater, H. A., 6, 10, 98
Gravitz, M. A., 109
Greely, A. T., 98
Greenson, M., 129

Grotevant, H. D., 100
Guba, E. G., 145
Guy, J. D., 99, 103, 122, 127, 129
Gysbers, N. C., 97

Hall, C. S., 101
Hallberg, E. T., 107, 108, 115
Handley, P., 3
Hardy, E., 3, 6, 9, 10, 12, 97, 98, 99, 101, 113, 124
Hart, L. E., 114
Hays, K. A., 102
Heibert, R., 108
Henry, W. E., 127, 129
Heppner, P. P., 3
Herman, B., 102
Herroid, D. J., 6
Hess, A. K., 3, 6, 11, 12, 113, 124
Hiebert, B., 107, 115
Hilgard, J. R., 4
Hill, C. E., 6, 8, 97, 98, 99
Hillebrand, E., 3
Hoffer, E., 38, 138
Hogan, R. A., 6, 7, 12, 98, 114
Holland, J. L., 23
Holloway, E. L., 130
Hoshmand, L., 143, 145, 146
Howard, G. S., 33, 143

Jablon, M., 6
Jennings, M., 102
Josselson, R., 136

Kaplan, B., 2, 3
Karpel, M., 101
Kaslow, N. J., 6
Killingmo, B., 129
Kivlighan, D. M., 108
Klein, E., 5
Knefelkamp, L., 58
Kohlberg, L., 5
Kraft, W. A., 115

Kvale, S., 145, 146, 147, 148, 149

Lamb, D., 102
Lambert, M. J., 3
Larsen, E., 134
Lawler, A. C., 101
Lee-Borden, N., 6
Lerner, R. M., 2, 3, 4
Levinson, D., 5
Levinson, M., 5
Lincoln, Y. S., 145
Lindzey, G., 101
Lisle, L., 131
Littrell, J. M., 6
Loganbill, C., 3, 6, 9, 10, 12, 97, 98, 99, 101, 113, 124
Lorentz, J., 6

McCarthy, P. R., 101, 140
McGowen, K. R., 114
McKee, R., 5
Malone, J., 102
Marcia, J. E., 32, 136, 137, 138
Marnell, Mats, 134
Marnell, Monica, 134
Martin, J., 107, 108, 115
Maslach, C., 133
May, R., 133
Miars, R. D., 3
Moon, Y. L., 5

Neimeyer, G., 143
Newman, J. L., 98, 121

O'Farrell, M., 3
Ogden, T. H., 129

Parker, C. A., 58
Patton, M. J., 143
Patton, M. Q., 144, 147, 148, 149, 153, 156

Author Index

Patton, S. M., 6
Perry, W. G., Jr, 5, 111
Piaget, J., 13, 132
Polkinghorne, D. E., 145

Quigley, S. T., 108

Ray, P. B., 3
Reed, K. G., 6, 8, 97, 98, 99
Reilley, R. R., 115
Resnikof, A., 143
Rest, J., 5, 150
Rodolfa, E. R., 115
Roehlke, H. J., 3
Rønnestad, M. H., 1, 3, 33, 97, 98, 121, 124, 130, 134, 149, 158
Rucker-Embden, I., 101

Sammons, M. T., 109
Schneirly, T. C., 3
Shontz, F. C., 143
Shostrom, E. L., 39, 121
Simono, R., 110
Sims, J. H., 127, 129
Skovholt, T. M., 1, 101, 124, 140, 149, 158
Slemon, A., 107, 108, 115
Snyder, J., 3

Spickelmier, J., 5
Spray, S. L., 127, 129
Sprinthall, N. A., 144
Stern, A., 3
Stierlin, H., 101
Stoltenberg, C., 3, 6, 12, 97, 98, 99, 113
Strauss, A. L., 144, 149, 153, 156, 157
Super, D. E., 5, 23

Tarule, J., 111, 145
Thomas, S. J., 5
Tracey, T. J., 3, 102

Vaillant, 5

Wachowiak, D., 110
Wallerstein, R., 3
Ward, G. W., 3
Wetzel, N., 101
Widick, C., 58
Wirsching, M., 101
Worthington, E. L., 3
Wrubel, J., 107

Yarris, E., 102
Yogev, S., 6

Subject Index

Accumulated wisdom, 77, 89, 94, 100, 107–108, 109, 115, 116
Anchoring, *see* Personal anchoring
Anxiety, 53, 98, 116, 124, 132
  as focus in supervision, 10
  Conditional Autonomy stage, 48
  Exploration stage, 52–53
  Imitation of Expert stage, 32, 36
  Integrity stage, 88, 89, 95–96
  performance, 23, 29, 36, 88, 122
  pervasive, 114–115
  post-traumatic, 48, 133
  reduction of, 89, 91, 93, 95–96, 105, 115–116, 122
  separation, 127–128
  Transition to Professional Training stage, 23, 24, 29
Apathy, 75
Authentic fit, 63
Autonomy, 7–8

Boundaries, 82
Burnout, 2, 11, 122, 126, 133, 149, 203

Central task
  Conditional Autonomy stage, 42
  Conventional stage, 17–18
  Exploration stage, 50–52
  Imitation of Experts stage, 30–31
  Individuation stage, 74–76
  Integration stage, 62–63

Integrity stage, 87–88
  Transition to Professional Training stage, 23
Clients as teachers, 118–119
Cognitive complexity, 5, 6, 130
Complexity, 20, 55, 83, 108
  awareness of, 124–127, 136, 140–141
  confusion of, 39
  disabling, 35
  focus of workshops, 38
  of job/work, 27, 54
  reduction of, 32, 36
Conceptual ideas used
  Conditional autonomy stage, 47
  Conventional stage, 19–20
  Exploration stage, 56–59
  Imitation of Experts stage, 36–38
  Individuation stage, 82–83
  Integration stage, 69–71
  Integrity stage, 93–95
  Transition to Professional Training stage, 27
Conceptual level, 4
Confidence
  experience of, 45
  lack of, 43
Confusion, 9, 10, 29, 39, 53, 60, 98, 133
Congruence, 93
Context-free theory, 57, 107
Continuity/discontinuity
  concept of, 3, 5, 75, 78
  descriptive/explanatory, 3, 4, 5

Subject Index

Contract, 2, 10
  developmental, 127, 133–134, 140
Countertransference, 72, 127, 128–129, 140
Cross-sectional design, 150

Definition of the stage
  Conditional autonomy stage, 42
  Conventional stage, 17
  Exploration stage, 50
  Imitation of experts stage, 30
  Individuation stage, 74
  Integration stage, 62
  Integrity stage, 87
  Transition to Professional Training stage, 22–23
Dependency, 7, 44, 51
Dependency/autonomy conflict, 7
Development
  concept of, 2–5
  general models of
    Dreyfus & Dreyfus, Freud, Erikson, Kohlberg, Rest *et al.*, Super, Levinson, 6–7
  professional models of
    the cognitive model of Blocher, 8–9
    the four-level model of Hogan, 7
    the integrated developmental model of Stoltenberg & Delworth, 12–13
    the model of Hill, Charles & Reed, 8
    the model of Loganbill, Hardy & Delworth, 9
    the psychoanalytic model of Fleming, 7
    the supervision focused model of Grater, 10
    the supervision focused model of Hess, 11
Didactic teaching, 3, 7, 8, 28
Discontinuity/continuity, *see* Continuity/discontinuity

Disillusionment, 3, 32, 51, 53, 56, 60, 64, 69, 113, 119, 130, 139
Divorce, 91

Exhaustion, 58, 75–76, 85

Feedback
  from clients, 8, 28, 32, 40
  from peers, 25, 40
  from supervisor, 24, 33, 40, 43
  role of, 3, 9
Flexibility, 10, 67, 105, 130, 144, 147
Foreclosure, 32, 35

Gender differences, 13, 111, 113–114
"Gloria" films, 121
Grief, 89

Hermeneutical circle, 148

Identification, 11, 19, 30, 39, 103, 121, 137
Identity, 11, 12, 32, 62, 80, 83, 99, 101, 104–105, 131, 136, 137–138, 141
Ideological arguments, 145–146
Ideological functioning, 100, 106
Imitation, 7, 47, 50, 95, 113, 120, 121
  as stage, 30–41
Individuation (*see also* Professional individuation), 5, 24, 87, 99–100, 113, 115, 117, 133–134
  as stage, 74–86
Integration, 9–10, 38, 82, 95, 99–100, 103, 131
  as stage, 62–73
Internalization, 30–31, 39, 127, 130, 140

Subject Index

definition, 131
Internship, 43–46, 49, 51, 53, 57–59, 102, 120, 132–133
Intuition, 46, 94, 108–109
Isolation, 79, 91, 92, 120, 127

Knowledge construction, 110–112

Laissez-faire orientation, 36
Learning process
    Conditional Autonomy stage, 47–48
    Conventional stage, 20
    Exploration stage, 59–60
    Individuation stage, 83–84
    Imitation of Experts stage, 39–40
    Integration stage, 71
    Integrity stage, 95
    Transition to Professional Training stage, 27–28
Life span, 1, 13, 114, 130

Measures of effectiveness and satisfaction
    Conditional Autonomy stage, 48–49
    Conventional stage, 20–21
    Exploration stage, 60–61
    Imitation of Experts stage, 40–41
    Individuation stage, 84–86
    Integration stage, 71–73
    Integrity stage, 95–97
    Transition to Professional Training stage, 28–29
Mentor
    as professional elders, 36, 91, 92, 98, 120
    as source of influence, 18, 32, 53, 64, 79, 89
    effect of role, 64
    feeling towards, 91
    impact of, 78, 112, 116, 136, 137
    internal, 105
    reliance on, 110
    role of, 53, 91
    search for, 71
Metagoal, 127, 131, 140
Modeling (*see also* Imitation)
    as learning process, 39–40
    characteristics of, 30–31, 47
    hazards of, 31
    positive effects of, 32
    relationship to self, 40
Models, use of, 32–33, 39–40, 42, 47, 48, 49, 71, 79
Moratorium, 125, 135, 137, 140–141
Motivation
    during study, 12, 34, 98
    for therapy, 139–140
    for work, 7–8, 54, 77, 84
    to enter profession, 22–23, 34, 73, 117–118, 122, 127–130

Narcissistic position, 122

Occupational counter transference, 125, 127–128, 140

Peers, 18, 28, 29, 36, 39, 60, 84, 101, 105, 106, 108
    as source of influence, 24–25 32–33, 44, 53–54, 64, 78–79, 89, 91
Personal anchoring, 52, 130–131
Predominant affect
    Conditional autonomy stage, 43
    Conventional stage, 18
    Exploration stage, 52–53
    Imitation of experts stage, 31–32
    Individuation stage, 76–77
    Integration stage, 63–64
    Integrity stage, 88–89

Predominant affect (*cont.*)
  Transition to professional training stage, 24
Premature closure, 124, 130, 135–136, 138–141
  definition, 135
Professional identity, *see* Identity
Professional individuation, 100, 109, 115, 117
  the post-training period, 103–105
  the pretraining period, 101
  the training period, 101–103
Professional self-confidence *see* Self-confidence
Pseudodevelopment, 103–105, 115, 124–125, 127–128, 135, 138–139
  definition, 124

Qualitative research, 143–148

Regret, 89
Research method
  description of method, 148–165
  questionnaire, 158–161
  reinterview form, 162–165
  sample description, 150–156
Responsibility
  for clients, 46
  for supervision, 10
  towards clients, 8–9, 46, 55, 59, 72, 82, 85, 121
Retirement, 87, 88, 91–92, 95, 114, 120, 126, 130
Rigidity, 66–67, 71, 84, 101–105
Role and working style
  Conditional Autonomy stage, 45–47
  Conventional stage, 19
  Exploration stage, 54–56
  Imitation of Experts stage, 35
  Individuation stage, 80–82
  Integration stage, 66–69

Integrity stage, 92–93
  Transition to Professional Training stage, 26

Self-confidence, 7, 8, 9, 98, 105, 111, 113, 115–116, 122, 130, 136, 168, 172, 195
  in Conditional Autonomy stage, 43, 45
  in Exploration stage, 52
  in Imitation of Expert stage, 38
  in Integration stage, 64
  in Integrity stage, 88–89, 91, 94
  in Transition of Professional Training stage, 28
Self-disclosure, 19, 65, 121
Self-protection, 11, 114, 121
Sources of influence
  Conditional Autonomy stage, 43–45
  Conventional stage, 18–19
  Exploration stage, 53–54
  Imitation of Experts stage, 32–35
  Individuation stage, 77–80
  Integration stage, 64–66
  Integrity stage, 89–92
  Transition to Professional Training stage, 24–26
Stage concept
  characteristics of, 3–5
  critique of, 4–5
Stagnation, 9–10, 124–142
Structuring factors, 132–134
  assimilation/accommodation balance, 132–133
  developmental contract, 133–134
  support/challenge balance, 133
Supervision
  among peers, 61, 106, 110, 111
  attitude towards, 10, 42, 44
  disappointments with, 35
  effects of, 31, 33, 36, 44, 66, 120
  expectations, 10
  feedback, 24, 33

focus, 9–12
goals of, 9–10
in group, 71
interventions, 8
non-confirming experiences, 43
relationship, 43
role of, 8, 38
structuring of, 134
theoretical controversies, 2
theoretical models of, 7–12
Support, 19, 31, 44, 46, 80, 119, 139
at transition prints, 120
of administrative/social structures, 132
of colleagues/peers/supervisors/mentors, 7–8, 24, 25, 33, 53, 79, 104, 120
of work environment, 9, 77, 106, 132, 141
role of, 3
social, 25
support/challenge balance, 127, 133

True believer, 38, 136, 138

Wounded healer, 117, 128

Zeitgeist, 24, 36